Texian Macabre

Texian Macabre

The Melancholy Tale of a Hanging in Early Houston

Stephen L. Hardin

Illustrated by GARY S. ZABOLY

State🦕House Press

Schreiner University · Kerrville, TX
325-660-1752 · www.mcwhiney.org

Copyright 2024, State House Press
All rights reserved

Cataloging-in-Publication Data

Names: Hardin, Stephen L., 1953- author.
Title: Texian macabre: the melancholy tale of a hanging in early Houston / Stephen L. Hardin; illustrated by Gary S. Zaboly.
Description: Revised edition. | Kerrville, TX: State House Press, 2024. | Includes bibliographical references, illustrations, maps, and index.
Identifiers: ISBN 9781649670229 (cloth)
Subjects: LCSH: Hanging – Texas – Houston – Case studies. | Houston (Tex.) – Social conditions – 19th century. | Houston (Tex.) – History – 19th century. | Zaboly, Gary S.
Classification: LCC HV9956 (print) | DCC 364.152

No part of this book may be reproduced in any form unless with written permission from State House Press, except for brief passages by reviewers.

First edition 2024

Cover and page design by Allen Griffith of Eye 4 Design

Distributed by Texas A&M University Press Consortium
800-826-8911
www.tamupress.com

This one is for Deborah, who, by filling the author's life
with sunshine and bluebonnets, allows him to ponder
ghastly topics without yielding to the darkness.

If you ever go to Houston
Boy, you better walk right,
And you better not gamble,
And you better not fight.

"Midnight Special"
Traditional folk song

Contents

Pen and Ink Illustrations	xi
Maps and Diagrams	xi
Photographs and Portraits	xiii
Acknowledgments	xv
Publisher's Introduction	xix
Introduction	xxv

Prologue   **They Swung Off at 2 O'clock**   A Hanging in Houston   xxxiii

1   **The High Merit of Service**   The Ordeal of David James Jones   1

2   **A Remnant of That Noble Band**   Flight and Fight   33

3   **The Most Miserable Place in the World**   The Town of Houston   57

4   **Vagabond Volunteers**   The Rowdy Loafers   99

5   **The Virtuous Part of the Community**   Houston's Gentry   129

6   **An Excellent Sentence**   The Reckoning   163

Epilogue   **Vengeance of the Public Hatred**   Legacy   193

Notes	219
Chronology	263
Bibliography	275
Index	289

Pen and Ink Illustrations

Frontispiece	
A Hanging in Houston	xxx
Escape	xl
Carnage	30
Splendor and Squalor	54–55
Drinking, Fighting, and Rangling	97
How Precious with Good Liquor in	126
Grave Robbers	160

Maps and Diagrams

The Texas Revolution	25
Houston Street Map, 1837–1839	59
Houston, Capital of Texas, 1837	64–65
Houston and Galveston	142

Photographs and Portraits

Henry Smith	9
Presidio La Bahía	16
James Walker Fannin, Jr.	19
The Goliad Massacre	34
Sam Houston	39
Thomas Jefferson Rusk	46
Goliad Burial Site	47
Anson Jones	61
Capitol Building, Houston	72
Samuel Augustus Maverick	73
Francis Richard Lubbock	81
Executive Mansion, Houston	82
Susanna Dickinson	89
Charlotte Allen	91
John Kirby Allen	92
Felix Huston	101
Albert Sydney Johnston	105
Francis Moore, Jr.	137
Mirabeau Buonaparte Lamar	143
Ashbel Smith	145

Acknowledgments

One of the joys of this project was the discovery of the Texas Room of the Houston Public Library. It is everything a research facility should be. Researchers find themselves ensconced in a resplendent space and pampered by an attentive staff. Would that all archival repositories followed their lead. While everyone at the Texas Room went out of their way to provide assistance, Jennifer Sheehan, Wendy Willeford, and Joel D. Draut deserve special mention. Thanks are also due to Jeffrey D. Dunn for calling my attention to this remarkable facility. Jeff is a fine attorney, but an even better friend.

Special thanks are due to independent researcher Mr. James L. Glass of Houston. He generously shared many of his own findings and sent me copies of his remarkable maps. Moreover, he offered to mail these items to Victoria and refused to accept even the cost of the postage. He is a gentleman and scholar of the old school.

As always, the professionals at the Texas General Land Office were convivial and cooperative. The entire staff stood ready to lend a hand, but I owe special thanks to Bobby Santiesteban, Galen D. Greaser, and John Molleston.

xvi   ACKNOWLEDGMENTS

In all of my previous books, the staff at the Texas State Library and Archives Commission has performed yeoman service, but never as much as with this one. Donaly Brice deserves special thanks for taking time out of his hectic schedule to track down a wayward document that proved crucial. John Anderson made selection of photographs almost effortless and Jean Carefoot talked me through the citation process and gave me some good leads to track down documents in other repositories.

It is always a treat to visit Elaine B. Davis and her staff at the Daughters of the Republic of Texas Library at the Alamo. Martha Utterback, Charles R. (Rusty) Gámez, and Debra Bryant spared no effort to make my time there fruitful. I was surprised to find this San Antonio library such a rich repository of rare Houston materials.

Almost twenty years has passed since I had last researched at the Catholic Archives of Texas and I had forgotten what a splendid facility it is. Thanks are due to my friend James L. Haley for reminding me of their rich Sam Houston collection. Archives Director Susan Eason was friendly, helpful, and professional. I will not wait so long before returning.

Sheron Barnes is the Special Collections Librarian at The Victoria College Library. She and her staff assist me on an almost daily basis. I take up so much of their time, I expect them to groan every time I darken their door. Yet, they never do, for which I remain grateful. More than once, Marie Adcock has helped me track down a wayward book or document. Bob Allen is a photographer without peer and always returns prints in a timely manner. I know how blessed I am to work with such good people.

Sandra Drozd reminds me on a daily basis why she is the "indispensable one." She is—and I state this with no fear of contradiction—the greatest secretary that ever lived. Without her assistance, I would be unable to get through a single day.

Friends and colleagues have read portions of the manuscript and offered valued suggestions. Among these are: Steve and Cynda Abolt, Bob Bethea, Dr. James E. Crisp, William C. Davis, Jim Green, Dr. Karen Hagan, Stephen Harrigan, Dr. Karen Hoblit, Colonel Alan C. Huffines, Dr. Robert T. Maberry, Scott McMahon, Lael Morgan, Frank Thompson, and David and Laura Vickers.

Writing a book is easy; publishing a book is hard. Even so, friends in Abilene made the process much less torturous. I offer heartfelt gratitude to Dr. Donald S. Frazier, President and Chief Executive Officer of the McWhiney Research Foundation. Thanks also to Dr. Robert F. Pace, Vice President and Chief Operating Officer, and Amy Smith, Executive Director and Treasurer. Carlyn Kahl, Managing Editor of State House Press, has tolerated this meddling author more that anyone has a right to expect. For that, my appreciation. While Dr. Grady McWhiney is no longer with us, I would be remiss if I did not acknowledge his friendship and support over the years. Doc, we miss you.

Finally, thanks and love for my wife, Deborah, and children, Walker and Savannah, who have suffered countless hours of neglect while Dad was out digging up dead Texians.

S.L.H.

Stephen L. Hardin, The Historian of Texas

I love this book. *Texian Macabre* is a deftly crafted tale. Get ready for a wild, weird ride of shocking twists and turns all leading to more than a touch or two of horror.

Now, History is not particularly mysterious. We know how it turns out! Which makes this work all that more amazing. I burned through the pages as I followed these larger-than-life characters along the dark paths leading them to their final cataclysmic intersection. Decapitated corpses of executed criminals? Yes, it's in there. The hairbreadth escape of a Texian from the Goliad Massacre? Absolutely. There is a lot of action in this history book, and the outcome of the journey always seems to be just over the bend—or next chapter.

Anyone who can make history interesting and engaging is always welcome at State House Press. That's why we have published two of Hardin's books—this one and *Lust for Glory*. When I learned that he was bringing out a new tome about the Runaway Scrape, *Texian Exodus* with The University of Texas Press, we decided it was time to bring out a new edition of *Texian Macabre*.

We are reprinting this to complete a chronicle of Texas Republic history. A grand epic.

For readers of Hardin's work on the Texas Revolution and Republic, his works might go in this order—*Texian Iliad* (UT Press), *Texian Exodus* (UT Press), *Texian Macabre* (State House Press), and *Lust for Glory* (State House Press). If you want to hear these Texas tales straight from the horse's mouth, you can check out his online presentations on The Texas Center's YouTube channel. I'll post a link below.

That said, let's talk about this great Texas historian—as writer, friend, and colleague. I met Steve back in 1988. He was finishing up graduate school at Texas Christian University while I was just getting started. He was living in Austin at the time, working for the Texas State Historical Association in their massive redo of the *Handbook of Texas*. When I made my first foray into research at the Barker Texas History Center—now the Briscoe Center for American History—I couched surfed at Steve's place. He was a gracious host, and a great advisor to a newcomer to the history business.

We had a lot in common, not the least of which was our mentor, Professor Grady McWhiney.

Steve was the epitome of a graduate scholar. He was a perpetual student. In his hometown of San Marcos (he claims that over his birthplace, McKinney) he earned a reputation. He took classes at Texas State University even though he had already graduated! He took them . . . because he just wanted to learn stuff. Finally, some good-natured professors took him under their wing. They introduced him to the master's degree program there which led him to his doctoral studies at TCU.

We did not have that trajectory in common. I was interested in getting into school, and out again. I had worked in the newspaper industry, the television sports industry, and the defense industry. None of these were conducive to the "life of the mind" that Steve epitomized. But I couldn't shake my history habit, so off to graduate school I went to see if I could make a living at it. Here is where we encountered each other, at good ol' Dave Reed Hall.

After having met Steve, I loved that I now knew a real scholar. Someone who took the craft seriously. He gave me a model of what a real historian should be. He was of a literary bent, and believed that the stories of the past should be good yarns, well told, and above all, accessible. Our task as historians was to write for the person down the street, not the professor down the hall. He didn't care for the petty variety of academics, but naturally gravitated to those who were affable. Of a similar disposition— and tastes in great food that was generally bad for you—we became good friends. McWhiney, also known for writing approachable history, had a great influence on us both.

Steve moved on to Victoria. My journey led me to Abilene.

Once there, Dr. McWhiney had asked me to start a non-profit to advance this concept of accessible history. What resulted was The Grady McWhiney Research Foundation. Then, we got busy, and before long had purchased State House Press that we merged with another publishing company we picked up previously. We joined the Texas A&M University Press consortium to market and distribute our books. Then, we took on the management of The Buffalo Gap Historic Village, an outdoor museum south of Abilene. Before long, we had become a 501(c)

xxii PUBLISHER'S INTRODUCTION

3 with several very involved enterprises. So, we changed the name to the McWhiney History Education Group to reflect this evolution.

As we grew, we needed reinforcements. When a position came open at the school where I served as faculty, I convinced Steve to leave his post at Victoria College. He joined me up north to lend a hand with the McWhiney Group. It was a pleasant time with him there. We were doing a lot of Texas history together. After his remarkably successful *Texian Iliad*, I was pleased that he opted to publish *Texian Macabre* with State House Press in 2007.

This book deserves a new, and greater, readership. That's why we are bringing out a second edition. So those that missed the chance more than a decade and a half ago can have a crack at it.

Steve has gone through and fixed a few typos and awkward sentences. Mostly this slightly redesigned work remains the essence of that first burst of genius. Every Houstonian worth their spurs should read this book. Everyone who likes a great true story with plenty of vinegar and twists should too. It is, to use a favorite Steve-ism, transcendent. Of course, he usually uses that word in connection to eating a ribeye.

The great Texas dreams we nurtured at that college in Abilene ultimately came to naught. In 2020, Schreiner University recruited me to create The Texas Center—similar at first to what Steve and I concocted up north, but now with the full faith and backing of the university administration. Steve lingered on a while—up north—tending to a history department that had been reduced from four fulltime faculty to just one—him. Then he retired.

Now he lives in Kerrville, his wife's adopted hometown. Once again, he is just a short drive away from me. Who knows what adventures may lie ahead for him here in the Hill Country. For me, I am certainly glad to have one of the best writers, historians, and friends close at hand—yet again.

Welcome to Kerrville, Steve.

Don Frazier

Introduction

This book traces the misadventures of David James Jones, a Texas hero who killed a man in Houston and paid for it at the end of a rope. Jones and John Christopher Columbus Quick, his companion on the gallows, represented a gang of troublemakers that the virtuous denounced as "rowdy loafers." The upper crust sought to demonstrate the fate that awaited the loafers that refused to change their rowdy ways or—preferably—that they leave town. This then is the story of a man who died for those he came to epitomize more than the murder he committed. It is also the story of early Houston, its citizens, and their peculiar notions of justice.

It remains one of history's sad ironies. Those who tame a land tend to embarrass those who follow. Early Texas was a hard country and the men who took it, held it, and broke it to their use were commonly crude, vulgar, lethal, loud-mouthed, pushy, immoral, and disagreeable. They were, as Frederic Remington termed them, "men with the bark on." They are the stuff of legend, and legends populate a mythic past. We might admire them less if we had to inhale the whiskey on their breath or suffer the stench of their unwashed bodies.[1]

xxvi   INTRODUCTION

Even so, the Texas Republic was always more than bloodshed and buckskin. The novelist John Graves observed another frontier type:

> Most Texans then as now were quiet people concerned with leading decent fruitful lives and building a future for themselves and their children. Among them from the very start were a good many broadly thoughtful men who believed that the use and development of people's minds could have great effect on that future. Texas may have been a frontier for a good long while, but during that same long while it was an outpost of a highly civilized world, and such men shared a widespread nineteenth-century conviction that intellectual curiosity, knowledge, and benevolent action could do much to lead society toward a better way of life—more, perhaps, than could battles, political maneuverings, factories, railroads, and the acquisition of goods. They believed in progress, but most passionately in a progress toward enlightenment.

Inevitably, the interests of the rowdies and the righteous diverged, and conflict ignited. The respectable class frequently sought to tame the tamers.[2]

The concept is not original. Historians, novelists, and directors—good and bad—have investigated the end of the frontier and men who have outlived their time. Sam Peckinpah made a career out of it. Therefore, there is no pretense of advancing a startling new interpretation or stretching the epistemological boundaries. This is a simple tale of men who came face to face with civilization—and wanted no part of it.

My first introduction to David James Jones had been in Andrew Forest Muir's beautifully edited 1950 article in the *Southwestern Historical Quarterly*. Yet, once I delved into the documents and discovered the multiple layers of the tale, it became darker, weirder, and more twisted. In a word, *macabre*.

I had never seen this side of the Texas Republic; I suspected most readers hadn't. Finally, it became a compulsion. This was not a story I wanted to write. It was a story I *had* to write.

This is not a biography of David James Jones. The documentation does not exist to support one. There is much concerning him I still don't know, cannot know. Historians reconstruct events from scraps of crumbling documents; there will always be loose ends. I could never discover which state he hailed from; I don't know his political affiliation; I never came close to unraveling the inner man. I can't even describe his appearance. He died a few years shy of daguerreotypes and people of his class did not sit for portraits. While extensive documentation concerning Jones's crime, trial, and execution exists, no one ever bothered to jot down a description of the man. No one considered him that important.

And that's the point. The rowdy loafers were the type of low-class rogues that almost never make it into the history books—which is not to say they never make history. The challenge of revealing people other historians had ignored appealed to me. While Jones provides the narrative thread, I never intended the book to be his story. Rather, it offers a vehicle to transport the reader to a lost time and place.

English historian Lord Acton observed: "History does not work with bottled essences, but with active combinations." Who best exemplified the Texas Republic? Was it David James Jones or Francis Moore, Jr.? Was it Susanna Dickinson or Mary Austin Holley? Was it a border lawyer or a rowdy loafer? All of them embodied early Texas. This dynamic mingling of personalities and interests made the time and place tremendously exciting. I wanted to examine these "active combinations": Jones simply provided the hook upon which I could hang their stories.[3]

My academic colleagues may find the style unconventional. So be it. Poet and recording artist, Bob Dylan described his approach to writing.

"You have to know and understand something," he avowed, "and then go past the vernacular." The "something" I have strived to know and understand is early Houston and its residents. I then attempted to get past the academic vernacular. Best-selling historian David McCullough probably said it best: "No harm's done to history by making it something someone would want to read." Whatever its faults—and doubtless there are many—I have tried to write a book someone would want to read.[4]

It is no accident that the folks at State House Press published this book. They have a tradition of supporting books that incorporate high standards of scholarship and readability. Their website states it succinctly: "We believe firmly in narrative history, in telling a good story, and telling it well—without losing sight of the people who made history and the events that changed a nation."[5]

In this case, the history makers are an unsavory mob of reprobates labeled the rowdy loafers. The events were a series of murders, trials, and hangings that followed. The country changed by these events was not, however, the United States of America. Rather, it was another sovereign nation: the Republic of Texas. If the reader closes this book with better understanding of, and an increased appreciation for, the people who inhabited that ephemeral empire, the author can enter his house justified.

xxx

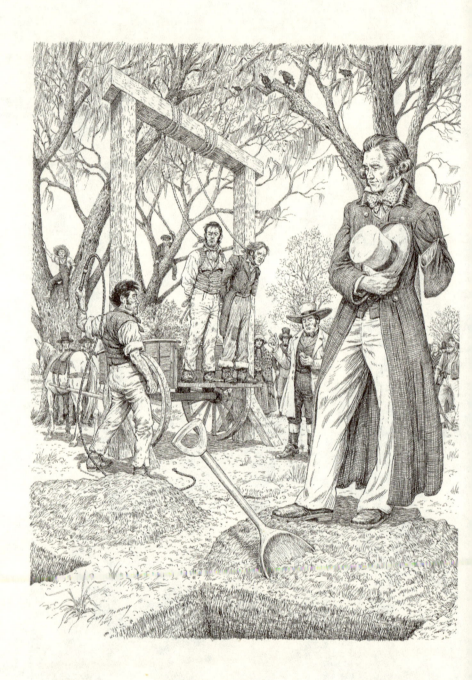

A Hanging in Houston

March 28, 1838

An expression of smug satisfaction cuts across the face of Mayor Francis Moore, Jr. He has worked for months to secure the conviction and execution of murderers John Christopher Columbus Quick and David James Jones; now he savors the amoment. A certifiable eccentric, the one-armed official wears the same ensemble every day: "the same Kentucky jeans pants, the same pair of stitchdowns, the same long and flowing blue green robe, the same redoubtable ancient drab beaver [hat]."

Sheriff John W. Moore, decked out in his finest foofaraw, checks his timepiece. Mayor Moore (no relation to the sheriff) has made it clear that he and all decent citizens expect the execution to proceed in a decorous and timely fashion. At the exact stroke of two o'clock, the lawman signals the hangman to flog the horse.

Quick and Jones, the central players of this morality play, stand perched precariously on a horse cart's tailgate. Houstonians cannot help but be impressed with Quick's demeanor, as he meets his fate "with great firmness and resignation." They are underwhelmed with Jones who appears "completely stupefied with fear or shame." Quick glowers at the hangman, who, his expression reveals, is unnerved.

In the background, a host that numbers between two and three thousand (witnesses on the ground could not agree) observe the proceedings with rapt attention. The theater is a "beautiful islet of timber," and children, more limber than their elders, secure choice seats in hovering oaks. Since murderers cannot lie in consecrated ground, open graves await their occupants under the gallows. Quick and Jones, however, have one consolation: Sheriff Moore has dipped into his pocket to assure that they meet their Maker wearing new socks. In Mayor Moore's Houston, one must observe the proprieties.

Prologue: They Swung Off at 2 O'clock
A Hanging in Houston

Between two and three thousand Houstonians watched enthralled as the hangman slipped nooses over the prisoners' heads. While crime and violence were routine in the fledgling capital of the Republic of Texas, the weight of law lay lightly on the ramshackle settlement. Judicial executions were rare and to witness two convicted murderers meet their Maker in a single drop—well, that was truly spectacular.[1]

Indeed, the city fathers intended an impressive demonstration. They wished to dispatch an unambiguous message to Houston's unruly underclass: break the law, disturb the peace, besmirch the reputation of our city, and we have rope enough to rein in such behavior. Officials were determined that the executions proceed without a hitch. On the day, Wednesday, March 28, 1838, they had drafted more than one hundred men from the town's militia companies to escort prisoners John C. C. Quick and David James Jones to the gallows. The militiamen imparted the "pomp of pow'r" to the proceedings. Or, perhaps, administrators feared the condemned's cronies might attempt an eleventh-hour rescue. If so, they had no cause to fret. Somber and dignified, the procession arrived at its destination without incident.[2]

The gallows stood "in a beautiful islet of timber, situated in the prairie about a mile south of the city." An overhead crossbeam lay across two uprights sunk into the earth, for this was to be a "horse-and-cart" hanging. The executioner backed the cart between the vertical timbers. He then carefully placed the prisoners on the cart's tailgate. Securing the nooses, he tied up to the crossbeam with but a sparse amount of slack in the rope.[3]

Early nineteenth-century officials considered the horse-and-cart hanging a progressive and benevolent innovation. Eighteenth-century judges never intended that hanging be a decorous process. Then, the hangman had helped the bound prisoner climb a ladder. After the executioner had secured the noose, he descended the ladder and yanked it away. Thousands experienced the misfortune of being "turned off the ladder." By 1800, allegedly for humane reasons, the cart had replaced the ladder in most judicial executions in both Britain and the United States. Even so, the drop from the cart was only a matter of inches, and many maintained that death came even slower than before. In the old days, the condemned at least had the opportunity to throw themselves off the ladder in an effort to crack their necks.[4]

Nineteenth-century gallows came in a variety of shapes and sizes— if the execution was a lynching any handy tree limb sufficed—but the design of the noose normally determined the efficacy of the hanging. Readers who grew up watching western movies will be familiar with the hangman's noose with its traditional eight coils. Executioners favored this knot for "long-drop" hangings when prisoners fell through the trapdoor of an elevated scaffold. The hangman typically placed the knot under or just behind the condemned's left ear. When he "reached the end of his rope," this knot, aided by the victim's body weight, brought tremendous force against the head and neck. If the hangman was a professional, the neck snapped like a twig and death appeared instantaneous.[5]

In 1838, however, the hangman's noose, the scaffold, and the long drop were all well in the future. Before 1850, the "short drop" was for all practical purposes universal in the United States. Hangmen employed a simple noose: a loop tied to one end of the rope with the other end passing through it. When the cart moved out from under the condemned, he—or, in many cases, she—tumbled mere inches. Such a minimal drop most often initiated a slow, strangling death from asphyxia.[6]

This was the moment gawking spectators savored. More often than not, victims would jerk, twitch, and twist on air. Englishmen wryly called these spasms "dancing the Tyburn jig" after the London prison where from 1571 to 1783 prisoners swung on the infamous "Triple Tree." As the noose tightened around the throat, victims convulsed and a bloody froth occasionally oozed from mouth and nostrils; women sometimes bled from the uterus. When hangmen refused the condemned a hood, spectators observed bulging eyes, protruding tongues, and various other manifestations of sluggish strangulation. One of these was especially incongruous: hanged men, while in the final throes of death, sometimes achieved an erection and, by some accounts, even ejaculated. Much to the pleasure of the howling mob, the condemned normally struggled from one to three minutes. Normally. Yet, there are cases on record where they thrashed about for five, ten, or even twenty minutes.[7]

On such occasions, women sometime ran forward to squash their faces and breasts against the bound hands. They believed the "dead man's hand" capable of curing blemishes and even illness. Another conviction was that perspiration from hanged criminals possessed curative powers. Consequently, it was common to see mothers rubbing their ailing babies against still-twitching felons. Superstitious customers believed lengths of hangman's rope and shavings from a busy gallows produced salutary effects. Hangmen, therefore, supplemented their earning by offering such items to the highest bidder.[8]

If victims jigged too long, the hangman or even the condemned's friends and relatives might tug on the prisoner's legs to allay his agony and relieve the mounting uneasiness of the crowd. This act of compassion was always dicey. As the body shut down, bladders and bowels released themselves, and these Good Samaritans had to jump back quick to avoid splashing excreta. Thus, the popular euphemism for being hanged: "pissing when you can't whistle."[9]

Less frequently, short-drop hangings resulted in a swift passage. In this event, pressure on the carotid arteries produced a sudden stoppage of the heart. That, in turn, brought about rapid unconsciousness. The victim was apt to slide into oblivion as the force of the tightening noose occluded the jugular vein, carotid arteries, and the trachea (windpipe) rendering breathing ever more difficult. Reports confirm that some prisoners gave up the ghost with little or no struggle. The lucky ones squirmed for an instant—in some cases, less than fifteen seconds—before hanging limp.[10]

The Quick–Jones execution went off with all the decorum and alacrity that the mayor and "certain officers of justice" might have wished. At the stroke of two o'clock, the hangman lashed the horse, the cart lurched forward, and Quick and Jones tipped off the tailgate. The slack in the rope allowed the pair to fall perhaps six inches. If the morbid horde hoped to enjoy the prisoners' death jerks, their serene departure surely disappointed.[11]

Old Testament tradition dictated that executed criminals could not lie in consecrated ground, so the executioner immediately buried the bodies at the foot of the gallows. That brought a satisfying finish to the final act of the performance, and Houston citizens, having enjoyed a splendid outing, began to stroll back into town.[12]

As jubilant spectators discussed the finer points of that day's hanging, they did not appreciate the multiple ironies that swirled around Jones's execution. Only a few of the city's elite knew that public relations had more to do with his death sentence than the pursuit of justice. The demands of municipal politics condemned Jones perhaps even more than the jury. All citizens knew, of course, that Jones had been a veteran of the Texian War for Independence. Truthfully, that was one of the reasons his hanging attracted such numbers. How often did they have the chance to see a bona fide hero strung up? Yes, his war record was a matter of public record. What the good people of Houston did not then comprehend was that the gentry had demanded Jones's death, not despite his hero's status, but *because* of it.

The lovely islet of timber was empty again. Quick and Jones were dead and planted. Sepulchral silence replaced the clamor of the mob. Houstonians in their hundreds ambled back into town believing that the hangman had well and finally sealed the fate of the prisoners: that they had suffered all possible degradation.

But it had only begun.

Texian Macabre

xl

Escape
Goliad, Palm Sunday, March 27, 1836

During the Goliad Massacre, David James Jones sprints for his life. A soldado of the Tres Villas Battalion fires at the fleeing prisoner, but the English designers of the smoothbore Brown Bess musket never intended it for aimed fire. Still, it does not miss by much, its .75-caliber ball just avoiding Jones and, instead, clipping his haversack strap. Jones's scarecrow appearance is no worse than most of his companions. J. C. Logan, a fellow member of Samuel O. Pettus's company, wrote of pantaloons made of tent cloth, and the illustration depicts Jones sporting such trousers. A cloth mechanic's cap flies off his head. Inexpensive to manufacture and purchase, this type of headgear found favor among laborers and immigrants. A blanket rolled across his body provides some comfort against cold Texas nights, but it also offers a modicum of protection from the saber strokes of Mexican cavalrymen.

The praying Texian behind Jones's left shoulder is Harvey Cox, a member of Captain Jack Shackelford's Alabama Red Rovers. Dillard Cooper, a comrade, escaped the slaughter. In 1874, the fifty-nine-year-old veteran filed an affidavit on behalf of Cox's heirs. Cooper swore he recalled, "Harvey Cox just before the firing took place fell on his knees and commence[d] praying, and, this is the circumstance which leads [the] deponent to remember said Harvey Cox so distinctly." The Mexican soldiers shot Cox as he prayed.

In 1870, Mrs. Fannie A. D. Darden interviewed Cooper and preserved his recollections. The dreadful events of 1836 had clearly left deep emotional scars. Mrs. Darden testified "for several years after the massacre [Cooper] could not recount it without shedding tears."

1

The High Merit of Service
The Ordeal of David James Jones

David James Jones's trip to the gallows had been meandering and unlikely. He was not a natural felon. His instincts were generous, even heroic, as nineteenth-century Americans defined the term. He had abandoned the safety of hearth and home to help strangers win their freedom. Even in the United States, Jones would have read about the Mexican province of Texas, for it had long stimulated the national imagination. It was a neighboring land, lying just across the Sabine River from Louisiana, but at the same time, it seemed distant, forbidding, and strange. From 1800 to 1820, several expeditions of American filibusters had tried to wrest the territory away from Spain and all had dashed on the rocks of their ambition. Jones would have been aware that most of his countrymen who had ventured into Texas with rifles in hand had died the same way.[1]

Yet, he would have also known that those Americans who traveled to Texas as peaceful settlers had thrived. In 1821—the year that Mexicans secured their independence from Spain—Virginia-born Stephen Fuller Austin brought the first of his colonists to occupy lands along the lower Brazos River. Austin became the leading *empresario* (immigration agent) and carefully administered every detail of his colony's progress. The earliest immigrants struggled at first but by 1829 Austin could boast to his brother-in-law: "This is the most liberal and munificent Govt on earth to emigrants—after being here one year you will oppose a change even to Uncle Sam."[2]

Austin did not exaggerate. The Mexican government was so openhanded that American newcomers could hardly believe their good fortune. A typical family, if farmers, received one *labor* (177.1 acres) or, if they were stock raisers, a *sitio* (a square league or 4,428.4 acres). Consequently, few immigrants admitted to being sodbusters. These land-hungry *norteamericanos* may have never owned a horse or punched a steer, but once in Texas they became "ranchers." In return, the Mexican government required American settlers to convert to Catholicism (at least on paper), provide evidence of their good character (again, on paper), and improve their grants within two years (in theory). That was it. Yet, some ingrates whined about the twelve and a half cents an acre Austin charged as a surveying fee. Even so, most colonists understood how good they had it. After paying all administrative fees, a league and labor together ran about thirty-eight cents an acre. If the grantee did not have that kind of money in pocket, he could pay it over time. The Panic of 1819 had devastated many American frontier families and, with land in the United States selling for about a $1.25 an acre, Mexican Texas proved a godsend for poor folks looking for a way—and a place—to begin anew.[3]

Mexicans were also attempting a new beginning. They had only recently thrown off the shackles of Spanish colonialism after a long and bitter revolution. During the 1820s, Mexico was a country struggling to find its footing and establish its identity. In 1824, Mexicans drafted a national constitution. While it differed in particulars, it embraced the basic principles of the U.S. Constitution. American-Mexicans looked forward to a bright future in a sister republic. To buttress the association, some Mexican officials termed the two countries as the United States of the North and the United States of the South.[4]

When word spread in the "old states" about the opportunities Mexican Texas provided, hundreds flocked to get in on the deal—and then the problems began. Many American immigrants, contemptuous of Mexican laws, did not bother working through empresarios, but simply squatted where they pleased. General Manuel de Mier y Terán observed, "The first news of them comes by discovering them on land already under cultivation." In 1828, he conducted an inspection tour of the faraway province, and what he found alarmed him. Writing from Nacogdoches, he discerned "as one covers the distance from [San Antonio de] Bejar to this town, he will note that Mexican influence is proportionately diminished until on arriving in this place he will see that it is almost nothing." Moreover, the Anglo-Celtic colonists he encountered failed to impress him:

> The North Americans are haughty; they shun society by inclination and because they disdain it. They devote themselves both to industrial enterprises and to the hardest labors—as well as the grossest vices— with exceptional ardor. They do not think they have relaxed from their grueling tasks until drunkenness dulls their senses, and in that state they are fierce and scandalous.

He voiced his recommendation in the strongest possible terms: "Either the government occupies Texas now, or it is lost forever."[5]

Terán's report resulted in the Law of April 6, 1830, the first of many attempts by the Mexican government to limit Anglo-American immigration. The new law slackened the pace of immigration into Texas, but just barely. Mexican administrators were too few to enforce it; American immigrants were too many to heed it. In the face of this demographic tidal wave, many Mexican leaders became resentful and suspicious. "Where others send invading armies," Minister of Foreign Relations Lucas Alamán grumbled, "[Americans] send their colonists." There was no sinister plot hatched on the banks of the Potomac; the American government was simply not that resourceful. It was more a spontaneous current of people chasing their aspirations. Nevertheless, the result was much the same. Between 1830 and 1834, the number of American immigrants to Texas skyrocketed. Although many of these immigrants were undocumented, making a precise census impossible, by 1834 estimates placed the number of Anglo-Americans and their slaves at more than 20,700. Conversely, the population of native Mexicans (Tejanos) remained stagnant around 4,000. Alamán's apprehensions were completely justified: the *norteamericano* population in Texas doubled every four years.[6]

If that were not disruption enough, rival factions threatened to rip Mexico asunder. Two political parties grappled for control. The conservative *centralistas* sought to unite the nation behind an authoritarian central government. Their liberal rivals, the *federalistas*, reasoned that unless officials disseminated power among the states, the ruling elite would strangle the infant republic in its crib. Federalists, moreover, supported American immigration for the prosperity it engendered. Centralists opposed it. One did not have to be Machiavelli to determine which side best protected the settlers' interests. Austin and the majority of the American colonists favored the federalistas.[7]

In 1834 Antonio López de Santa Anna, a putative liberal, brokered a Faustian bargain with the centralists, emerged as a military dictator, and abolished the Constitution of 1824. In October 1835, a centralist congress dissolved state legislatures and reduced the states to military departments commanded by Santa Anna's handpicked cronies. When federalists resisted the centralist coup, Mexicans plunged into civil war.[8]

Even after Santa Anna overthrew the Constitution of 1824, American colonists remained remarkably indifferent. They had come to Texas to improve their lot, not to involve themselves in Mexican domestic squabbles. About those, they knew little and cared less. During the summer of 1835, a centralist force under Brigadier General Martín Perfecto de Cos arrived in Texas and finally captured the attention of the Anglo-Celtic colonists. Not until the centralists threatened their communities did they rally behind the federalists. Even Stephen F. Austin, who had always preached cooperation with the Mexican government, could not stomach the thugs who had hijacked it. He determined that the centralists had but one goal, to "destroy and break up the foreign settlements in Texas." There seemed but one conclusion: "Conciliatory measures with Genl. Cos and the military at Bexar are hopeless. WAR is our only resource—there is no other remedy but to defend our rights, our country and ourselves by force of arms."[9]

The American colonists soon had occasion to apply Austin's remedy. On October 2, 1835, conflict ignited at Gonzales when centralist forces demanded a cannon that federalist authorities had supplied the settlement years before. Instead, "Texians," as American colonists now styled themselves, deployed the ordnance to drive the centralist detachment off the field. By the end of October the "Army of the People" had marched on San Antonio, besieged the town, and bottled up Cos and his eight hundred-man force.[10]

Mexican centralists saw the source of the conflict in a different light. Acting President Miguel Barragán allowed only one cause for the war—gringo in gratitude:

To the Texas colonist, the word **MEXICAN** is, and has been, an execrable word. There has been no insult or violation that our countrymen have not suffered, included being jailed as "foreigners" in their own country.

The Texas colonies have been considered, for a long time, as general quarters for the enemies of the Nation; where all the bums and adventurers from the whole world have been gathered to revolt against the generous nation which has tolerated their insolence.

Soon, Texian officials would also have cause to bewail the hordes of "bums and adventurers" that plagued Texas.[11]

In the United States, newspapers followed the events in Texas with rapt interest. Many adventurous souls, however, were not content simply to read about them. No less a distinguished herald than Andrew Jackson's protégé and former Tennessee governor, Sam Houston, sounded the clarion. Its meaning was shrill and clear:

War in defence of our rights, our oaths, and our constitutions is inevitable in Texas.

If volunteers from the United States will join their brethren in this section, they will receive liberal bounties of land. We have millions of acres of our best lands unchosen and unappropriated.

Let each man come with a good rifle and one hundred rounds of ammunition,—and to come soon.

Our war cry is "LIBERTY OR DEATH!!" Our principals are to support the constitution, and down with the usurper!![12]

Men heard the call—and rallied to it. Like David James Jones, most U.S. volunteers were young, single, and, in equal measure, idealistic and opportunistic. Away from families and unburdened by regular jobs, they were more boisterous than the earlier Texian settlers. In the beginning, the old colonists welcomed these high-spirited immigrants. In November 1835, Governor Henry Smith praised their selflessness. "No sordid or mercenary considerations have induced them to leave their homes and share our fate," he prattled. That would have surprised Alabama Red Rover Abishai Dickson, who assured his wife, "I have some hopes of making a little fortune." Still, others did have altruistic intentions. "Permit me, through you, to volunteer my services in the present struggle of Texas without condition," James Butler Bonham wrote Sam Houston. "I shall receive nothing, either in the form of service pay, or lands, or rations." Nevertheless, as the war dragged on and volunteers became more assertive, some Texas politicians began to wonder if they had grabbed a wolf by the ears. Shortly after San Jacinto, ad interim President David G. Burnet questioned the wisdom of inundating "our country with an unprofitable tribe of needy adventurers." With the passage of time, the bonds between the Texas establishment and U.S. volunteers began to fray.[13]

David James Jones arrived in Texas in December 1835, but not in time to participate in the taking of Béxar. He joined the Auxiliary Volunteer Corps on December 21, probably in Nacogdoches. Members of that organization consisted of men who tendered their services "for and during the war." Jones seems to have fallen in with an ad hoc band of recruits headed for the front. His activities during the entire month of January 1836 remain cloudy. That month was a chaotic time for officials of the provisional government, who were embroiled in a bitter wrangle over the proposed Matamoros Expedition. Until they sorted out the mess, there was no point in the Nacogdoches recruits heading southward. No one knew exactly where the army would require soldiers, so the volunteers likely sat tight awaiting orders. By early February, however, Jones and his companions were on the road to San Felipe on the Brazos River. There, officers would assign them a duty post.[14]

By February 9, 1836, Jones had arrived in the frontier settlement of San Felipe, Stephen F. Austin's hometown and then the site of the provisional government of Texas. Here Jones first encountered one who would loom large in his future: Acting Governor James W. Robinson.[15]

Robinson, who carried some troubled personal baggage, found himself governor only by the strangest of circumstances. A native of Indiana, he was then forty-six years of age. As a young man, he practiced law in his home state and, in 1820, married Mary Isdell. Their union produced five children. Nevertheless, when Robinson moved to Arkansas in 1828, he ditched his wife and brood. Mrs. Robinson later secured a divorce on the grounds of abandonment. In Arkansas, Robinson had moved on, marrying Sarah Snider. They had one son.[16]

In January 1833, Robinson and his new family arrived in Texas. They settled in Nacogdoches, where Robinson made a favorable impression. Citizens of the Redlands community chose him as their delegate to the Consultation of 1835. Delegates of that body elected Robinson lieutenant governor of the provisional government. As a member of the General Council, he would participate in some truly disastrous decisions.[17]

Active from November 14, 1835, until March 1, 1836, the provisional government failed to provide unified leadership when Texas desperately needed it. From the beginning, factionalism directed its proceedings. Henry Smith, an independence advocate, served as governor, assisted by Robinson, his lieutenant governor. The General Council consisted of one representative from each municipality and acted in an advisory capacity. This arrangement was doomed to failure. Most members of the council were moderates who opposed an immediate declaration of independence, arguing that such a move would alienate Mexican federalists. Smith did not give a two-penny damn about Mexicans of any stripe, and the council's temperate stance did not endear it to the zealous governor. To exacerbate tension, no one had bothered to define the governor's powers, and Smith was not shy about assuming them whenever convenient. Naturally contentious, Smith wielded his veto power like a club, but by December the council unceremoniously overrode him and rejected his appointments. Increasingly, Smith found himself without friends, support, or any real power.[18]

The biggest cause of disagreement was the Matamoros Expedition. This was a quixotic scheme to mount an offensive against the Mexican town on the far bank of the Rio Grande. How the government would supply a Texian army at such distance was not an issue of concern. Although Smith and the council favored the broad notion, they could not agree on a commander. General Sam Houston was a Smith crony, but believed (correctly) that the council would not support him. Houston offered

Henry Smith was not as pleasant in person as he looks in this portrait. As ad interim governor of Texas in 1835–1836, his venomous tongue and his unwillingness to negotiate provoked discord with the council, brought about his impeachment, and contributed to the military disasters at the Alamo and Goliad. He, nevertheless, served in President Houston's first administration as secretary of the treasury. Yet, Smith failed to balance the Republic's budget or bestow value to its near worthless currency. Infected with Gold Fever, he died in a California mining camp in 1851. *Courtesy Texas State Library and Archives Commission.*

command to James Bowie, who refused it. The council appointed Francis W. Johnson, who first rode to San Felipe seeking sanction for the expedition. Once receiving an ironclad endorsement, he began to have second thoughts. While Johnson dithered, council members tapped James W. Fannin to command, but he was unable to attract a sufficient number of volunteers. Houston and Johnson again offered their services, seeking the consent of both Governor Smith and the council. Yet, like a recurring nightmare, neither prospective leader could recruit enough men. Dismayed with the backbiting and ineptitude, Houston withdrew his name from consideration and accepted an appointment as commissioner to the Cherokees. Smith and the council were at loggerheads. Soldiers in the field awaited instructions from officials who appeared incapable of making any decision. Johnson camped at San Patricio with some one hundred volunteers, while Fannin took up winter quarters at Refugio.[19]

On January 6, 1836, Houston informed Smith that Johnson, before retiring to San Patricio, had stripped the Béxar garrison of supplies. In Houston's opinion, gallant soldiers had suffered depredations at the hands of one who was little better than a bandit chief:

> The brave men who have been wounded in the battles of Texas, and the sick from exposure in her cause, without blankets or supplies, are left neglected in her hospitals; while the needful stores and supplies are diverted from them, without authority by self-created officers, who do not acknowledge the only government known to Texas and the world.[20]

Smith erupted like Vesuvius. On January 9, allowing his rhetoric to run away with him, his anger flowed over the council like lava:

> Look around upon your flock, your discernment will easily detect the scoundrels. The complaint; contraction of the eyes; the gape of the mouth; the vacant stare; the hung head; the restless fidgety disposition; the sneaking sycophantic look; a natural meanness of countenance; an unguarded shrug of the shoulders; a sympathetic tickling and contraction of the muscles of the neck anticipating the rope; a restless uneasiness to adjourn, dreading to face the storm [they] themselves have raised.

This was but a prelude to the substance of his tirade. "I consider as the devisers of ways and means," Smith explained, "you have done all contemplated by the organic law. That your services are now no longer needed, until the convention meets; I will continue to discharge my duties as Commander-in-Chief of the army and navy, and see that the laws are executed."[21]

Smith had thrown down the gauntlet—and the council took it up. Two days later, members issued a proclamation to the "People of Texas." In it, they reviewed their rancorous relationship with Governor Smith. They complained that Smith, who had consistently demonstrated "stubbornness and perverseness," had also unleashed the "vilest and most uncouth anathema, couched in the most vulgarly abusive language." The governor was, they concluded, nothing more than a two-bit tyrant who had attempted to usurp the peoples' power. Referencing Smith's meltdown, the offended officials posed a series of rhetorical questions:

> By what sort of delusion could he have been so blindly actuated, as to put forth a document so degrading to himself, so mortifying to

his countrymen and disgraceful to the office he holds! Could his success in imposing himself upon the people as their Governor, encourage him to attempt the assumption of all the power, authority and dominion he now claims? Heaven forgive his delusion! And may he learn from this act, that a gallant people, engaged in a perilous contest for right, with a foreign foe, cannot be thus gulled and cheated of their liberties at home, under the immediate superintendence of their agents.

Council members asserted that his actions left them but one option; "they have preferred charges of impeachment against Governor Smith, for the manifest injuries and difficulties he has endeavored to bring upon his country; that country which raised him to the high and responsible station of her Governor. Yes, the council met the occasion firmly." Governor Smith fired the council; the council fired him right back.[22]

Conditions then became genuinely confusing. The council declared Smith's lieutenant governor, James W. Robinson, to be "acting" governor. Moreover, military commanders in the field, agents in the United States, and, henceforth, all Texas officials would report to him. On January 18, Smith dispatched a pathetic letter to Robinson in which he declared the "Council did not make, nor can they break me; nor can you, with all the plastic power of your council chamber, upon what you may vainly conceive to be my ruin. You, as a legal and sensible man, ought to know better." For all his bluster, Smith was whistling past the graveyard. Still, he continued to insist that he was the true governor and refused to hand over the archives. For its part, the General Council ignored Smith and continued to meet sporadically. Texians were not certain who possessed the legal authority and few seemed to care. They had always done much as they pleased anyhow.[23]

Newcomers to Texas and its muddled politics, Jones and his companions had no way of knowing what they were getting into. They reported to the Council Hall in San Felipe, where the chair of the Advisory Committee, Don Carlos Barrett, greeted them. The volunteers must have been a sorry-looking lot because Barrett recommended to acting president Robinson that officers arm and outfit them from the "public stores":

Council Hall, San Felipe

February 9th 1836

To the Acting Govr

The advisory committee, are of opinion that ten volunteers, whose names are herewith, should be furnished with the enclosed articles, to be receipted for by the Commander, Saml Sprague,—and that they be ordered to Copano, there to report to the commanding officer, for orders to join the Matamoras expedition—and that they be furnished with an order to the com[man]d[an]t at Goliad, & all other places, where public stores are kept, to be furnished with the necessary & proper supplies in the usual measure & form—

D. C. Barrett, *Chn*

J. D. Clements

Alexr Thomson

G. A. Pattillo

Approved Feb 9, 1836

James W. Robinson

Acting Governor[24]

14 THE HIGH MERIT OF SERVICE

The following statement accompanied Barrett's letter:

> We the undersigned do agree to proceed on to the Army of Texas under the direcktions of the Governor & Council. Samuel Sprague has bin releckted to head the company whose names are attached to this Paper. Samuel Sprague, Daniel Murphey, John W. Thomson, Nathaniel Hazen, Charles Linley, R. K. Petty, G. F. Pittman, C. S. Hardwicke, David J. Jones, A. B. Hannan.[25]

Thus, Sprague's squad made its way toward Copano Bay. It is unlikely that they ever reached that destination, however, for events were unfolding that altered the Texians' strategic initiatives. On February 4 and 5, Fannin had transferred the companies under his command to Refugio to better facilitate his movements toward Matamoros. On February 7, Tejano federalist Plácido Benavides galloped into Refugio with intelligence that Santa Anna had arrived on the Rio Grande and was poised to drive into Texas and attack Béxar and Goliad simultaneously. This news, of course, quashed all the Matamoros schemes, and Fannin began to scramble. He dispatched Captain William G. Cooke with two companies to reinforce the Irish settlement of San Patricio and removed his own headquarters to the Presidio La Bahía at Goliad. He left Captain Amon B. King with a small garrison at Refugio. He also placed John Chenoweth and a few mounted scouts to guard the vital port at Copano. On February 12, Captain John Shackelford and his Alabama Red Rovers joined Fannin at the presidio, which the rebels renamed Fort Defiance. On February 16, Mexican Generalissimo Antonio López de Santa Anna crossed the Rio Grande and drove the bulk of his army toward San Antonio de Béxar along Camino Real. The following day, Brigadier General José Urrea forded down river at Matamoros at the head of five hundred infantry and cavalry. Barreling up Atascosito Road, his mission was to retake Goliad. David James Jones and his companions had no way of knowing it, but they were marching into a maelstrom.

Acting Lieutenant Sprague's squad arrived in Goliad on or about February 20; they were certainly present by the 24th. The squad did not remain intact as Colonel Fannin dispersed it among previously existing units in need of reinforcements. Charles Linley, for example, fell in with Captain David N. Burke's Company of Mobile Grays. One surmises that Samuel Sprague lost his acting commission and returned to the ranks upon his arrival at Fort Defiance. His name and those of G. F. Pittman and C. S. Hardwicke fail to appear on any company roster and may have remained unattached to any particular unit. The muster rolls later compiled by surviving Texian surgeon, Joseph Henry Barnard, and the *Telegraph and Texas Register* specifically list Daniel Murphy, Nathaniel Hazen, and Rufus R. Petty—as it turned out his name was actually Jetty —as "unattached."[26]

The most intriguing case is that of John W. Thomson, who may have abandoned Sprague's squad to join his friend David Crockett at Béxar. His name appears on the list of the Alamo slain, but the evidence for that assertion is flimsy. He might just as easily have remained with Sprague's squad and died later at Goliad. As the foremost authority of the Goliad garrison Harbert Davenport concluded: "There is no certain proof." All this confusion suggests the disorganized state of Fannin's Goliad command.[27]

Fortunately, the disposition of David James Jones is more certain. Once in Goliad, he joined Major Benjamin C. Wallace's Second (or La Fayette) Battalion as a member of a battle-tested unit, the "San Antonio Greys." Led by William G. Cooke, the unit was one of two companies that constituted the New Orleans Greys, organized in the Crescent City on the evening of

The northwest bastion of the Presidio La Bahía (Fort Defiance) as it appears today. In the background is the fort's chapel, where the Mexicans confined David James Jones and the other Texian prisoners before the Goliad Massacre. *Photograph by Deborah Bloys Hardin. Author's Collection.*

October 13, 1835. Cooke's company had so distinguished itself in the bitter street fighting during the December assault on Béxar that its members began to style themselves as the San Antonio Greys. By February 1836, the company prepared to march on Matamoros. On February 15, Captain Cooke resigned as company commander and departed on a special assignment to the Washington Independence Convention. There he received an appointment on General Houston's staff. As the coming weeks demonstrated, his timing had been impeccable. Following Cooke's departure, Fannin consolidated the San Antonio Greys with Captain John E. Grace's fifteen-man company.

This reconstituted company required a new commander. On the same day that Captain Cooke resigned, the men elected Virginian Samuel O.

Pettus to take his place. Pettus was the kind of born leader much esteemed by Jacksonians. He had joined the New Orleans Greys on October 22, 1835, as a private in Cooke's company and later participated in the siege and storming of Béxar. His courageous conduct so impressed his comrades that they elected him first lieutenant of Cooke's Company on New Year's Day, 1836. Thus, when Cooke resigned, the men viewed Pettus as his natural replacement. That Pettus had no formal military training did not bother them in the least. Captain Grace, living up to his name, generously accepted demotion and served as the company's first lieutenant. Since there were so many new faces in company, Jones probably did not feel as much the new guy as he might have otherwise.[28]

Jones arrived in Goliad without a weapon, without a uniform, and without knowledge of the muddle into which he was sinking. Back in San Felipe, D. C. Barrett had recommended that the military officials outfit Jones and his companions from public stores. Conditions were, however, actually worse at Goliad. On February 24, J. C. Logan, another member of Pettus's company, described the hardships his unit had endured:

> Our Company has just returned to this [post] from San Patricio on the fronteer of Texas & in a few days [we] are Going to march to Bexar[.] [W]e have seen some Hard times in the country[.] [F]or the last 2 Month[s] we have ben living Entirely on beef & We are all most naked as we are cutting Up tent cloth to make us Panteloons & Every man is his own Taylor in this Army & a good many of us are bare footed & worst of all the Schooner that was bringing provision & clothes has been wrecked[.] She was from New Orleans & bound to Copeno & we all undergo fatigue that we would not do if [we] wer in the U.S. & all for the chance of triping a few mexicans.

If Jones reached Goliad looking like a scarecrow, once there he likely preserved his ragamuffin appearance. Yet, as most other volunteers were as tatty, he had no reason to feel conspicuous.[29]

Notwithstanding the privation they had suffered, Jones's messmates placed tremendous confidence in Captain Pettus, but the private soon heard whispers concerning Colonel Fannin. Camp gossip claimed that he was cracking under the strain of command. Having jockeyed, plotted, and connived for a field command, he found himself wholly unsuited for it. On February 21, Fannin entreated Robinson, "I hope you will soon release me from the army, at least as an officer." The following day, he wrote Robinson with a final appeal. "I am a better judge of my military abilities than others," Fannin lamented, "and if I am qualified to command an Army, I have not found it out." Such an outlook must have inspired enormous confidence in Jones and the rest of the garrison.[30]

But the time for whining had passed. Jones learned that on February 23, Santa Anna had arrived in Béxar and opened the siege of the Alamo. Co-commanders William Barret Travis and James Bowie dispatched a letter that pressured Fannin even more. "In this extremity, we hope you will send us all the men you can spare promptly," they pleaded. "We have but little provisions, but enough to serve us til you and your men arrive." Bowie and Travis, knowing Fannin's nature, concluded with words that seemed to question his honor—or, perhaps, merely his resolve: "We deem it unnecessary to repeat to a brave officer, who knows his duty, that we call on him for assistance." His volunteers begged Fannin to rush to the aid of their comrades in Béxar, but Robinson and the council had been unequivocal. Fannin was to hold Goliad. The situation required a swift decision and a steely resolve, but confronted by events, Fannin did what he did best. He vacillated.[31]

West Point dropout, failed planter, and successful slave trader, James Walker Fannin, Jr. was wholly out of his depth as a field commander. His indecisiveness was in large measure responsible for the Texian defeat at Coleto Creek. Knowing that most of his command had already preceded him in death, he was the final victim of the Goliad Massacre. *Courtesy of the Dallas Historical Society.*

His adversary, Brigadier General José Urrea, seemed not to know the meaning of that word. The general's scouts had told him that rebel commanders Francis Johnson and James Grant had taken position in the village of San Patricio. Urrea drove northward to the Nueces River to strike before the Texians could shake off their listlessness. Urrea led 320 infantry, 230 dragoons, and a 4-pound field piece. He left behind about 200 soldados in Matamoros. They could follow later, but now speed was critical and he could travel faster with fewer men.[32]

Oblivious of Urrea's approach, Grant and a mounted detachment had left Johnson with his garrison in San Patricio. At 3:00 A.M. on February 27, Urrea launched his attack behind a bucketing rainstorm. The centralists fell upon Johnson's men with such swiftness and surprise that the Texians never had an opportunity to rally. Dawn revealed that Urrea had taken the town, killed twenty rebels, and captured another thirty-two. Only eight, including Colonel Johnson, had escaped. Urrea lost one man killed and four wounded.[33]

20   THE HIGH MERIT OF SERVICE

In San Patricio, Urrea learned that Grant's detachment was approaching the town. He led eighty dragoons to a mott about twenty-five miles southwest of the captured settlement. Urrea understood that Grant and his men must ride through the coppice called Los Cuates de Agua Dulce. "I divided my force into six groups," Urrea later recorded, "and hid them in the woods."[34]

On the morning of March 2, Grant and his party rode into Urrea's trap. The action unfolded as if the centralist general had scripted it himself. Indeed, his diary entry seemed almost apathetic:

> Between ten and eleven in the morning, Dr. Grant arrived. He was attacked and vanquished by the parties under my command and that of Colonel Francisco Garray. Dr. Grant and forty of the riflemen were left dead on the field and we took six prisoners besides their arms, munitions, and horses.

Among the rebels who escaped was Plácido Benavides, who rode hell-for-leather to Goliad to inform Fannin of Urrea's victory.[35]

While Dr. Grant lay dying on a lonely South Texas prairie, delegates at the Town of Washington were declaring Texas a free and sovereign republic. On March 4, the politicians reached a decision that Jones and the other hapless members of Fannin's Goliad garrison considered of even greater import. The convention appointed Sam Houston commander-in-chief of all Texian forces under arms. For the first time, the rebel army experienced true unity of command. At last, Fannin might benefit from supervision.[36]

Jones and the others soon realized that Fannin was having trouble reaching any decision. On February 26, the colonel had bowed to the demands of his men and led 320 men and four cannon to relieve the Alamo garrison. Still in sight of Fort Defiance, a wheel came off a supply wagon. About the time the men repaired the first wagon, two more wagons fell apart. The oxen were too weak to haul the heavy artillery. Then a blue-tailed norther blew through, freezing man and beast. As the sun sank, Fannin properly concluded that his men could not march in the dark, so he ordered them back to the warmth of their barracks. Disgusted soldiers returned to the fort, but Fannin did his best to maintain morale. He cheerfully declared that they would make a fresh start on the dawn.[37]

Yet, the new day brought only additional obstacles. The oxen had wandered off during the night. Fannin dispatched riders to round them up, but it was noon before they returned with the wayfaring animals. Disconsolate, Fannin called a council of war. During the meeting, a courier arrived with news that Urrea had wiped out Johnson's command. The assembled officers, sobered by that intelligence, decided to remain in Goliad and defend their fort. The Alamo garrison would have to fend for itself. Fannin, who had questioned the wisdom of a relief effort, was palpably relieved.[38]

Fannin's stock was rapidly falling with the men, who daily witnessed demonstrations of his indecisiveness. J. G. Ferguson, an Alabama Red Rover, described his disdain in a letter to his brother: "Our number of men consists of about 400, all of which are volunteers from the States, with the exception of 30 regulars. Our commander is Col. Fannin, and I am sorry to say, the majority of the soldiers do not like him, for what cause I do not know, without it is because they think he has not the interest of the country at heart, or that he wishes to become great without taking the proper steps to attain greatness." Captain Burr H. Duval observed, "much dissention prevails among the Volunteers[.] Col. Fannin, now in command (Genl. Houston being absent), is unpopular—and nothing but the certainty of hard fighting, and that shortly, could have kept us together so long."[39]

Fannin understood that a retreat was inevitable and began to consolidate his forces. On March 11, he dispatched Captain Amon B. King's company to evacuate stranded Irish families in Refugio. Fannin's orders emphasized the need for speedy action. Instead of quickly removing the families, King took it upon himself to terrorize local centralist *rancheros*. Whilst doing so, he and his men stumbled onto one of Urrea's advance cavalry detachments. The Mexican horsemen withdrew following a brief skirmish. King could have grasped the opportunity to retire to Goliad with the noncombatants. He dispatched a courier to Fannin requesting reinforcements. Fannin foolishly hastened William Ward's Georgia Battalion to assist King: the first in a series of appalling command decisions.[40]

Advancing on Refugio, Urrea subsequently encountered, killed, or captured not only King's company, but also Ward's Georgia Battalion. Instead of consolidating his forces, Fannin had flung them out for Urrea to defeat piecemeal. Ensconced in Goliad, Fannin had no way of knowing the fate of King and Ward's units and impatiently awaited their return.[41]

On March 13 or 14, the Goliad commander received orders that relieved him of the burden of making a command decision. Letters from the newly appointed Commander-in-Chief Sam Houston had arrived. Dispatched from Gonzales, they informed Fannin that the Alamo had fallen and Travis, Bowie, and all their men lay dead. Houston instructed Fannin to immediately abandon Fort Defiance and retire to Victoria on the Guadalupe River. The general insisted that Fannin act "as soon as practicable." Seemingly doubting Fannin's ability to grasp the need for alacrity, Houston repeated his directive in the strongest possible terms:

"The immediate advance of the enemy may be confidently expected, as well as a rise of water. Prompt movements are therefore highly important." Notwithstanding Houston's orders, Fannin felt compelled to remain at Goliad until King and Ward in Refugio returned to the fold. It would be a long wait.[42]

On March 17, Fannin, Jones, and the other members of the Goliad garrison learned the fate of King and Ward. Instead of retreating immediately, Fannin spent all of March 18 preparing to retreat. He insisted on hauling nine cannon and about five hundred spare muskets. Lacking sufficient draft horses, the garrison relied on oxen to haul baggage and artillery.[43]

On March 19, Fannin finally began to retreat toward Victoria. Even then, it was at a snail's pace. Jones fell in with Captain Pettus's company and made ready to hike the twenty-six miles to Victoria. But the oxen were unruly, and before they had traveled four miles, they stubbornly stopped to graze. Texian teamsters could only curse and wait. Then a howitzer broke down, costing more valuable time. The column had traveled only six miles when Fannin ordered a halt. Captain Jack Shackelford of the Alabama Red Rovers "remonstrated warmly," but Fannin laughed off his fears. He reassured the captain that Mexicans would never dare attack a force of more than four hundred Texians.[44]

General Urrea was about to justify Shackelford's concerns. Following the fall of the Alamo, Santa Anna had dispatched elements of the Morales and San Luis battalions to Urrea. On March 18, those troops joined Urrea on the outskirts of Goliad. These reinforcements increased Urrea's force to at least 1,400 soldados—a figure that did not include the some 200 Tejano rancheros that had flocked to his banner. Urrea now had numerical superiority, momentum, and the element of surprise. It was time to spring his trap.[45]

Meanwhile, Jones and the other members of the Goliad garrison resumed the march after an hour's rest. They had proceeded only a few miles when they observed a large force of centralist cavalry emerging from the timber two miles behind. Even then, Fannin insisted that the Mexican horsemen could do nothing but harass the Texian retreat. Since his own cavalry had galloped off toward Victoria, Fannin placed two gun crews to the rear with orders to delay the centralist cavalry until his infantry could reach Coleto Creek, some two miles ahead. Captains James Holland and Stephen Hurst unlimbered and loaded their guns as the bulk of Fannin's column plodded forward. While Jones and the others directed their attention to the enemy cavalrymen advancing on their rear, other units appeared to the north and west.[46]

The rebel gunners tried to buy their comrades some time. "The effect of our artillery fire was immediate and horrible," New Orleans Grey Hermann Ehrenberg recalled. "Many of the Mexicans were thrown off their saddles, and their riderless horses galloped aimlessly across the field, while wounded men and beast lying prostrate in the dust were trampled upon by the advancing or retreating cavalry squadrons. The confusion which ensued checked the enemy's onset to some extent, and the short respite enabled us to resume our march."[47]

But not for long. Fannin recalled his guns and advanced toward a stand of timber about a mile to the northeast. Urrea's cavalry beat him to it. Seeing that the enemy had taken possession of the cover he sought, Fannin cast about for any advantage the terrain might offer—and found it. Some five hundred yards to his front he detected a suggestion of a rise that might provide some benefit on the utterly flat ground. He shouted for his men to make a dash for the slight elevation. As they did so, however, an ammunition wagon broke down. Fannin would not abandon his ammo

and directed his men to rally around their disabled wagon. This was the nightmare scenario for the Texians: caught in the open without cover and surrounded by Mexican lancers.[48]

Fannin shouted to his company commanders to form square. Captain Pettus echoed the order and Jones and his companions formed ranks at right angles in a defensive box to protect the wagons and the draft animals. Fannin placed his cannon on each corner, as the Mexican cavalrymen swirled around the Texians. Having pinned down Fannin's command, Urrea ordered the Mexican infantry forward. He gave his *cazadores*, light infantrymen armed with Baker rifles, specific targets: the draft animals. Urrea had Fannin and his rebels exactly where he wanted them, and without oxen to haul their wagons, there the Texians would remain. Once Mexican snipers dropped the oxen, they shifted their sights to the rebel artillerymen and then the officers. Fannin went down as a ball lodged in his thigh, but he was soon on his feet, shouting orders. James Walker Fannin, Jr., was no Napoleon, but neither was he a coward.[49]

Repeatedly loading and firing their muskets, Jones and his fellow rebels fought with a valor born of desperation. While they displayed an abundance of courage, they lacked almost everything else. Gunners ran short of water to swab their cannon. Expecting to arrive in Victoria by nightfall, the garrison had packed little food. To add to their desperate situation, their tactical position was the worst imaginable. By nightfall, the "cowardly" Mexicans had fought them to a standstill, killing nine Texians and wounding another fifty-one.[50]

Jones and the other rebels knew that the enemy had them surrounded. The blast of bugles and the derisive catcalls of enemy soldados concealed in the inky darkness confirmed their tactical dilemma. That night Fannin, Pettus, and the other company commanders took stock of their situation. In the gloom, the garrison might be able to cut its way through to the timber along the banks of Coleto Creek, but that meant abandoning the wounded. The enlisted men refused that option. As if to douse any flicker of hope, pouring rains ruined remaining stocks of gunpowder. The men constructed an effective, if gruesome, barricade. "We took the dead mules and horses," Able Morgan recounted, "and laid round and made breast works by ditching and throwing dirt on them. Even our knapsacks were piled on to help, and some trunks." Fannin had his men dig shallow trenches around the square. Scraping sod at least kept the men warm as they toiled through the night.[51]

Dawn on March 20 revealed even more clearly the bleakness of their position. During the night the rest of Urrea's troops had arrived on the field. He recorded, "One hundred infantry, two-four-pounders, and a howitzer were added to my force." Armed with a howitzer, Urrea could stand well beyond rifle range and pound the Texians to oblivion. If the Texians broke and ran, the Mexicans lancers stood ready. Had the two commanders been playing chess, Urrea would have shouted, "checkmate."[52]

Fannin hobbled forward under a white flag to discuss terms. General Urrea made it clear that any surrender would be unconditional. Fannin returned to the square to confer with his officers. He assured his men that he had received the best possible terms. Under such doleful circumstances, he was doubtless correct. David James Jones and the rest of Fannin's command laid down their arms.[53]

The Mexicans marched Jones and the other able-bodied Texian prisoners back to the Presidio La Bahía; few of its former inhabitants would have now had the heart to call it Fort Defiance. They left the wounded on the field under the care of the Texian surgeons. Dr. Barnard recorded that Captain Francis J. Desanque, Captain Hugh McDonald Frazer, and Captain Pettus stayed behind to help him with the wounded. He also mentioned "two or three other men who had been left with me on the ground." Since Jones served under Pettus, there is a possibility that he may have been one of those that lingered to assist Barnard.[54]

Barnard and his assistants finally arrived back at the fort on March 22. "It was late when we reached the fort," he recorded in his diary, "and we were sent into the church, where we found all the prisoners were placed,

28   THE HIGH MERIT OF SERVICE

and crowded up in a very uncomfortable manner, and strictly and strongly guarded." John Crittenden Duval, a member of the company commanded by his older brother Burr H. Duval recalled, "We were so crowded we had hardly room to lie down at night." Not only did Jones and the other Texian prisoners feel cramped, but they were also starving. Duval reported that their Mexican captors had reduced the rebels' rations to "five ounces of fresh beef a day, which we had to cook in the best way we could and eat without salt." Some captives were so ravenous that they ate their meat raw. Jones and his fellow prisoners endured such conditions for a week.[55]

On March 27, conditions seemed to improve when Mexican soldados released their prisoners from confinement. Mexican officers lifted the prisoner's spirits further when they told the Texians to gather wood or round up cattle. They even told some prisoners that a ship awaited them on the coast to transport them to the United States. "This, you may be sure, was joyful news to us," John C. Duval asserted, "and we lost no time in making preparations to leave our uncomfortable quarters. When all was ready we were formed into three divisions and marched out under a strong guard. As we passed by some Mexican women who were standing near the main entrance to the fort, I heard them say 'pobrecitos' (poor fellows), but the incident at the time made but little impression on my mind."[56]

What the women meant soon revealed itself with all the force of unbridled barbarity. Singing as they marched, the captives set out in different directions. When the columns reached a point some half a mile from the fort, their sentries ordered them to halt. Then, on signal, the Mexican infantrymen methodically gunned down the unarmed Texians. "They were within three or four feet of us when they fired," Charles B. Shain recounted. Most of the astonished prisoners fell under the first volley. Among the dead was Abishai M. Dickson, who had earlier written his wife that he had "some hopes of making a little fortune." Fired at point-blank range, a .753-caliber musket ball dashed all of his hopes. Centralist lancers cut off those who avoided the repeated fusillades, while infantrymen finished off the wounded with bayonets and butcher knives. Amidst the mayhem, twenty-eight fugitives escaped into the brush or into the San Antonio River.[57]

One of them was David James Jones.

Carnage
Goliad, June 3, 1836

Following the Goliad Massacre, Mexican soldiers tried to destroy the evidence of their handiwork. The pyres smoldered but refused to ignite properly, producing stacks of charred corpses. Stymied, soldados dumped the bodies in a shallow trench and haphazardly covered them with dirt. Attracted by the smell, roving dogs and coyotes located the mass grave, unearthed the cadavers, and ate their fill. On June 3, 1836, Texian soldiers reached the spot and encountered the gnawed, rotting remains of their slaughtered comrades.

General Thomas Jefferson Rusk and Private David James Jones survey the carnage. The general brings his handkerchief to his nose to hamper the tang of decomposing flesh. Jones reflects upon the twisted circumstances that spared him the fate of his messmates. Rusk issues orders for a formal military funeral to take place the following day.

In an effort to carry out these orders, Texian soldiers collect the bones—and body parts that are not yet bones. Overcome by emotion and the stench, one man falls to his knees and surrenders the contents of his stomach. To Rusk's left, the kneeling Texian recognizes a thing that was once his kinsman. Texians in the background remove the bodies, some of which fall apart in their hands. Bandannas cover noses to defend against the stink of putrefaction.

The presence of men fails to deter nature's scavengers. Overhead, a kettle of turkey vultures relishes the carrion-rich environment. In the putrid trench, a cur more daring—or perhaps simply hungrier—than others in his pack, chews the shriveled arm of a partially buried victim of Santa Anna's callous brutality.

2

A Remnant of That Noble Band

Flight and Fight

ineteenth-century commanders called it the "fog of battle," the pea soup of black-powder smoke. After continuous fire, a soldier could barely see the men standing next to him, much less the enemy down field. On March 27, 1836, David James Jones may have employed the cover of this "fog" to sprint out of range and conceal himself. May have, but one cannot know. That is the most frustrating element of his story. Almost every Goliad survivor later left an account of his experience, narratives that formed the basis of future knowledge. Yet, when Jones tipped off that horse cart in Houston two years later, all he knew, all he could have shared, was lost. And each of us is poorer for it.[1]

History remembers the slaughter of the Texian prisoners as the Goliad Massacre. One man bears the blame for this outrage, Antonio López de Santa Anna. He could have employed discretion, but chose not to. He would have done better to dump the defeated and demoralized volunteers on U.S. shores. Their stories of Mexican clemency and Texian neglect might have dissuaded others from volunteering. The Mexican commander could have gained the moral high ground; instead, the world came to view him

American illustrator Norman Price's pen-and-ink sketch of the Goliad Massacre captures accurately the disbelief of the Texian prisoners as their Mexican guards fire a volley into them. The captives believed that they were being marched to the coast where they would board ships bound for the United States. Some 342 fell victim to Santa Anna's barbarous order. *Courtesy of Texas State Library and Archives Commission.*

as a bloodthirsty butcher. As one European diplomat rebuked, "great and lasting disgrace must fall upon the nation under whose flag such atrocities have been committed."[2]

Of the forty-one men in Pettus's company, six escaped the massacre. The soldados of the Yucatán and Tres Villas battalions, who carried out Santa Anna's order, took no pleasure in their assignment. They were horrified that he demanded that they perform this ghastly deed on a holy day—Palm Sunday. Consequently, one suspects that they did not pursue the escapees with the murderous fervor that their generalissimo might have wished.[3]

While Jones died without leaving his account, his story mirrors that of Kentucky survivor, Charles B. Shain. When the soldados opened fire,

Shain darted toward the San Antonio River, plunged in, and swam to the opposite bank. In the process, he lost both of his shoes. "[Daniel] Murphy and myself met as soon as we crossed [the river]," Shain later reported. The two fugitives hid in the bushes until the Mexicans ceased firing, a duration of two and a half hours. Later, the pair made their way to a clump of timber where they found another escapee, John Williams, up a tree. The three men concealed themselves throughout the night. The following day, they traveled northeastward until the sky became so cloudy they could no longer determine directions. Consequently, they rested along Coleto Creek until morning. Now barefooted, Shain's every step became a form of torture. Shain, Murphy, and Williams trudged through the next day and night, although, "it was so cloudy we knew not which way we were traveling." During the course of that overcast day, the trio came across two more fugitives: "On that day we fell in with two more of our companions, one of whom belonged to the first, and *the other to the second division*" [emphasis added].[4]

One wishes, of course, that Shain had recorded the names of "our companions." Even so, he provided an illuminating detail: one of them belonged to the second division. Recall that Jones was a member of Pettus's Company, which was part of Major Benjamin C. Wallace's *Second Battalion*. Since Jones later arrived in camp with Shain's group and was also a member of the "second division," it is almost certain that he was the fellow who joined Shain's party on March 29.

Shain's account, while no literary tour de force, is nonetheless, remarkably rich in detail. It recounts many narrow escapes and provides the level of immediacy that only a personal account can. He described one uncomfortable circumstance as six Mexicans pursued his party along the west bank of the Guadalupe River. "We thought we would hide in the bushes, but we found a very large Panther in the bushes. The Mexicans in

A REMNANT OF THAT NOBLE BAND

our rear, a large river before us, a Panther in the bushes. Of the three dangers we took to the river and all got over safely and hid in the bushes on the other side until night." Eating turtles and hogs that they found along their path, the escapees reached the Lavaca River where they were taken in by a Texian settler.[5]

Shain, Jones, and the others had endured the most treacherous part of their journey, but many hazards still lay ahead. In abandoned cabins along the Lavaca River, the fugitives ate their fill and rested four days. "The people," Shain later described, "had left all their chickens which we killed and ate." The men continued their northward trek, alert for Mexican patrols. "We traveled two days from the Labaca before we got to the San Felipe and Gonzales road. The road looked very much like an army had a few days before, passed along there. We had not traveled very far before we saw two men on horseback coming toward us. We dodged out to one side of the road until they passed. We found them to be Mexican spies."[6]

Near the Colorado River, the survivors encountered a German settler who knew even less than they did about the progress of the war. Shain's wrote:

> Before reaching the river, we met an old Dutchman, and brought him along with us. He was going directly towards the Mexican army. We told him of the butchery of all of Colonel Fannin's men, but he could not understand it. He said that he had heard there was to be war six months ago, but had never heard any more about it. He said all his neighbors had removed, and he was afraid of the Indians. When we got to the Colorado river, Murphy, Kemp, and myself, swam the river, and went to Lacy's four miles distance to kill a hog while the others made a raft to get the Dutchman across the river.[7]

Once across the Colorado River, the escapees again ran into elements of the Mexican army. Shain recounted the circumstances:

We had not traveled far when we saw about 600 Mexican soldiers: we then got into the woods about half a mile off and staid there until night. That night we came upon the Mexicans encamped on the San Bayard [San Bernard] river, and went up that river about five miles before we could get across on account of quicksand. We got in the road again and had come within four or five miles of San Felipe, when we came on a Mexican picket guard lying asleep in the road. We left the road without disturbing him, and went out in the prairie about two miles from where we had seen the picket. It being very cloudy we could not travel so concluded to lie down in the prairie until the moon rose, but we went to sleep and did not wake till sunrise. Then we had about five miles to travel before we could get into the woods on the Brazos river. In doing this we went in sight of the Mexicans at San Felipe, who were sounding their bugles, beating their drums, and firing their cannon. We went through the timber on the Brazos to the river, which one of our company said he could not swim. We then went into the prairie along the edge of the woods which were too thick for us to pass through.[8]

Jones and the others resolved to slog to the Town of Washington, ford the Brazos River there, and attempt to discover the location of the Texian army. To reach Washington, however, they had to swim flooded Mill Creek. Still dripping, they reached the public house operated by John Cummings. There, Jones and the other refugees could have met John's sister, Rebecca Cummings, who had been engaged to William Barret Travis. But, perhaps not. Still in deep mourning, Miss Cummings would have violated decorum had she received visitors.[9]

Moreover, the fugitives did not stay at the Cummings place long enough to visit. As Shain told it, "We had not been there more than an hour when we saw one of our spies. I called to him but he was a little backward at first, being some distance off at the time. He came up to us, and that night, rode back to Campana, and sent us horses. That night we staid in our picket guard camp, four miles from Cummings' and four miles from General Houston's camp." The Goliad survivors that Houston's scouts found at Cummings's house were William Brenan, Nat Hazen, Thomas Kemp, Daniel Murphy, Charles Shain, and David James Jones. Ironically, three of the six—Hazen, Murphy, and Jones—had been members of Acting Lieutenant Sprague's squad during their journey from San Felipe to Goliad.[10]

The following day, April 11, the six Goliad fugitives rode into the Texian camp on the Brazos River opposite Jared Groce's plantation. Nicholas Labadie, a Texian army surgeon, described the men as "wounded, barefooted, and ragged." Major Robert Coleman, an inveterate Houston rival, noted, "six of the unfortunate men belonging to Col. Fannin's command, reached the camp, and immediately detailed to the General the particulars of that unfortunate affair." This occasion was their introduction to Sam Houston. Jones and his comrades must have thought him an odd character, for they found him in a somewhat compromising posture. He was lying in his tent, his head in the lap of Pamelia Mann, a Runaway Scrape refugee (and, according to camp scuttlebutt, a woman of accommodating morals) who was lovingly combing the general's curly locks. (To be fair, his intimates claimed the general was also constitutionally inclined toward vice.) Spotting the pitiable survivors approach his tent, the general leapt up "as if he had received an electric shock."

"Why, General," Mrs. Mann teased, "you nearly made me put the comb into your head. You must certainly be frightened."

"Who, madam," he retorted, "would be otherwise than frightened, when not only his own destruction, but that of his country, stares him in the face."

The massacre survivors must have found Houston's behavior disturbing. Had they merely replaced one wavering commanding officer with another?[11]

While in camp on the Brazos, Jones likely came across an old acquaintance. James W. Robinson, the former governor who had dispatched Jones to Fannin's command with Acting Lieutenant Samuel Sprague on February 9, had quit politics. Now a republic with an ad interim president, Texas no longer needed an acting governor. Robinson, however, accepted his downgrade with good grace and joined the ranks as a private in Company J, Second Regiment, a mounted company. It would not be the last time the two men would cross paths.[12]

The remnant of Fannin's Goliad command settled in with their new units. The quartermaster outfitted them with new shoes and clothing, which all desperately needed. Shain was in especially bad shape. "I am well with the exception of very sore feet occasioned by walking through the prairies barefooted," he wrote his father on April 11. "Tomorrow I shall go over the river to a farm to stay until I get entirely well." Brenan, Hazen,

This portrait depicts the "Sword of San Jacinto" and the Republic's first elected president, Sam Houston, as he appeared during his first term. Although his alcoholism worried his closest advisors, his fondness for the bottle never dulled his political instincts. He was a staunch supporter of his namesake city. *Courtesy Texas State Library and Archives Commission.*

40   A REMNANT OF THAT NOBLE BAND

Kemp, Murphy, and Shain later fell in with Colonel Sidney Sherman's Second Regiment of Volunteers as members of Captain William Patton's Columbia company. United by bonds of shared adversity, all those who made the trek from Goliad to the Texian camp on the Brazos River opted to serve together. That is to say, all but one. David James Jones joined Captain Joseph Bell Chance's Washington Guards, a ranger unit. Jones must have held on to the horse he received at John Cummings's public house on April 10, or perhaps Captain Chance supplied him with a spare mount. Had Jones done something on the trail that alienated him from the others? Alternatively, did they do something to rile him? Shain did not mention such an incident, but neither did he mention Jones by name. Such an omission might be an indication of bad blood between Jones and the others, but without supporting evidence, this conclusion is merely speculation.[13]

Worn out and footsore, Jones did not enjoy much of a breather. On April 12, Houston issued orders to break camp. Around 10:00 A.M., the army began crossing the Brazos aboard the steamboat *Yellow Stone*, a process that continued until the afternoon of April 13. The rangers, no doubt, swam their horses across. When Captain Chance assembled his men and mounts on the east bank of the river, they rode to Jared Groce's Bernardo plantation where they camped for the night.

On April 14, Houston broke camp and led his men eastward. The soldiers did not know their destination, as Houston had not deigned to share his thoughts with the rank and file. That uncertainty encouraged conjecture and disgruntlement. For thirty-five days, all Houston had done was alternately retreat and drill. The men doubted his will to fight, and many called for his dismissal. The dissatisfaction came to a head on April 16, when the army approached a fork in the road. One prong led to Nacogdoches and American Louisiana, the other toward Harrisburg and the enemy. Many of the soldiers insisted that if Houston took the road of continued retreat, they would mutiny. "So great became the excitement among the Captains commanding companies," Jesse Billingsley recounted, "that many of us signed an agreement to support each other and take the road leading in the direction of the foe, whatever the order might be." It did not come to that. As the army drew near the fork, a bellow sounded through the ranks, "To the right, boys, to the right!" Musicians marching at the head of the column struck up a lively tune and took the southern path. So did the rest of the army. Houston said nothing and followed behind. Without orders, the soldiers took the route that would ultimately lead them to San Jacinto. Historians, however, still debate if it was the path General Houston truly intended. No doubts existed in the mind of Texian volunteer Jonathan Hampton Kuykendall: "I do not believe that Gen'l Houston gave any order whatever as to which road should be followed, but when the head of the column reached the forks of the road it took the right-hand without being either bid or forbid."[14]

Now that each step brought them closer to combat, the men marched with hardened resolve. On the night of April 16, scouts arrived at camp to inform Houston that units of the Mexican army under the personal command to Santa Anna were in Harrisburg, less than twenty-five miles away. The army broke camp at first light and marched fifteen miles that day. The men pitched camp that night about six miles north of Harrisburg. Around noon on April 18, the army arrived at a point on Buffalo Bayou opposite the town. Gazing across the muddy stream, the Texians could see that Santa Anna had burned the town before his departure. The mounted scouts of Erastus "Deaf" Smith and Henry Karnes swam the bayou and rode to locate the enemy. Dog tired, the rest of the army crumpled at their camp below Harrisburg. They had marched some sixty miles in two days. Late that evening, Deaf Smith returned with vital intelligence from a captured Mexican courier with dispatches for Santa Anna. From these, Houston learned that Santa Anna's division was at New Washington on Galveston Bay. To rejoin the bulk of his forces at Fort Bend, Santa Anna must take the road that led to the ferry operated by Nathaniel Lynch. If Houston's embittered Texians arrived there first, they might present the "Napoleon of the West" with a Waterloo of his own.

To accomplish that goal, however, the army had to travel light and fast, leaving the baggage in camp. Those too ill to march and most of the medical staff stayed behind as well. Houston also ordered all of Chance's thirty-seven mounted rangers to remain with the baggage. In the event the enemy attacked the camp, they were to shoot their two Mexican prisoners and blow up the Texian ammunition wagon.[15]

Orders be damned. David James Jones was having none of it. He had lost too many friends, slogged too many miles, and suffered too many hardships to miss his chance for payback. Whether he requested Chance's permission, or simply went absent without leave is anyone's guess. D. J. Jones appears on the muster roll of Captain Chance's company in the General Land Office. Beside his name is the annotation "in the battle."[16]

On April 20, Jones and the rest of Houston's Texian army would finally confront Santa Anna's detachment. Marching at a killing pace, the Texians arrived at Lynch's Ferry at the junction of Buffalo Bayou and the San Jacinto River about 10:00 A.M. The Texians claimed possession of the strategic ground. Santa Anna arrived on the field around 11:30 A.M. and received the shock of his life when he found the path to his main army blocked by Houston and his men—rebels he thought were retreating northward toward Nacogdoches.

Following an indecisive artillery duel, Colonel Sherman volunteered to lead a cavalry charge to capture the Mexicans' single field piece. Houston expressed little confidence in the design, but finally granted permission.

Sherman rode at the head of some seventy mounted riflemen, one of whom was former governor James W. Robinson. The Texian horsemen charged, and the Mexican artillerymen withdrew their cannon behind the cover of a hill. Having gained nothing, Sherman's men withdrew to reload. That meant dismounting, and when they did, the Mexican lancers replied with a charge of their own, supported by four companies of infantry. Major Lysander Wells later described the action: "Finding ourselves exposed to the incessant fire of an unequal number of cavalry, their artillery, and two hundred infantry, and our own infantry not having come up to engage theirs, as expected, we were at length obliged, reluctantly, to retire, leaving two fine horses dead upon the field."[17]

The inactivity of the Texian infantrymen may have disturbed Major Wells, but he praised the heroism of one Texian in particular. "One of Fannin's men, who had been led out to be shot, but made his escape, was on the right of the division, and behaved most gallantly." This daring fellow was almost certainly David James Jones. Of course, other of "Fannin's men" were on the field that day, but Brenan, Hazen, Kemp, Murphy, and Shain had all joined Captain William Patton's Columbia company—an infantry unit. As a member of Captain Chance's ranger company, Jones would have been the only one of the Goliad survivors able to participate in the cavalry skirmish.[18]

The following day, however, Jones was on foot. Having achieved such distinction as a mounted rifleman on the twentieth it seems odd that he would serve as a footslogger on the twenty-first. Still, Jones could have behaved a tad too gallantly, for his may have been one of the "two fine horses dead upon the field." If so, Jones would have had no choice but to stow his saddle and trail a musket.

Whatever the reason, Jones fell in with Company H, First Regiment Texas Volunteers. Captain William Warner Hill had commanded the unit since its formation on March 1 in Washington County. He had fallen seriously ill, however, and had remained at the camp below Harrisburg. Irish-born First Lieutenant Robert Stevenson, therefore, took Hill's place as acting company commander. When the Texian line stepped off around 4:30 P.M., Private Jones marched in line with Company H. A fellow company member, the seventeen-year-old Private John Milton Swisher, recalled the scene:

> The troops marched with alacrity to a distance of about a quarter of a mile from the Mexican encampment, where we were formed in line of battle and ordered to charge, having reserved our fire till within point-blank range. Thick and fast flew the bullets! In less than 20 minutes from the time we commenced firing we were in possession of the enemy's breast-works with all their camp equipment, baggage, etc., and before the sun sank on the western horizon 630 Mexicans had been killed, 208 wounded, and 730 taken prisoners.[19]

As they shot, stabbed, bayoneted, and clubbed hapless Mexicans, Texian troops roared, "Remember the Alamo! Remember Goliad!" For most, it was only a vengeful battle cry. David James Jones really could remember Goliad, however, and one can only imagine the emotions that raged through him as he closed upon the enemy. Jones's feelings reflected those of fellow massacre survivor, Charles B. Shain, who stated in a letter to his father shortly before the battle, "I will try to avenge the death of some of my brave friends."[20]

Santa Anna was a captive and the Mexican army was in full retreat, but Texians still faced a real and present danger. Notwithstanding Santa Anna's assurances, the Mexican Congress resolved to continue the war against Texas. On June 5, that body placed General Urrea in command of a new campaign.

He told Matamoros officials that he stood ready to lead soldados across the Rio Grande the instant he received orders from the central government. Such reports naturally alarmed Texians, who made plans to defend against another onslaught.[21]

Following San Jacinto, Jones remained in the army. He did not have much of a choice, as he had no home or family to retire to and most of his Texas friends were dead. Jones now followed a new general. Sam Houston had traveled to New Orleans to receive treatment for the wound he received at San Jacinto. Thomas Jefferson Rusk resigned his post as secretary of war to accept the rank of brigadier general and took command of the army on May 4. Following the victory at San Jacinto, many of the Texian volunteers had melted away. With Rusk at their head, some three hundred men pursued the retreating Mexican army to assure that they really did abandon Texas. General Rusk established his headquarters in Victoria on the Guadalupe River.

When Rusk's scouts ventured into Goliad—the first Texians to arrive there since the March massacre—what they discovered shocked and sickened them. The Mexicans had placed the bodies on pyres of mesquite brush doused with tallow. The grease on the pyre flared bright for an instant, but the green wood refused to ignite, leaving a pile of half-roasted cadavers. When the Texians arrived late in May, they found the festering remains in a partially filled trench, where the Mexicans had dumped them. Dogs, wolves, and coyotes had made a feast of the corpses. Gnawed bones littered the ground for yards.[22]

On June 2, General Rusk ordered a parade for the following day to inter the remains of the Goliad garrison "with all the honors of war." He organized the funeral down to the smallest detail. "Those of Fannin's command who are in the army," he directed, "and have so miraculously escaped, will attend as mourners." On Friday, June 3, Rusk delivered

Thomas Jefferson Rusk took command of the Texas army following the battle of San Jacinto. Troops under his command discovered and buried the remains of the Goliad Massacre victims. He later served as a Texas senator. *Author's Collection.*

an impassioned eulogy that began, "FELLOW SOLDIERS: In the order of Providence we are this day called upon to pay the last sad offices of respect to the remains of the noble and heroic band, who, battling for our sacred rights, have fallen beneath the ruthless hand of a tyrant." Later in the address, Rusk extolled the "mourners": "A small number of them now stand by the grave—a bare remnant of that noble band. Our tribute of respect is due to them." Emotion overcame Rusk, and he handed his address to an aide to finish. The general was not the only one who felt the power of the moment. One of the survivors cried out, "Remember Goliad!" Was the man David James Jones? Records of the event do not say, but he certainly stood among those Rusk designated as the "mourners."[23]

Throughout the summer of 1836, volunteers from the United States continued to arrive in Camp Victoria. By August, Rusk's once piddling thee hundred-man force grew to around twenty-five hundred. Rusk welcomed these new arrivals. The more soldiers under his command, the better his chances of halting the anticipated Mexican invasion. Even so, more men also meant more mouths to feed, and Texian logistics, never efficient at the best of times, became even more unreliable. Moreover, larger numbers of men in camp increased the opportunity for epidemics, the bane of all nineteenth-century armies.[24]

Robert Hall, one of the American volunteers who joined Rusk's command, saw no combat but learned that peril and death nonetheless hounded Texas soldiers. The Tennessean enlisted on June 1 and served until November 7, 1836, at which time he bribed a surgeon to receive a medical discharge. Hall left a vivid description of the privation that Jones and his messmates suffered during the summer and autumn of 1836:

Texans gather to honor those killed at the battle of Coleto Creek and the Goliad Massacre. The 1936 monument marks the spot where soldiers under Thomas Jefferson Rusk buried the remains of Colonel Fannin and his men. Mexican soldados stripped the bodies and placed them on a pyre. The wood, however, was green and the flames died out, leaving the charred corpses to the vultures, curs, and coyotes. *Photo by Newton M. Warzecha. Courtesy Presidio La Bahía.*

A REMNANT OF THAT NOBLE BAND

> The army was at that time about 2000 strong, but very poorly equipped, and with scarcely any commissary supplies. We were there nearly four months, and during all that time I never saw a piece of bread. We lived entirely on beef, but the soldiers were in good spirits until something like dysentery broke out and a great many died. I think at least 300 brave fellows were wrapped in their blankets and laid away in the earth of that camp.[25]

Following San Jacinto, Texas commanders restructured the army to accommodate the influx of American volunteers. By August 1836, Private Jones had become a member of Captain W. J. Elliott's company of volunteers. The remarks on the muster roll, dated August 31, 1836, indicate that Jones joined the unit on August 13. The muster roll also specified that he had signed on for a three-month hitch. That notation was significant, as Republic officials had offered a bounty of 320 acres to those who served at least three months.[26]

But Jones did not make three months in Elliott's company. On October 3, he received an honorable discharge from the army of the Texas Republic. No Texian soldier could have claimed to have endured more adversity, risked more danger, or lost more friends than David James Jones.[27]

But what now? Jones left the army armed with a bounty certificate, which stated that he was entitled to land in any Texas county for his military service. Through an act passed by the council on December 5, 1835, "permanent volunteers," those who served for the duration of the war or those discharged sooner by reason of disability, were due 640 acres. The bounty donation, however, was different from the headright grant. Under the Constitution of 1836, all heads of families living in Texas on March 4, 1836 (except blacks and Indians, of course), could receive "first class" headrights of one league and one labor, a total of 4,605.5 acres. Unmarried men seventeen years of age or older who met those terms were entitled to one-third of a league, or 640 acres. Jones received headright and bounty grants. As a single man, he had 1,280 acres coming to him.[28]

Having the certificates, however, did not grant title to the acreage. Rather, they simply stated that Jones was entitled to the land. For a soldier to take possession of his grant was an involved process. Once the veteran decided on the county in which he wanted to live, he then presented his certificates to the county surveyor. George B. Erath, a San Jacinto veteran and a surveyor, described how the system worked:

> A county surveyor was elected by congress for every county, but was not really to practice in the field. He was the recorder of field notes, keeper of maps, reporter of what was done, but, under the first principles of the land law, was not expected to survey, except in the smaller interior counties where there was little business. Deputies did the field work; they were distinct officers, giving bond and security to the president and after annexation to the governor.

The county surveyor consulted a plat map to determine the location of unclaimed land. When a veteran selected his acreage, county officials then charged him surveying fees. The fees were not exorbitant, but it was still more than many ex-soldiers possessed. Knowing the straits of many of the veterans, some surveyors took pity on them. "It was considered all right by people of the frontier for a man to do work and wait two years or more for his pay," Erath recollected. "I may add, too, that such a thing as interest was unheard of in those days."[29]

Then as now, it took money to make money. Even if a man could swing the surveying fees, he might not be able to afford the stock or seed required for the land to return him a living. Moreover, many U.S.

volunteers were city slickers who knew nothing about working the land. Others had no desire to tie themselves to a plot of ground, no matter how substantial—and, even in 1836, most folks considered 1,280 acres substantial. After all Jones had just been through, farming or ranching may have struck him as a bit humdrum. Land was for men who were ready to settle down, get married, and rear families. Clearly, many of these youthful blades were not prepared for that.

Fortunately (or in many cases unfortunately) established and well-heeled Texians stood ready to exchange currency for certificates. It seemed like a good deal for veterans who did not have a use for the certificates, but always needed cold cash. It is not clear what Jones did in the months after he left the service, but by February 20, 1837, he had landed in Washington County. On that date, he signed over his headright certificate to New Jersey native David Ayres for the sum of three thousand dollars. Ayres had been a close friend of William Barret Travis, who had left his son, Charles, in the care of Ayres and his wife, Ann. In February 1836, Travis, on his way to the Alamo, had stopped to visit his son for the last time at the Ayres's home. Travis addressed one of his last, and certainly most poignant, letters to Ayres:

> Dear Sir:—Take care of my little boy. If the country should be saved I may make him a splendid fortune. But if the country should be lost, and I should perish, he will have nothing but the proud recollection that he is the son of a man who died for his country.[30]

Ayres was the embodiment of the Texian gentry. He was a respected merchant, and his forty-four years placed him well into middle age. In 1832, he arrived in Mexican Texas with a full purse, intent on buying property and building a home. Early in 1833, he landed at the mouth of the Brazos River and made his way upstream. He secured a tract some thirty miles west of the Town of Washington, where he built a stone house he called Montville. Then he went back to New Jersey. He returned in May 1834, with his brother and both their families. A devout man, Ayres hauled what he claimed to be the first crate of Bibles ever brought into Texas and a supply of books from the New York Sunday School Union. He and his family first settled in the Irish community of San Patricio on the Nueces River, but their stay was brief. In November 1834, he moved his family to Montville. He gave away Bibles to any who asked for them. While Mr. Ayres operated his mercantile business, Mrs. Ayres and Lydia Ann McHenry taught school out of Montville. Indeed, Travis had enrolled Charles in this academy. Ayres honored Travis's final request to "take care [of his] little boy." Following his father's death, Charles remained with the Ayres family for two years.[31]

Deafness prevented his active service during the Texas Revolution, but Ayres provided rations to the Texian army. During the Runaway Scrape, General Houston appointed him to look after fleeing families. Following the victory at San Jacinto, Ayres offered his services to ad interim President David G. Burnet. "I am unable on account of my health to turn out and perform the duties of a common Soldier," Ayres wrote, "[but] I wish to be in the service of my country if there is any post of any kind that my health will permit me to fill." Ayres returned to Montville, which he found in ruins. Consequently, he moved his family and his business into the Town of Washington. Business thrived. By 1837, his fortunes had recovered enough for him to buy an extensive tract near Bellville, in Austin County. He also bought Jones's headright certificate that year.[32]

Around this time, Jones transferred his bounty certificate to another prominent Texian. Successful land speculator James Morgan purchased the certificate for an undisclosed amount. Morgan had lived in Texas for a number of years and understood the lay of the land. After an 1830 visit to Brazoria, he determined to open a mercantile company in Mexican Texas. Returning to North Carolina, Morgan bound his slaves as indentured servants for ninety-nine years to subvert the Mexican government's ban of the "peculiar institution." He then set out for Texas with his wife, a son, two daughters, and their sixteen "servants." Opening a store in Anahuac, he soon involved himself in the War Party. In 1835, Morgan became an agent for the New Washington Association, a land speculating concern organized by Mexican empresario Lorenzo de Zavala and a cabal of New York investors. On behalf of his backers, Morgan bought hundreds of acres in the Harrisburg and Liberty municipalities. At the mouth of the San Jacinto River, he laid out the settlement of New Washington. Seeking to inhabit the town, the company imported a diverse assemblage of Scottish highlanders along with free blacks from New York and Connecticut. Among the latter, was Emily D. West, better known in Texas folklore as the "Yellow Rose of Texas." By the time Jones transferred his bounty certificate to Morgan, the speculator was one of the richest men in the Republic. Indeed, his prosperity derailed his political aspirations. When Morgan sought election to the Republic's Congress, voters rejected him because they were wary of his fortune.[33]

Never in his life had Jones possessed so much money. Well set, he could have returned to the United States in high style. Yet, he now had a stake in the republic. He had earned the respect of his fellow soldiers, he was a survivor of Goliad, and he was a hero of San Jacinto. It would have meant little back in the "old states," but in Texas that conveyed singular status.

Thinking back on his time in Texas, Jones counted himself blessed. He had fought at the battle of Coleto Creek and emerged unscathed. At least 342 of his comrades had fallen in the Goliad Massacre, yet he was one of only 28 who escaped. On numerous occasions during the agonizing tramp to the Texian camp, he had evaded capture. At San Jacinto, he was in the thick of the fight on both April 20 and 21, and yet remained untouched by enemy lead or steel. In the perilous days in Camp Victoria, he had dodged the invisible organisms that had caused him to wrap so many of his messmates "in their blankets." Jones had every reason to look to the future with confidence. He was young, lucky, and alive. He had some jingle in his pocket and a spring in his step. Like many combat veterans, he likely had a difficult time relating to civilians. He wished to mix with other young men who knew the bitter taste of war. He wanted to be where the action was. In the spring of 1837, that meant the newborn capital.

After all that he had survived, David James Jones could not have imagined that Houston City would prove the deadliest place he had ever seen.

55

Splendor and Squalor
Houston, March 5, 1838

Following a night of wild carousing, a trio of rowdy loafers lounges outside their favorite grog shop. Their behavior, their very presence, is an affront to members of a virtuous Houston family.

These loafers are fair representatives of their ilk. The reprobate sitting on the porch (sitting, because he is too sozzled to stand) nurses a bottle of Irish whiskey, which the sign above him publicizes. The idle brute standing closest to the door wiles away the time whittling with his gargantuan Bowie knife. Having lost his brogans to a winning hand, he now goes barefoot. He may have handed over his footwear but his blade stays keen, his pistol primed and loaded. Clearly, he keeps his priorities straight. Straight, at least, for Houston City. The wretched fellow at the foot of the steps brazenly answers nature's call on a public street, in full light of day. Did his mother teach him no better manners? Of course, she did. This vulgar exhibition flaunts his scorn for the gentry, all the effete coxcombs and dainty ladies who high-hat veterans down on their luck.

It has the desired effect. The wife averts her eyes from this unseemly spectacle; her husband shouts fury at the scum who dare insult his family. A gloved hand, ready to avenge outraged honor, grips the hilt of his Bowie knife. Their little girl, ignorant of the male anatomy, wonders aloud, "Mommy, what is that man doing?" Walking behind at a deferential distance, a slave woman prudently attempts to conceal her amusement. Her efforts are largely unsuccessful.

Tree stumps, horse droppings, dead cats, and assorted garbage litter muddy streets, all lending to the putrescence that exemplifies the Republic's capital.

3
The Most Miserable Place in the World
The Town of Houston

The Brothers Allen—Augustus and John—possessed vision, optimism, and, above all, salesmanship. All those talents were evident in their public notice touting the infant town of Houston. They assured potential investors there was "no place in Texas more healthy, having an abundance of excellent spring water, and enjoying the sea breeze in all its freshness." The siblings never doubted that providence and location had tagged Houston as the "great interior commercial emporium of Texas." They continued:

> Nature appears to have designated this place for the future seat of Government. It is handsome and beautifully elevated, salubrious and well watered, and now the very heart or center of population, and will be so for a length of time to come. It combines two important advantages: a communication with the coast and foreign countries, and with different portions of the Republic. As the country shall improve, railroads will become in use, and will be extended from this point to the Brazos, and up the same, also from this up to the head waters of San Jacinto, embracing

THE MOST MISERABLE PLACE IN THE WORLD

> that rich country, and in a few years the whole trade of the upper Brazos
> will make its way into Galveston Bay through this channel.

It would be inaccurate to dismiss the Allen brothers as mere land speculators. Superb entrepreneurs, they claimed to offer investors health, happiness, and prosperity. Along with the town lots, the New York natives sold nothing less than John Winthrop's vision of a "golden city on a hill"— or, in this case, a glittering burg on the bayou. Hundreds, then thousands, rushed to claim their portion of that dream.[1]

Yet, on August 30, 1836, the date on which the *Telegraph and Texas Register* ran the Allens' grandiloquent ad, all they had to sell was smoke and mirrors. The "Town of Houston," as they boldly titled the notice, was at the time nothing more than stakes in the dirt and marks on a chart. It was perhaps natural that the Allens would have entrusted another pair of brothers, Gail Jr. and John P. Borden, to survey the site. A Borden surrogate, Moses Lapham, appeared to have done most of the actual labor. As he explained from Columbia in an October 1, 1836, letter to his father, "I shall leave here (my home at present) early in the morning to go lay off the town lots of the town of Houston, that you see advertized in the Telegraph. It lies on Buffalo Bayou, eight miles above Harrisburg." Following the brothers' plan, Lapham laid out the town in a grid, running the streets parallel and perpendicular to Buffalo Bayou. As that waterway provided the chief transportation artery, he anchored the town upon it.[2]

Together, the Allen brothers forged an impressive team. Augustus was a dour bookkeeper, the meticulous one who handled all the minutiae. He was also a patriot. During the War for Independence, he served as a Texas agent in the United States, where he purchased the schooner *Brutus* and sold it to the provisional government virtually at cost. Little brother John was gregarious, brazen, and political—the ideal pitchman. As a member of

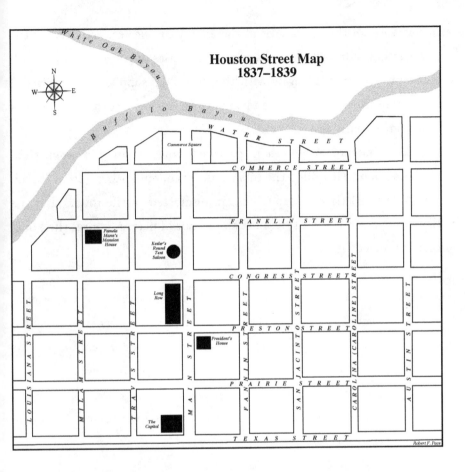

the Texas legislature, he worked assiduously to convince fellow lawmakers to proclaim Houston the temporary seat of government. He understood that their collaboration would assure the town's future—and the Allen brothers' fortune. On October 3, 1836, the First Congress gathered at Columbia where the twenty-six-year-old real-estate dealer addressed its members. He made a fervent case for his Houston site, citing twin concerns of trade and security: "I consider that the seat of government ought to be on the coast because it combines the advantages of a safe and speedy communication with the United States and the interior of the country at the same time; because we will have more speedy and certain information of the operations of the enemy on the sea, and because the government will possess so many more facilities of communicating with the army and furnishing it with the necessary supplies. What place, I would inquire, possesses more advantages in this respect than the town of Houston? I boldly assert, None."[3]

Boldly, indeed. Allen then parroted lines from his August 30 advertisement. He culled the bits about "excellent spring water," "bayou navigable at all times," "capitalists are interested in the town," and the like. No matter; a good spiel never went out of date. Allen set the hook, then he reeled them in:

> Should the Congress see proper to locate the seat of government at Houston[,] I offer to build a State house and the necessary offices for the various departments of the government, and to rent them to the government on a credit until such time as it may be convenient to make payment. Or, if the government sees proper to erect the buildings, I propose[,] when the seat of government is removed[,] to purchase the said buildings at such price as they may be appraised at.

Allen's clincher was an appeal to self-interest: "I assure the members that houses and comfortable accommodations will be furnished at Houston in a very short time. And if the seat of government is there located no pains will be spared to render the various officers of the government as comfortable as they could expect to be in any other place in Texas." Were these none-to-subtle bribes? Surely not. Call them "flattering inducements."[4]

Whether bribes or blandishments, they worked. On November 30, 1836, Texas officials finally succumbed to the dubious lures of the Houston site, but even more to the Allen brothers' relentless lobbying. As one early settler recounted, "these thorough-going business men" had by their "enterprise and influence ... succeeded in getting the seat of government removed" from Columbia. Others, however, suggested that personal ambitions had colored the deliberations. "[T]he vanity of the successful conqueror was appealed to, many lots were granted to those who would immediately build on them; a splendid map of the city was carried on the wings of the wind to distant places to catch in time the greedy speculator and allure the uninitiated," carped one critic of the deal, "and in a few brief months the bait had been successfully offered to a sufficient majority of the members of Congress." Congressman Anson Jones was even more direct. In his opinion, the bill to transfer the capital to Houston "constituted a perfect 'selling out' of Texas to a few individuals." Despite the dubious ethics of the process, legislators selected Houston over fifteen other better-established locations and proclaimed that it would serve "as the seat of government for the republic of Texas until the year 1840." Had the Allen brothers bought off the Texas Congress? If they did, they received good value for their money.[5]

Congressman Anson Jones was never fond of Houston—at least as the seat of government. In his view, the transfer of the capital from Columbia "constituted a perfect 'selling out' of Texas to a few individuals." Jones, however, survived his time there and, as the last president of the Texas Republic, oversaw its annexation to the United States. Notwithstanding his ambivalence toward the city, he was living there when he committed suicide in 1858. *Courtesy Texas State Library and Archives Commission.*

62   THE MOST MISERABLE PLACE IN THE WORLD

By year's end, would-be Houstonians had begun to make their way toward the new capital but found the journey difficult. South Carolina native Francis R. Lubbock recalled that Buffalo Bayou boasted "plenty of water and breadth." Nonetheless it took three days for the crew and passengers aboard the steamboat *Laura* to drag her twelve miles over or around numerous obstacles. As Lubbock recalled:

> We had to rig what were called Spanish windlasses on the shore to heave the logs and snags out of our way, the passengers all working faithfully. All hands on board would get out on shore, and cutting down a tree would make a windlass by boring holes in it and placing it upon a support and throwing a bight of rope around it, secure one end to a tree in the rear and the other to the snags or fallen trees in the water. Then by means of the capstan bars we would turn the improvised capstan on land, and draw from the track of our steamer the obstructions. Capitalists, dignified judge, military heroes, young merchant in fine clothes from the dressiest city in the United States, all lent a helping hand.[6]

Dr. Francis Moore, Jr., an erstwhile surgeon in the regular Texian army and the new editor of the *Telegraph and Texas Register*, described the excruciating journey from Lynchburg to Houston aboard the steamer *Yellow Stone*. A "great part of the ensuing day was spent in groping (if a steamboat can grope) at the rapid rate of one or two miles an hour," he wryly observed, "to the very crown of the 'head of Navigation' of Buffalo Bayou at the city of Houston." Moore later identified what he perceived to be the greatest impediment to Houston's progress. "The principle objection to this place," he complained, "is the difficulty of access by water; the bayou above Harrisburg being so narrow, so serpentine and blocked up with snags and overhanging trees, that immense improvements will be required to render the navigation convenient for large steamboats."[7]

Dr. John Washington Lockhart recalled the travails of a journey he made in the autumn of 1837. "Buffalo bayou was then a miserable stream for navigation," he affirmed. "Our [steam] boat showed that on a former trip she had run foul of an overhanging tree, which had pulled nearly half of her cabin off." Like Lubbock, Dr. Lockhart described the Herculean efforts required to pilot a vessel along the treacherous channel—especially when the gloom was darker than boot blacking:

> [N]ight overtook us as we entered the narrows of Buffalo bayou. It seemed our boat entered with a very tight squeeze. We made very little headway from there to Houston. Captain Sterett had two huge bonfires made, one on each side of the bow of the boat of pine knots. These fires were made in iron baskets, supported on iron rods attached to the bow, so that the boat in moving along carried its own light. These lights in straight parts of the bayou lit it up for some distance, but when the boat would have to make short curves in following the winding stream the bow would frequently appear to rest on one bank of the bayou and the stern on the other, and then the lights would make it appear as if we were about to take to the woods. All trace of water was gone until the deck hands with their long poles would, by pushing against the bank, turn the prow of the boat into the stream again. At these times the boat, gliding smoothly and almost without noise along the banks, the torches casting grewsome shadows of the big trees here and there, the thumping of the machinery, the ringing of the bells signaling the engineer to "go ahead" or "reverse," mixed with the wild refrain of the boat hands singing their chorus songs; the darkness and stillness of the night outside, except when broken by the occasional howl of some wild animal, made one feel as if he were wandering in a dreamland.[8]

64 THE MOST MISERABLE PLACE IN THE WORLD

TEXIAN MACABRE

KEY
1. Capitol Building
2. President's House
3. Liberty Pole
4. Henry Kesler's Round Tent Saloon
5. Cruger & Moore "Telgraph" Office
6. A.C. & Charlotte Allen's Home
7. Elisha Floyd's City Hotel
8. Pamela Mann's Mansion House
9. To the Jockey Club Race Track
10. William Fairfax Gray Law Office
11. Lt. John Hall Tent Store
12. Kelcy & Hubbard Store
13. To San Jacinto Battleground
14. To Hangman's Grove

Houston, Capital of Texas, 1837

In their August 30 advertisement, the Allen brothers had declared, "Vessels from New Orleans or New York can sail without obstacle to this place [Houston], and steamboats of the largest class can run to Galveston Island in 8 or 10 hours, in all seasons of the year." The exhausted and mud-caked passengers of vessels that plied the waters of that turbid bog must have recalled this claim with considerable bemusement and not a little resentment.[9]

By New Year's Day 1837, the snail's pace so frustrated Lubbock that he sought another means of conveyance; as he approached Houston, however, he discovered its trace so faint that he almost missed it:

> Just before reaching our destination a party of us, becoming weary of the steamer, took a yawl and concluded we would hunt for the city. So little evidence could we see of a landing that we passed by the site and run into White Oak Bayou, realizing that we must have passed the city when we struck the brush. We then backed down the bayou, and by close observation discovered a rod or street laid off from the water's edge. Upon landing we found stakes and footprints, indicating that we were in the town tract.[10]

As Lubbock explored the town site closely he discovered that his first impressions had deceived him. A few citizens were constructing frame buildings on newly acquired lots. Other enterprising Houstonians, unable to afford lumber, had pitched tents and conducted business under canvas. Prophetically, one of the larger tents functioned as a saloon; Houston had already begun to assume its distinctive character.[11]

On January 18, 1837, Captain Robert Boyce arrived in town after walking from Columbia. As he described it, the settlement "consisted of clapboard camps and tents; not even a log house was finished." The next morning the captain discovered that a New Orleans merchant had recently opened an emporium in a dazzling white tent. "Here, for $4," he recalled, "I purchased an outfit and dressed up like a gentleman." In 1837, it was important that a man of substance dress the part, no matter how coarse his surroundings.[12]

Captain Boyce got quite a deal. Apparently, he arrived before the inflation common to most boomtowns began to spiral skyward. Later that year, an American traveler observed that Houston prices climbed beyond those most folks could afford. "Cloth, which did not cost originally more than three dollars a yard and which retailed in the United States at from five to six, was selling here from fifteen to twenty. Hats which did not cost more than two or three dollars at wholesale were selling from ten to fifteen," he protested, "and it was common for boots not worth more than five to six dollars anywhere else to bring eighteen dollars a pair."[13]

Merchants and stockmen far outside the town hauled their wares into Houston to receive maximum profits. Dr. John Leonard Riddell told of his experience with one hard-nosed farmer who lived near the frontier settlement of Seguin. "[W]e came to the woods and to a rude log house where we found an old man with plenty of poultry, hogs, cattle, cheese and garden sauce [vegetables for the table]. The old curmudgeon would in no wise part with anything," the good doctor recounted, "although in remuneration I offered him silver money." Riddell complained that he had offered to pay the farmer double the "current Houston price" for a rind of cheese and a few hens. Even so, the old man refused to part with these precious commodities. He curtly informed the doctor that, "by & by," he intended to offer his goods in Houston where the "whole would amount to something." Small wonder that produce sold at a premium. Visitor Mary Austin Holley confirmed there was, "No garden in Houston—none but imported vegetables."[14]

In March 1837, the first court under the Texas Republic brought some semblance of law to Houston. Dilue Harris recounted that John W. Moore, the sheriff of Harrisburg County, summoned her father to serve on the grand jury. The court convened in circumstances less majestic than some sticklers might have wished. "The jury," she recalled, "sat on a log under an arbor of pine bushes." Jurymen heard the case against James Adams, on trial for theft. They ordered that Adams restore to Lawrence Ramey $295.00, and notes mentioned in the indictment that he receive thirty-nine lashes on his naked back and have the letter T branded on his right hand. The court further decreed that, on March 31, the sheriff or his deputy should carry out the sentence in some public place inside the town of Houston. Defendant Joseph T. Bell stood trial for murder, but, upon hearing the evidence, jurymen concluded that he had acted only as they would have done in similar circumstances. The verdict: justifiable homicide. This was not Bell's first encounter with the law: "He had been tried at Harrisburg for the same crime before Judge David G. Burnet in '34 and pronounced not guilty." Mrs. Harris recollected that the exonerated party had endured "so much trouble he decided to leave that part of Texas." No doubt prudent; a third murder charge would have likely proven fatal.[15]

The town and the Allen brothers enjoyed a powerful advocate in President Sam Houston. Elected in September 1836, he had worked behind the scenes to transfer the seat of government to his namesake city. The Allens took pains to persuade the "Sword of San Jacinto" to cut in their favor. Not only did they name the city in his honor, a move calculated to massage his gargantuan ego, but also transferred several town lots to him. Consequently, Houston became a tireless booster of the eponymous city. On April 28, 1837, the president wrote his friend Robert A. Irion expressing his amazement at the settlement's astounding growth. "On the 20th of January," the president recounted, "a small log cabin & 12 persons were all that distinguished it from the adjacent forests, and now there are upwards of 100 houses finished, and going up rapidly (some of them fine frame buildings) and 1500 people, all actively engaged in their respective pursuits. It is remarkable to observe the sobriety and industry like we see in the North—I have not seen a drunken man since my arrival." This last aspect would not last. Soon the city would provide the president with the opportunity to view more tosspots than even he would have thought possible. By November 19, when Methodist minister Littleton Fowler arrived in Houston, his impression was far different: "Here I find much vice, gaming, drunkenness, and profanity the commonest." He also found "many stores, and any number of doggeries." Doggery was a synonym for saloon.[16]

The Allen brothers assured their slice of the action. Early in 1837, the brothers oversaw the construction of an extended, one-story building stretching along the west side of Main Street from Congress Avenue to Preston Street. The Allens intended that "Long Row," as locals came to call it, house government offices until the Capitol reached completion, although the structure seemingly never served that purpose. Instead, the Allens divided the long building into shops that they rented to local merchants. It became a social and business hot spot. Sometimes called "Mercantile Row," most of the establishment's customers preferred the original moniker, "Long Row."[17]

Late in 1837, an American visitor noted the dramatic proliferation of residents. "[W]hen I arrived," he observed, "Houston was not only the center of most of the spirit and enterprise of Texas, but it seemed to be the focus of immigration from all directions, as it continued to be during the summer. Persons came pouring in until, in a short time, a floating population had collected some four or five hundred people." He further explained, "houses could not be built near as fast as required, so that tents were pitched in every direction over the prairie, which gave to the city the appearance of a Methodist campground." Her friends assured Mary Austin Holley that she "should not know Houston, [as] it has grown so much since I was there."[18]

On April 1, contractor Thomas William Ward and a crew of laborers began work on the nation's capitol—a sprawling, two-story wooden structure at Main and Texas Avenue. On May 9, torrential rains struck Houston, damaging the partially constructed building. True to their word, the Allen brothers picked up the tab (and astutely retained title to the building). They did not skimp on materials, going so far as to import the lumber from Maine. Considering the chaotic and ephemeral nature of the business that transpired in that structure, it was perhaps appropriate that its construction began on April Fool's Day.[19]

While Rome was not built in a day, much of early Houston was. Dr. Moore reported the phenomena: "We frequently notice on our way to breakfast a quantity of lumber thrown carelessly in a heap, and, upon returning in the evening, are greeted with the surprising appearance of a house." The effusive editor pitied the "poor Indian who strolls about the streets amazed to see white men gathering, thick as leaves of the forest, and rearing a mighty city where so recently they hunted the prairie deer and the buffaloe. The Capitol but yesterday was merely framed, now lifts its towering form above the puny buildings round, like a gigantic oak amid the prairie bushes."[20]

What began as an impromptu hamlet had morphed into an ad libbed metropolis. In July 1837, Connecticut native Ashbel Smith boasted Houston "was a perfect wilderness in February last, now it contains a handsome Capitol, about 200 houses and more than 2000 inhabitants; and it is increasing with wonderful rapidity." Mary Austin Holley described the scene on Christmas Eve:

The main street of this city of a year extends from the landing into the prairie—a beautiful plain of some six miles wide & extending, with points and islands of timber, quite to the Brazos. On this main street are two large hotels, 2 stories, with galleries (crowded to overflowing) several stores—painted white—one block of eleven stores (rent $500 each)—some two story dwelling houses—& then the capitol—painted peach blossom about 1/4 mile from the landing. Other streets, parallel, & at right angles, are built on here & there, but chiefly designated by stakes. One story dwellings are scattered in the edge of the timbers which form an amphitheatre round the prairie, according to the bend of the Bayou, which being wider, would render this a most eligible town site. As it is, it is too inconvenient, besides being unhealthy & a removal of the government is talked of.[21]

The city suffered all the ills of desultory development. By 1838 the Allen brothers' dream had become a nightmare. Houston resembled not so much a city as a perverse burlesque of one. Even the most zealous booster had to admit that much of the year it was a contaminated cesspit. In the summer, swarms of flies carried the bacteria that caused dysentery. Winter brought typhus, influenza, cholera, and tuberculosis. Almost yearly yellow fever epidemics swept through the city claiming vast numbers of victims. A ghastly assortment of detritus littered the muddy streets. One official was dead on target when he referred to "this detested, self-poluted, isolated mudhole of a city." Mrs. William Fairfax Gray averred that she "never saw anything like the mud here. It is a tenaceous black clay," she continued, "which can not be got off of any thing without washing—and is about a foot or so deep." Francis R. Lubbock recalled Houston as a "very muddy place, almost the entire town tract being black, stiff land, and with poor drainage, so that, with the immense wagon trade, the roads

Constructed of timber imported from Maine and "painted peach blossom," the capitol building was the largest and most impressive structure in early Houston. Its chambers, nonetheless, frequently emptied amid shouts and gunfire. *Courtesy Texas State Library and Archives Commission.*

and streets, although wide and handsome, were almost impassable in wet weather." So too, were the "roads from Houston to the country in almost any direction." Likewise, Samuel Maverick of San Antonio mocked the "seat of Government" as a "wretched mud-hole." Dr. John Washington

Lockhart recalled the avenues were "very muddy, and it was not an unusual thing then and long afterward to see ox wagons bogged down on the principal streets." Frequent rains liquefied the black dirt and horse droppings. Wagon wheels further whipped the mixture into a putrid slime. With good reason, "the Father of Texas Medicine" Ashbel Smith requested a New Orleans friend to procure for him a "pair of India Rubber overshoes." And never ending, like a symphony of squalor, the maddening buzzing of the flies. As night draped its cloak over Houston, citizens endured another

Houston's allures held no charm for Béxar resident, Samuel Augustus Maverick. Writing his wife Mary in 1838, he derided the town as a "wretched mud-hole." Many visitors shared his opinion. *Courtesy Daughters of the Republic of Texas Library at the Alamo.*

one of nature's recitals: "the howling of wolves." Many shared Nacogdoches Representative Kelsey H. Douglass's opinion that Houston was, "the most misera[b]le place in the world."[22]

It was no mystery why Houston was so muddy. Much of the land the Allen brothers selected for the town site was swampland. One of their nephews, O. F. Allen, later depicted the difficulties involved in reclaiming the area. "One could hardly picture the jungle and swampy sweet gum woods that a good portion of the city is built upon." Allen claimed the "southwestern portion of the city was a green scum lake, studded with giant sweet gum trees, and water from one to two and a half feet deep." Reflecting the racial sensitivities of his day, Allen recalled the backbreaking and deadly work required to drain these wetlands. "The labor of clearing the great space was done by negro slaves and Mexicans, as no white man could have worked and endured the insect bites and malaria, snake bites, impure water, and other hardships." The slaves could not either, for as Allen reproached, "many of the blacks died before their work was done."[23]

The rancid streets functioned more as obstacle courses. Because of the Borden brothers' prescience, streets measured eighty feet wide and ran ramrod straight. The exception was Water Street. It was one hundred feet wide and mirrored the meanderings of Buffalo Bayou. Even so, "streets and squares," one resident reported, "were still covered with trees and stumps that obstructed the way, especially at nighttime." If that were not enough, stray horses, dogs, cats, rats, and even hogs ran feral through the streets.[24]

Dead animals posed an even greater hazard than live ones. The carcasses lay where they fell and festered alongside the refuse that littered Houston boulevards. "[I]t was said that enough oxen had been killed on the roads from Houston to the high rolling country to build the first twenty-five miles of the Houston and Texas Central railroad," recalled Dr. Lockhart. He was not certain if such claims were factual, but he did know that he had personally seen "the roads lined with carcasses." Add horse droppings and raw sewage, and the stench was nauseating. The place smelled less like a town than a charnel house.[25]

More than animal carcasses sullied the avenues. Dr. Moore recalled that "instances have been known when three or four dead bodies have been picked up of a morning in the street, and that sickness and death visited almost every family." He noted that these fatalities were "more owing to the exposed situation of the inhabitants than the unhealthiness of the climate."[26]

Moore took the board of health to task for their negligence. He upbraided the members for the offal that "has been suffered to lay unremoved in our vicinity, so near as to impregnate the atmosphere with its putridity." He further excoriated officials for allowing the "washings of the kitchens and back yards of the whole city . . . to be thrown into the streets and gutters, there to rot and emit a stench disgusting and poisonous in the extreme." Shamefaced, Congressman Douglass admitted to his wife, "we liv like hogs."[27]

Naturally, citizens sought to avoid the fetid quagmires that passed for roads, but that produced another quandary. The city council subsequently approved an ordinance that forbade local jehus from riding horses or driving carriages and wagons on the sidewalks.[28]

Then there was the vermin. Traveler C. C. Cox decamped in the loft of a Houston home. His bed consisted of a few blankets thrown upon the hard plank flooring, which the Ohio native allowed would have been adequate but for "other company": "The fleas were as thick as the sands of the sea. Our clothes were actually bloody, and our bodies freckled after a night of warfare with the Vermine."[29]

Nor could Houstonians elude the maddening attention of flies and mosquitoes. An American tourist reported the ravages of the "blister fly" that he "found along the waters of the lower country, where they lie in wait for horses and cattle in such numbers that, when they light, they literally cover their victim and drive it to distraction." He swore that he had seen flies terrorize a horse until it was "covered with gore and champ his bit in the agony of torment." It was, of course, not only mounts that suffered. "Musquetoes and other insects," the author of a popular emigrant's guide asserted, "annoy the over-heated emigrants by day and night." An English traveler noted the "myriads of mosquitoes, which are so venomous and troublesome as to render exlstence hardly endurable." On a business trip, Francis Lubbock became lost and had to spend the night in the Brazos bottom. "The darkness," he recounted, "was made hideous by the yelping of wolves, the cries of the Mexican panther, and the never ending hum of mosquitos." He survived his night in the woods, but upon returning to his boarding house discovered his face "so disfigured by mosquito bites that my wife scarcely recognized me."[30]

THE MOST MISERABLE PLACE IN THE WORLD

If Houstonians suffered a dazzling assortment of vermin, rats were the worst. As soon as Houstonians snuffed their candles, the skitter of rats lulled them into slumber. Gustav Dresel, a young German immigrant, described the scourge of these loathsome creatures:

> Thousands of these troublesome guests made sport by night, and nothing could be brought to safety from them. All the provisions were soon begnawed by them, and the best rat dog became tired of destroying them because their number never decreased. Human corpses had to be watched during the whole night because otherwise these fiends ate their way into them. The finger of a little child who lay alone in the cradle for a few hours was half eaten away. This I saw myself. . . . Rats often dashed across me by the half-dozens at night. In the beginning this proves annoying; of course, later one gets accustomed to it.

One might accuse Dresel of exaggeration were his observations not corroborated by others. "I cannot convey an idea of the multitude of Rats in Houston at that time," C. C. Cox recollected. "They were almost as large as Prairie dogs and when night came on, the streets and Houses were litterly alive with these animals. Such running and squealling throughout the night, to say nothing of the fear of losing a toe or your nose, if you chanced to fall asleep, created such an apprehension that together with the attention that had to be given our other Companions made sleep well nigh impossible."[31]

The oppressive heat and humidity were also well nigh impossible to endure. From the beginning, the city achieved a reputation for its astronomically high temperatures. The summer of 1980 registered temperatures that *exceeded* one hundred degrees for fourteen consecutive days. Modern Texans can hardly imagine how debilitating such heat would have been before the advent of air conditioning. Numerous citizens of the Texas Republic cursed the hellish Houston summers. One reporter proclaimed the atmosphere "dry, hot, and oppressive." Citizens thought it paradoxical that streets were quagmires when it rained and "dusty and disagreeable" when it did not. Edward Stiff claimed that the climate was "decidedly unfriendly to health; quite as much so as New Orleans. . . . The morning sun beams down with scorching and sickly heat; and

From mountain dell or stream,

Not a fleeting zephyr springs;

Fearful lest the noontide beam

Scorch its soft, its silken wings.

President Houston learned that the privileges of his office did not include relief from the summers in his namesake city. On an especially blistering day, he beseeched: "God keep me clear of the heat of the natural as well as the political season." Physician John H. Bauer remembered one summer so hot that "we worked in Genl. Houston's house in Houston until early morning—stripped of all clothing except our shirts."[32]

So crushing was the heat and humidity that the entire city seemed to sink into a slough of lethargy. Ashbel Smith bemoaned, "the heat is so severe during the middle of the day, that most of us lie in the shade and pant—morning and evening." The editor of the *Morning Star*, left a vivid record of the misery:

Oh for a good cold norther! one of your real old-fashioned ones, early though it be for them. We are tired of gazing upon burning, brassy skies; upon hot looking clouds, and parched earth. We are weary of throwing

78   THE MOST MISERABLE PLACE IN THE WORLD

open all the doors and windows, and placing ourself in the draught, in hopes to catch one breath of cool air to cool our fevered brow. We are weary of staying at home in the day time, lest we should be scorched with intense heat; and of being obliged to remain within our mosquitoe-bar at night, lest we be devoured by the mosquitoes. We are weary of feeling the perspiration coursing down our cheeks as we sit at our desks puzzling our brains, or rummaging over the mails, in order to present something interesting to our readers. We are weary of this lassitude, and languor; this constant relaxation of mind and body, which incapacitates us alike for mental and physical labor. We want something to brace us up. And what is better for that purpose than a good cold norther?[33]

The sweat-soaked editor should have been careful what he wished for. Winters proved as frigid as summers were charring. Again, Houston's location was a factor. Buffalo Bayou provided the city's northern boundary; to south and west, "stretching far in the distance," recounted one resident, "is an extensive prairie with here and there a grove of timber." (Indeed, one of these groves would be the site of the gallows that feature so prominently in this unfolding morality play.) "The country westward of Houston for some thirty miles or more, is a level prairie," observed A. B. Lawrence, "with scarcely a sufficient inclination to carry off the water of the rains that fall upon it." All this wide, open space allowed icy winds to sweep through unimpeded, cutting scythe-like through dwellings and clothing The buffeting winds made the city cold; the marshy bayou rendered it damp.[34]

Hearty Houstonians might have endured the cold and abided the dampness, but the combination proved lethal for great numbers of them. Dr. John Washington Lockhart recalled that two consecutive winters were especially vicious. "In 1837 and 1838 there was a sleet," he recounted, "that broke all the large limbs off the old trees; and after melting, left the appearance as if a great cyclone had devastated the forest." The *Telegraph* noted that on February 16, 1837, the city experienced "Remarkably cold weather," with the mercury plummeting to "within ten degrees of zero." Dresel explained that residents were ill equipped for such conditions. "When fall came with its northers and there were only three stoves in the whole of Houston, we used to light fires in front of the saloon in the evening, stand around them and enjoy—not excepting the President— hot drinks with merry speeches." Lubbock concurred: "Stoves at that time were very seldom if ever seen." Even the president's cabin had no fireplace, "nothing but a small clay furnace in the room for him to get over and warm his fingers, Indian fashion." Writing his wife, Congressman Douglass grumbled, "The room that I occupy has no fire and I all most frose Last night." He cut his letter short: "I am quite cold so farewell." John Hunter Herndon bewailed the city's "cold disagreeable weather," which was, he believed, "worse than Kentucky." On 4 February 1838, his diary entry was laconic in its melancholy: "Several persons freeze to death."[35]

Describing the winter of 1838, Mary Austin Holley lamented: "The excessive bad weather for a month & a half past has defeated all objects, & interfered with all business. The few who could get about have had their labor for their pains," she concluded. "It has been truly unfortunate having such a winter—a thing unheard of before—so different from what the early season promise[d]. There has been no getting about for storms— Every body had to stop just where they were overtaken by them & use the best shelter they could." If winter proved a hardship, on occasion it at least provided spectacular landscapes. On February 16, Mrs. Holley noted, "Water froze solid in my room during the night. The prairie was like a sea of glass, glittering in the sunshine. It continued shining & freezing all day. As cold as Boston Commons."[36]

Most of Houston's dwellings—makeshift, ramshackle, and foul—did little to protect their inhabitants from the ravages of the weather. While barely fit for human habitation, vermin felt perfectly at home. Rats in their thousands, having feasted on the putrescent offal in the streets, then disputed possession of the shanties. On January 23, 1838, John Hunter Herndon received his first view of the city. "Arrived at Houston at 3 O'clock P.M.," he recorded in his diary. "Formed bad opinion of the place which time will correct or confirm. The buildings are all indifferent, some small, unfinished frames, the rest of boards and shantys." Dr. Smith admitted, "few of our houses have chimnies. And, indeed, we have as yet in this country but few of the comforts of civilized life." The small clapboard house belonging to Francis R. Lubbock and his French Creole wife, Adele, was typical of those throughout the city. It was constructed of "three-foot pine boards and covered with three-foot pine boards, and contained all told one room about twelve feet square and a smaller shed room. There was one door leading into the main room and one door from that room into the shed room, both of three-foot boards, with all the hinges made of wood. There was no window in the house," Lubbock recalled. "When air and light were wanted, a board was knocked off." San Jacinto veteran Moseley Baker and his wife also lived in a two-room clapboard house. In the larger room a carpet covered the dirt floor, which he explained, "gave an air of comfort contrasting strongly with the surroundings."[37]

With memories of the Runaway Scrape still fresh, Houstonians were hesitant to invest in permanent dwellings when they might have to abandon them at a moment's notice.

"Apprehensions of another invasion not having yet wholly subsided," Smith reported, "the improvements are for the most part of a temporary and unsubstantial nature."[38]

The twenty-year-old Francis Richard Lubbock was among the earliest residents of Houston. He aspired to become a wealthy merchant and sold the first barrel of flour and bag of coffee in the settlement. Yet, while living in the capital, he caught the political bug and began a life of public service that spanned sixty years. During the War Between the States, he served as Governor of Texas, at which time he sat for this portrait. *Author's Collection.*

President Houston was not one to put on airs—at least, when it came to his quarters. When ornithologist James J. Audubon visited him on May 4, 1837, the famed naturalist observed that the residence was a "small log house consisting of two rooms and a passage through, after the Southern fashion." Nor did Houston's billet impress visitor Mary Austin Holley. As her diary noted: "The President's cabin has no glass—slats across the windows with blankets interwoven supply the place." Francis Lubbock recalled the presidential mansion as a "small rough log cabin about twelve by sixteen feet, with probably a small shed attached." Notwithstanding his grubby surroundings, "Ol' Sam Jacinto" dressed to impress, and largely succeeded. Audubon thought the president striking in his "velvet coat and trousers trimmed with broad gold lace."[39]

Houses were so few and immigrants so many that the unprincipled began to prey on the unsuspecting. In April 1837, Gail Borden and Dr. Francis Moore, Jr., proprietors of the *Telegraph and Texas Register*, resolved

President Houston's Executive Mansion. The style of the building was typical of many in early Houston. They "contained all told one room about twelve feet square and a smaller shed room," which this photograph shows to great advantage. Since many witnesses recalled visiting the president in his "log cabin," this clapboard shanty may have been his second abode—and a considerable improvement over the first. *Courtesy Texas State Library and Archives Commission.*

to transfer their newspaper from Columbia to Houston. They arranged with a Houston contractor to build an office that was to be completed, or almost so, by the time of their projected arrival. After "groping" their way down Buffalo Bayou, the partners rushed off the *Yellow Stone* and, taking "time by the forelock," hurried to inspect their new office building. Disillusionment awaited them. Instead of a "nearly finished building," they discerned "like others who have confided in *speculative things*, we have been deceived. No building had ever been nearly finished at Houston intended for the press."[40]

Determined to proceed in the face of all obstacles, Borden and Moore rented a shanty, the "only convenient building obtainable," installed their press, and began production. Despite everything, Moore managed to retain his sense of humor—and the poetic—as he depicted the hovel in a couplet:

Without a roof, and without a floor,

Without windows and without a door.

The paper's new headquarters proved far from satisfactory. "The shanty is falling about our ears," Moore reported, "the massive beams have dropped upon the stands, made a most disgusting pi, and driven the workmen to seek safety outside, the devil alone looks smiling on the mischief." Yet his calamities had only begun. "The heavy rains of Monday night poured torrents into our shanty and transformed the floor to a bed of mud in which our journeymen stuck so fast that they could not stick to their business," Moore related a few days later. "We are obliged to suspend our operations." He was determined, however, that the interruption would be brief. Moore bought a house and shifted press and printers into drier offices.[41]

Gustav Dresel's introduction to Houston's architecture was both startling and cacophonous. In August 1838, when the young German arrived in the city, he encountered his business associate Robert Levenhagen. Since Dresel had not yet arranged for his lodging, Levenhagen proposed that he flop in his office until the new Houstonian could secure better accommodations. Dresel was unprepared for his first sight of his friend's corporate headquarters. "It was a little wooden hut, on four posts, about one and a half feet above the ground," he recalled, "and it contained not more floor space than fifteen feet square. Next to it was another building, namely, a rickety barn in which corn and corn meal were stored." In the weeks that followed, Dresel became acquainted with various members of

Houston's German community. Among his new friends was the Gerlach family, who operated a popular boardinghouse. The Gerlachs managed to find space for him in their attic "by the side of thirteen companions." Notwithstanding the cramped conditions, Dresel found his new bedmates an improvement over those at Levenhagen's office. As he explained it: "Pigs regularly held a party under the office during the night, so that we had to go to sleep to the melodious grunting of these unbearable animals; the change of lodgings was, therefore, not disagreeable."[42]

The flood of immigrants pouring into Houston soon learned that housing was limited and amenities minimal. Even government officials were not immune. As late as 1839, Congressman Douglass bemoaned, "I am unhaply situated hear for want of Room Lodgin." Inadequate space required that several men share the same room and frequently even the same bed. Many had to settle for a pallet on the floor. Recall Gustav Dresel's thirteen attic mates and C. C. Cox's flea infested loft; such accommodations were by no means extraordinary. Even John Hunter Herndon, a young gentleman imbued with well-developed notions of his dignity, had to bunk with a friend: "Took lodgings at Floyd's Hotel. Invited by Jackson Smith Esq. to take part of his room and bed."[43]

Matilda Houstoun left a delightful description of the snares awaiting both the patrons and proprietors of Houston hotels:

> There are plenty of inns at Houston, such as they are, and we took up our quarters at the "Houston House," a large shambling wooden building, kept by Captain or Colonel Baldwin, one of the most civil, obliging people I ever saw. We had a sitting room which was weather proof, though to keep out the intense cold was impossible. It was said that our landlord was anxious to add to the comforts of the house, but he had a great many bad debts; it was, he told us, a loosing concern altogether; more went out

than came in, and only that morning, having asked a gentleman to pay his bill, the reply was, "If you come to insult me again, sir, by God, I'll shoot you, sir."

The dining at the Houston House was nothing like that the English couple might have enjoyed in London. Having had enough of Texas table manners, "Our dinner we had in private." A contrite Colonel Baldwin allowed as how the hotel was "in a fix." Notwithstanding the landlord's regrets, Mrs. Houstoun recalled "our fare was not bad of its kind, there being 'pork dodgers' and 'dough doings,' (corn bread) chicken fixings, and sausages." The inn's wait staff was attentive, in their fashion: "Rossetta, a negress with rings on every finger, waited upon us, and a hideous creature she was: Jerry, too, the black porter, and a great thief, assisted."

Being foreign visitors, paying customers, and persons of obvious quality, Mrs. Houstoun and her husband were able to secure a room entirely to themselves. Such arrangements, however, offended the egalitarian sensibilities of one fellow who considered it outrageous that one couple should hog so much prime sleeping space. "We were disturbed . . . in the course of the night by the importunities of an unfortunate man, who could not find a bed," Mrs. Houstoun recounted, "and who kept knocking at all our doors, saying he was very cold and must come in." The mortified innkeeper again offered his apologies and explained that the lout belonged to a breed that was, sadly, all too common in the Republic of Texas: "He was what the landlord called a 'rowdy loafer;' not a pleasant companion, as it is by these people, and by these alone (who are not Texans be it said) that gouging and bowie knifing are practiced."

Colonel Baldwin sent the "rowdy loafer" packing, but the nocturnal travails of the Houstouns were far from finished. "The weather had by this time changed, and a cold sleety rain was falling," Mrs. Houstoun

86   THE MOST MISERABLE PLACE IN THE WORLD

remembered. "Our ceiling was of canvas, and in the night we were obliged to "fix" an umbrella over the bed, while I watched the feet of a restless cat as she wandered over our heads; her paws finding their way through the holes, which time had worn in our sail cloth covering." One may, at least, hope that the peripatetic feline enforced some degree of population control over the hotel's rats.[44]

This was Houston, where temperance was at best a hope and inebriation was always an option. While residents lacked most of the creature comforts, one frontier preacher chided that they always appeared abundantly supplied with "John Barley Corn and cigars." An array of saloons and grog shops stood ready to supply both, along with a glut of rotgut guaranteed to lift spirits and wreck health. Deputy Constable Edward Stiff cataloged Houston's public buildings. Among these were "forty-seven places for selling intoxicating drinks, most of which are gaming dens." Deputy Stiff, who visited these enterprises in a professional capacity, witnessed firsthand the corruption such places encouraged. "No wonder," he suggested, "that the habits of the people are dissolute." By August 1837, Ashbel Smith likened Houston to "a sort of Babel of persons of every degree of morality."[45]

The most notorious of the gin palaces was Henry Kessler's Round Tent, located on the west side of Main Street and a stone's throw from Congress Avenue. It was difficult to miss, for its perimeter measured more than a hundred feet, and it stood between thirty and forty feet high. To be situated in such improvised accommodations, Kessler offered a remarkably refined selection. In addition to the "bust-head" whiskey, he provided the gentry with "brandy cocktails, gin toddies, claret punches, cherry-brandy de la forêt noir, etc."[46]

The habitués of Houston's forty-seven saloons swilled in quantities that would have proven lethal to those with less tolerance for it. Indeed, rotgut had proven fatal for "scores of young men who died from intemperance." A censorious American tourist confessed "a few" residents did not "exceed the limits of moderation," but that a "large majority knew no restraint to their appetites." He expounded:

> The extent to which this vice was carried exceeded all belief. It appeared to be the business of the great mass of the people to collect around these centers of vice and hold their drunken orgies, without seeming to know that the Sabbath was made for more serious purposes and night for rest. Drinking was reduced to a system and had its own laws and regulations. Nothing was regarded as a greater violation of established etiquette than for one who was going to drink not to invite all within a reasonable distance to partake, so that the Texians being entirely a military people not only fought but drank in platoons.

Dresel also mentioned the conviviality of Houston bibulousness. "In Texas barrooms," he affirmed, "one cannot in decency order a drink without inviting all one's acquaintances and their friends who happened to be present. This is, of course, reciprocated, and thus there are frequent occasions to take a drink."[47]

Young men, flowing liquor, and abundant weaponry proved a deadly combination. Audubon expressed his amazement to discover a gang of Indians, "drunk and hallooing," staggering down the streets of the capital. One Englishman found Bowie knives the "tenant of every Texan's bosom." "There were frequent brawls," Dresel related, "pistols were drawn, bowie knives flashed, and as everyone walked about well armed, these incidents looked rather dangerous. I twice witnessed scenes where first in the barroom and afterwards in the street, men were wounded in this manner." These conditions compelled John Hunter Herndon to conclude that Houston was the "greatest sink of dissipation and vice that modern times have known." Universalist minister Erasmus Manford concurred. He depicted the town as, "a moral desert—a hell on earth," where "vice of most every name and grade reigned triumphantly."[48]

Not content to pummel each other, inhabitants also assailed the King's English. British tourist Nicholas Maillard discovered that Houston's working class affected a "flash," or slang, vernacular. "When speaking of those men who have been fortunate enough to gain their esteem," he documented, "they say, 'He's an up-street man, that,'—'A right smart man,'—'A pretty considerable of a man,'—'A tarnation tall man': this last expression, when applied to some of their eminent men who happen to be considerably under the middle standard, is far more amusing than all the rest of their peculiarities, and cannot fail to probe the gravity of a stranger."[49]

Prostitutes, inevitable wherever large numbers of single men flock, contributed to the air of debauchery. By 1840, Houston's Cyprians had become so brazen, that city officials decreed that any woman strutting her wares in a style "not usual for respectable females," would suffer a fine of not less than fifty dollars and a jail term of ten to thirty days. The ordinance had little effect, for the following year another demanded a twenty-dollar bond for any "female of ill fame" discovered in a public place after 8:00 P.M. Because of this crackdown, many strumpets moved their activities indoors. Most worked out of local boarding houses, the most notorious being Pamelia Mann's Mansion House. In 1837 and 1838, however, most of Houston's harlots plied their trade in the open air.[50]

One of the women working the squalid Houston streets was Alamo widow Susanna Dickinson. The death of her husband, Almaron, left her with few friends, few marketable skills, and a toddler to feed. By 1837, desperate for a provider and protector, she had taken up with an unsavory fellow named John A. Parker, who lived near Harrisburg. Gossips whispered behind their hands that Mrs. Dickinson had begun to practice the oldest profession. Sam S. Smith, who later served as San Antonio alderman, treasurer, and mayor, testified that she was "living in open concubinage with the said Parker." Smith surmised that Parker hired out his common law wife and further asserted, "Mrs. Dickinson was generally considered a strumpet." Smith claimed to have particular knowledge of her activities, as seen in his affidavit:

> Sam S. Smith also says that on one occasion he personally witnessed Mrs. Dickinson, in flagrante dilecto, with a man boarding at Parker's house; That the connection took place in a log barn in daylight, and that he (Sam S. Smith) was summoned by another man to see the assignation, which he did by looking between the logs of the barn.

Alamo widow Susanna Dickinson had few pleasant memories of Houston. During her time there, she struggled to feed herself and her daughter, divorced an abusive husband, and practiced the oldest profession. Later in life, she found a good man, made a true love match, and moved to Austin where she won respect as a pioneer matron and an accomplished businesswoman. She was about twenty-four years of age in 1838. Years later, during her respectable period, she sat for this photograph. *Courtesy Texas State Library and Archives Commission.*

90   THE MOST MISERABLE PLACE IN THE WORLD

This assignation was typical of most in Houston: a quick rut behind the boarding house, in a ratty shack, in a dark alley. These were slam-bam grinds; speedy, sordid, and, for both the trollops and their johns, ultimately soul-killing.[51]

Houston's manners slowly changed as "respectable females" made their appearance. The first to arrive was Charlotte Allen, wife of Augustus. The only accommodation in town fit for the occupancy of a lady was a newly built log cabin. When its owners learned of Mrs. Allen's circumstances, they graciously vacated the cabin and offered it for her use. In March 1837, President Houston was able to tell a friend, "I am informed that many ladies are coming to Houston and that society will be fine." Nor was he deceived. On July 16, Harrisburg County officials issued Houston's first marriage license to Hugh McCrory and Mary Smith. Methodist Minister Z. H. Matthews joined the happy couple on July 23. Even Susanna Dickinson acquired respectability. By June 1837 she had cut loose from Parker, moved to Houston, and was cohabitating with John Williams. On or about November 27, 1837, the couple made their union legal. Williams may have made an honest woman out of the widow Dickinson, but she would learn that her new husband had brought his own baggage to the marriage. Her wedded bliss would be brief.[52]

By Christmas Day 1837, Charlotte Allen was out of the borrowed cabin and in to her new home. That day Mary Austin Holley made an entry in her diary: "Staid all night with Mrs. Allen—very hospitably entertained—a new good house—well—even elegantly furnished." The presence of ladies provided some modicum of gentility, but their numbers were too few to implement significant improvement.[53]

Christmas Day 1837, was memorable for reasons other than Mrs. Allen's furnishings. The night before, a rider galloped into Houston with news that a Mexican army was mustering below the Rio Grande.

Charlotte Allen, wife of Augustus, was the first woman to arrive in the ramshackle settlement of Houston, earning her designation as the "mother of Houston." By Christmas, 1837, she was able to receive guests in a splendid home, which Mary Austin Holley described as "elegantly furnished." She was thirty-two-years-old at the time; she obviously sat for this photograph many years later. *Courtesy Texas State Library and Archives Commission.*

Observing the scene from the Allens' gallery, Mary Austin Holley witnessed the "whole town in motion like bees swarming." Even so, Houstonians had heard such warnings before. "Nobody was afraid," Mrs. Holley recorded, "but everybody was busy." The Allens refused to allow such distractions to ruin their celebrations, and guests took their fill of eggnog. As eggs were demanding prices as high a fifty cents each, such hospitality was all the more impressive. Still, as Mrs. Holley explained in a letter to her children, the Allens were "very genteel people & live well. [They] have a good house & elegant furniture (mahogany—hair sofas—red velvet rocking chairs &c) all nice and new, & in modern style. Here we were most kindly entertained for two days." The invasion rumors proved baseless, and citizens shifted their attentions to bringing in 1838 in high style.[54]

The juxtaposition of splendor and squalor jarred the senses, but a few Houstonians made the effort to acquire and display works of art. During Mrs. Holley's December 1837 visit, President Houston took her on a tour of a gallery

In September 1836, Nacogdoches voters elected twenty-six-year-old John Kirby Allen to represent them in the Texas Congress. Yet, once in office, he influenced fellow congressmen to transfer the seat of government to the then non-existent town of Houston. The move greatly bolstered the fortunes of the Allen brothers. John K. Allen did not long enjoy the benefits of his machinations; he died in Houston in 1838. *Courtesy Houston Public Library, Houston Metropolitan Research Center.*

in the new capitol building. All this presidential attention appeared to have flattered her. Writing to her children, she bragged how the "Sword of San Jacinto" had "gallanted us to the Capitol, in one wing of which is a gallery of portraits of distinguished characters of the last campaign. You see the arts flourish in this new land already."[55]

Notwithstanding a few cultural pretensions, for the next several years Houston remained nasty, brutish, and propelled by testosterone. In the "whole population of Houston," an American visitor remarked, "I doubt whether there were more than sixty or seventy females, both married and single. Some of the immigrants had left their wives behind until the country became more settled," he explained, "and many had never had any. For the benefit of the ladies, I would mention that speculations are to be made in Texas." On March 15, 1838, John Hunter Herndon "saw thirteen ladies at one time on the street," an event so unusual that he recorded it in his diary. That number, he proclaimed, was "more than I supposed were in the city." The first site of the "precocious city" almost overwhelmed

Millie Gray, a daughter of Virginia society. She felt like a peacock trapped in a chicken coop. "[M]y heart feels oppressed & it requires an effort to wear the appearance of cheerfulness," she explained. "I could (if I were a weeping character) sit down & fairly weep."[56]

John Allen's early death shattered his dreams of wealth and fame. According to one admirer, Allen had lived "long enough to see his city lots commanding prices equal to any city lots in America; and was beginning to enjoy the blessing of a fortune, when his earthly career was stopped, and he was suddenly called to the bar of his God." In this Age of Romanticism, ladies and gentlemen of a certain class adulated on the altar of sensibilité. The Romantics valued feeling over reason and held that all human experience was to be savored—even death. Indeed, mortality with all its trappings fascinated them. They viewed mawkish mourning of the departed as full expression of true feeling.[57]

A common mosquito demolished all of Allen's schemes, all his talent and energy, everything he was and everything he might have been. He died of "congestive fever," what modern readers know as malaria. And therein an irony. No one had done more to envisage, invent, and promote the city of Houston. Indeed, the triumph of that enterprise became his obsession. Allen had asserted that there was "no place in Texas more healthy" than Houston. But it was he who had placed the town beside a mosquito-infested "green scum lake," a decision that cost the lives of hundreds of the city's residents—including his own. "There is no motion visible in the waters of [Buffalo] Bayou for nearly two-thirds of the year," an English visitor observed, "which is supposed to render its banks most insalubrious." There was, of course, nothing malevolent in Allen's actions; in 1836, no one understood that malarial infection began with a mosquito bite. Nor should one fault Allen for creating a great city or assuring that his venture would be lucrative. But flourishing communities, those that provide affluence and quality of life, do not simply happen. One must design them. Many cities have, of course, evolved with a discernible absence of urban planning, but they tend to function like, well, Houston. One may reasonably rebuke Allen for neglecting to foster carefully the municipality he established. If John Kirby Allen was the "Father of Houston," he ultimately proved a deadbeat dad.[58]

Mary Wollstonecraft Shelley's *Frankenstein; or, The Modern Prometheus* revealed the Romantic essence with all its passion and pathos. Published in 1818, the book attracted audiences on both sides of the Atlantic. The tale revolved around Victor Frankenstein, a brilliant Swiss physician in his twenties, who fashioned an artificial life. The manufactured man, however, repelled his creator who rejected his experiment and turned the creature out of doors, ignoring his responsibility for the not quite human being he had created. Although a giant in stature, the creature was in the true sense a babe in the woods, without love, without care, without direction. The creature became a murderous misanthrope and swore vengeance against the father of his misery, a mania that by the end of the novel had wrecked the lives of both Frankenstein and his creature.[59]

Did John Allen ever read the novel? No one knows, but it would have appealed to his temperament. If he had, it is difficult to imagine that, as he lay dying at the age of twenty-eight, he did not see in himself elements of Victor Frankenstein. Moreover, if one can extend the allegory further, he was surely perceptive enough to recognize that Houston had been his "creature."

Drinking, fighting, and Rangling
Houston, December 10, 1837

Representative Kelsey Harris Douglass can scarcely suppress his disdain for Houston City. On December 10, 1837, he writes his wife in Nacogdoches complaining, "Drinking, fighting, and rangling is the order of the day at this place." This illustration provides a sampling of various frontier types that constitute the "rowdy loafers" and depicts one of the grog-house brawls that have so alienated the congressman.

A disagreement over a card game has erupted into a personal affray: an all too common occurrence. The dapper fellow aiming a flintlock pistol in his right hand and wielding a massive Bowie knife in his left, represents a Southern planter. His opponent, a U.S. Army deserter, retains his regulation wheel-cap and roundabout jacket. His weapon—borrowed from the U.S. arsenal—is an Ames M1832 Foot Artillery sword. The nefarious-looking veteran with the eye-patch affects a Mexican serape and vaquero spurs, souvenirs from San Jacinto. Against the left wall, a top-hatted gentleman struggles with a backwoods leatherstocking. The city slicker brandishes an "Arkansas toothpick," the buck skinner a Bowie knife. The Mexican bus boy in the far background is one of the some seven hundred prisoners of war taken at San Jacinto. As Mexico's politicians promise further hostilities, Texas officials refuse to release their prisoners. Feeding and housing them, however, is a problem—one solved by hiring out hapless captives as unpaid "servants" to local citizens. Having survived the battlefield carnage, this despondent underling finds working in a Houston gin joint almost as dangerous.

Notwithstanding the brouhaha, a scruffy tomcat stands guard over his dinner—one of the thousands of rats that run riot through the town's squalid streets and shanties.

4
Vagabond Volunteers
The Rowdy Loafers

No one knows exactly when David James Jones turned up in Houston, but he most certainly arrived as an outcast. He was not alone. Hundreds of young men found themselves in similar straits. Later generations might label them "hobos," "bums," "transients," "indigents," "vagrants," or "the homeless." In 1838, however, Texians of good reputation scorned them as "rowdy loafers." Whatever one called such fellows, they were, in a word, undesirables: "rowdy" because they were young men with too much time on their hands and "loafers" as a result of government policy.[1]

During their struggle for independence, Texians had begged American volunteers to assist them. The penniless provisional government could not provide cash incentives, so officials promised the one commodity that Texas had in abundance: land. Many came, many served, and many received munificent bounties of real estate. An act of the provisional government gave 640 acres to each soldier in the regular army; another granted 8,640 acres to volunteers who enlisted for the duration of the conflict. Even those who served for three months could expect 320 acres. Word crackled in the "old states" like flame through dry grass. During the summer of 1836, hundreds of Americans flocked to Texas seeking adventure, glory, and renown. To their annoyance, they found that Santa Anna was a prisoner; the enemy was in retreat; and the fighting, for the moment anyway, was finished. Even so, Texians expected Mexicans to launch a new campaign and enlisted newcomers into their ranks. So it was that the cast of the army transformed from settlers fighting for hearth and home to one three times as large consisting primarily of American volunteers with few ties to the Republic they had sworn to defend. And the most fractious of these American volunteers was Felix Huston.[2]

One historian described General Huston as a "true friend of Texas." An influential Mississippi politician and slave trader, Huston was practicing law in Natchez when the Texas revolt ignited. He had anticipated the event. On July 14, 1835, almost three months before the Gonzales "Come and Take It" fight, the prescient attorney organized a meeting in Natchez to promote Texas independence and secure money to achieve that goal. An effective fundraiser, he mustered men and money in Mississippi and Kentucky. He invested his own capital, incurring a personal debt of forty thousand dollars. On May 5, 1836, he and Rezin P. Bowie, who many claimed was the inventor of the infamous blade most often associated with his late brother, left Natchez at the head of five to seven hundred American volunteers. Unfortunately, the climatic battle at San Jacinto had occurred thirteen days before. The doughty band finally arrived in Texas on July 4, 1836. Notwithstanding his dreams of martial glory, Huston was a season late and a battle short.[3]

Huston performed his best service to Texas while still in Mississippi. From the moment he set foot in the Republic, he became an inconvenient "friend." He embroiled himself in local politics, aligning himself against ad interim President David G. Burnet. When Burnet replaced General Thomas J. Rusk with Mirabeau B. Lamar, Huston protested the administration's "interference." When Lamar arrived in camp, Rusk called for a popular vote. Notwithstanding the troops' overwhelming support of Rusk, Lamar blithely continued to issue orders as commander in chief. Just as blithely, the independent volunteers (by a vote of 1,500 to 179) elected to ignore them. Huston and other officers finally persuaded Lamar to step aside. It was a humiliating episode for Lamar, Burnet, and the rule of law.[4]

In September 1836, Sam Houston became the Republic's first elected president; he soon learned, however, that tribulations involving the army robbed much of the joy from his victory. General Rusk, who had taken command of the army after Houston received a serious wound at San Jacinto, won appointment as secretary of war. The post of army commander remained unfilled, but legions stood ready to fill Rusk's boots. "There were very few above the rank of captain," one spectator jibed, "who

Attorney, opportunist, and would-be conqueror, Felix Huston was an insubordinate thorn in President Houston's flesh. Historian Eugene C. Barker accurately observed that his Texas service was "more obstreperous than effective." Huston wounded Albert Sidney Johnston in a duel, but later persuaded him to support plans to invade Mexico. When President Houston furloughed the Republic's unruly volunteers, he relegated Huston to a general without an army. Many of those unemployed soldiers descended on the new capital where they achieved a reputation as "rowdy loafers." In 1857, Huston died in Natchez, Mississippi, without achieving his dreams of glory. Courtesy Texas State Library and Archives Commission.

did not aspire to be commander-in-chief!" In December 1836, Houston lamented: "The curse of the country has been an excess of officers." When he took office, "the force in the field was reported at six hundred and fifty, and the number of officers commissioned five hundred and ninety two." The president may have said this with tongue firmly fixed in cheek, but the statement accurately described his frustration. On December 20, 1836, President Houston appointed Felix Huston junior brigadier general and *temporary* commander of the army. President Houston never had any intention to retain Huston, a newcomer with scant military experience, in command. Nevertheless, shortly thereafter Huston started speaking of "my army."[5]

From the instant he took temporary command, Huston demonstrated that his ambition leapt far beyond his ability. Impatient to realize his dreams of conquest, he proposed an invasion of Mexico that would culminate in the capture of Matamoros. The men admired their thirty-six-year-old commander for he *looked* every inch a hero. Attorney William Fairfax Gray recorded his initial inklings of the man: "Here is a General Felix Huston, dressed *a la militaire*. He is tall and well made, rather slender. Has the bearing of a proud, ambitious man, evidently making an effort to be free and easy, so as to win popular favor." The volunteers nicknamed their youthful chief, "Old Long-shanks"—referencing his height—or "Old Leather-Breeches"—denoting his rough and rowdy manner. How could his men fail to love him? In his rebellion, insolence, and sedition, Huston was a mirror image of themselves.[6]

The soldiers Huston found in camp did not match the splendid specimens of his Napoleonic vision. "At the time I took command the camp was flooded with whiskey and even retail shops made of the tents— and quarrelling and fighting and noise was heard all over camp."[7]

Much quarrelling, fighting, and noise also surrounded the proposed Matamoras operation. President Houston opposed it. As early as August 1836, he had expressed reservations: "I have always abhored the thought of attacking Matamoras, for the reason that no benefit could result to us from it." Instead, he stressed that Texians should "husband our resources, and act defensively, and our independence will be established."[8]

General Huston bemoaned the lack of fundamental supplies. "I must mention a matter of *immense* importance," he wrote to the president; "We have not cartridge paper or flints. And it would be really ridiculous if we were cut to pieces for want of such articles—or compelled to retreat. The waste paper of the printing office would be thankfully received." The courage of the troops meant little if they had no flints for their flintlock muskets.[9]

Notwithstanding the president's resistance, Huston's schemes seduced the troops, most of whom had also missed the fighting. As Huston admitted, they were not of the highest caliber. As one piece of period doggerel expressed it:

> To reckless spirits journeying from afar
> 'Tis Texas yet presents a Polar Star
> By misfortune, crime and oppression driven,
> From every State and Kingdom under heaven.

The volunteers may have represented "every State and Kingdom," but the majority hailed from southern states and reflected southern culture and traditions. English gentlewoman Frances Trollope recorded her impressions of these boisterous swains. Southerners were a "most disorderly set of persons, constantly gambling and wrangling, very seldom sober,

104 VAGABOND VOLUNTEERS

and never suffering a night to pass without giving practical proof of the respect in which they hold the doctrine of equality, and community of property."[10]

These "reckless spirits" were bored and eager for glory. Two soldiers had died in a "drunken debauche," General Huston disclosed. "The army was proportionably large," one old Texian recorded, "and most of its members had come to reap fame and distinction. The elements, though calm, were not cohesive. A single spark would inflame the entire body." An Ohio visitor explained that as "many of the men and some of the officers were not actuated by the most honorable motives, either in coming to the country or in joining the army, mutiny, insubordination, and difficulties of all kinds among one another were the natural consequences." One authority that knew more of the character of these rascals than most (and better than he might have wished) left a vivid portrait of this disparate rabble:

> Here were gathered those indomitable men of battle whom Santa Anna pointedly characterized as the *tumultuario* of the Mississippi Valley; the ardent youth of the South, burning for glory and military enterprise. Here enthusiasts of constitutional freedom were mingled with adventurous soldiers from Europe; and souls as knightly, generous, and unstained as Bayard's, with outlaws and men of broken and desperate fortunes. Some of the best and some of the worst people in the world were thrown into contact; but in one quality all were alike, a hardihood that no danger could check.

Seldom had the character of a general so matched that of his soldiers.[11]

President Houston had already decided that General Huston had to go, at least as army commander. The Chief Executive offered command to

An older Albert Sidney Johnston here wears the uniform of a Confederate general. Felix Huston seriously wounded him in an infamous duel but he, nevertheless, came to support his assailant's scheme for an invasion of Mexico. Johnston died heroically on the field at Shiloh in 1862. *Courtesy Texas State Library and Archives Commission.*

General James Hamilton, former governor of South Carolina and a firm supporter of Texas. Hamilton prudently refused. Houston then settled on West Point graduate Albert Sidney Johnston, an "officer of experience and high reputation." On January 31, 1837, Johnston won appointment as senior brigadier general in command of the army. He was three years younger than Huston but years ahead in maturity, intelligence, and ability. Johnston was an adult; Huston would always behave like a petulant adolescent. It looked as if Huston's days as temporary commander were numbered.[12]

Yet, on February 4, 1837, when Johnston arrived in camp to take lawful command of the army, General Huston refused to stand down. Instead, citing his refusal to be "overslaughed under humiliating circumstances," he challenged his replacement to a duel. Years later Huston told Jefferson Davis, the future president of the Confederate States of America, that since he "could not fight the President, Sam Houston"—the one actually accountable for his removal—"he was glad to have a gentleman to hold responsible." Johnston accepted the challenge; to do otherwise would have

106   VAGABOND VOLUNTEERS

damned him forever in the eyes of the troops. The antagonists exchanged six shots on the banks of the Lavaca River. Huston's last bullet tore through Johnston's hip, rendering him unable to assume command. Besides, Huston was now more popular than ever. When he returned to camp following the duel, one witness observed that a "thousand soldiers rushed forward to congratulate him." The raucous throng would never have countenanced his removal. Both General Huston and the mutable, rank-scented mob he led had spun wildly out of control. Neither seemed willing to follow the orders of the duly elected civilian authorities. By a calculated act of violence, Huston had extended his tenure as "temporary" commander and President Houston was powerless to do anything about it—for the time being.[13]

The president had no choice but to retain Huston. The temporary commander may have been a querulous fool, but he was the only man the volunteers seemed willing to follow. Besides, the more professional officers had already resigned their commissions in disgust. "The best and most intelligent officers absent themselves," General Huston acknowledged, "and leave but indifferent materials." President Houston knew how he felt. The Republic needed an army to defend it against Mexican invasion, which reliable agents reported to be in the offing. There were also political considerations. The president required the backing of the army "party" to preserve control of the government. Most of his opposition came from those with army ties or who harbored military aspirations themselves. Thomas J. Green and Moseley Baker were chief among the president's political rivals, men whose dislike of Houston stemmed from his conduct of the San Jacinto campaign a year earlier. So President Houston had to bide his time and give General Huston just enough rope to hang himself.[14]

Following the duel, conditions deteriorated even further. Under Huston's command the army fell victim to hunger, disease, and death. He knew how to inflame a mob but not how to feed it. In a letter to President Houston dated March 5, 1837, Colonel Henry Teal, one of Huston's field officers, bemoaned the deprivation soldiers had to endure. "[W]e have not one mouthful of bread Stuffs," the colonel explained in an inimitable syntax entirely his own, "nor hav not had for ten days and beef is verry Scears and hear [hard?] to get and when got verry pore and bad." Upon receiving such reports, Houston wrote to Texian agents in New Orleans, urging that they immediately dispatch provender to the soldiers in the field. "The supplies, sent for are indispensable to the salvation of the army," he wrote. "Unless our friends now sustain us, [they] will leave Texas in a situation as deplorable, as it was on the 20th of March last year," during the height of the Runaway Scrape. President Houston had already received reports that bands of soldiers were ransacking supplies from citizens without offering even the promise of compensation. "My object," he explained to one officer, "is to have the Army supplied regularly and prevent all future impressments of supplies or any thing else which may belong to the citizens."[15]

The volunteers not only failed to observe the regulation and routine of a military organization, but also openly mocked such notions. "They would have marched unmurmuringly into the open jaws of death," one old Texian declared, "rather than yield a point of pride, or of their idea of honor." He added that the recalcitrant volunteers were "without discipline, subordination, or effective organization, so obedience was a mere matter of choice." Colonel Teal complained, "I am adoing evry thing in my power for to disiplin my command . . . [but] it is verry hard for to command men that is bear footed and naked and hongry." Still, Colonel Teal did not have long to suffer the indignity of commanding such slothful soldiers. Two months after penning this dispatch, the colonel was shot in his sleep by a brute who resented the officer's efforts to enforce "disiplin."[16]

Learning of Teal's murder, Houston dispatched a sharp-worded communiqué to the troops. He sugared the pill by lauding their service under difficult conditions: "Posterity will number you amongst the proudest spirits who have dared to strike for liberty." But then he denounced Teal's murder and urged the volunteers to maintain order: "It was a felon deed; it was no soldier by whom it was perpetrated; it was a miscreant." General Huston did not seem overly concerned; boys, after all, would be boys. Moreover, he had no wish to share Teal's fate.[17]

With the Johnston problem solved, Huston pushed ahead with his invasion schemes. President Houston, however, recalled how the Matamoros Expedition of 1835–1836 had almost doused all hope for Texas and prompted the needless loss of life at the Alamo and Goliad. He had no intention of reprising those debacles. While Huston agitated, Houston stalled. The general finally absorbed that the president did not support him or his machinations. He shared his frustration in a March 28 letter to Albert Sidney Johnston. Huston asserted that it was "entirely useless to argue or reason with the President on this subject. . . . As to our waging war, he will not hear of it." He closed on a dejected note: "I am in low spirits as to our prospects, and deem Texas in a very critical situation." Did he really expect sympathy from the man he had attempted to kill just weeks earlier? Remarkably, Johnston had discounted his injuries for the good of the service. He also believed an offensive would force the Mexican Congress to finally recognize Texas independence.[18]

Huston did not sit idle while his aspirations faded like the mist; a bold stroke could salvage a "critical situation." As early as March 16, Huston had applied for a ninety-day leave to Mississippi to arrange his private affairs. The president immediately granted the request. Here, at last, was a way to get this mettlesome upstart out of his hair. Huston, however, delayed his departure believing himself indispensable. He had acquired an unlikely ally. Now, both he and Albert Sidney Johnston pressed the case for a new Matamoros Expedition. Recovered from his wound and willing to forgive the attempt on his life, Johnston finally took command of the army. But Huston remained as his right-hand man. This improbable duo believed that they needed more men to assure the success of the proposed invasion. It was not Houston, but Johnston and Huston who first advanced the notion of a temporary furlough for the army. The pair failed to date their joint petition, but clerks noted that it arrived in the president's office on May 24. The Johnston–Huston plan released all but three hundred of the Republic's soldiers. Both generals proposed traveling to the United States, where they planned to recruit six thousand American volunteers who would arrive in Texas by November 1. Huston and Johnston intended to launch their invasion on December 1.[19]

President Houston perceived a problem with this extravagant design: if the Republic could not feed the two thousand troops already in ranks, how ever would it supply an additional six thousand? It was an absurd proposal, but it did provide Houston an opening. As early as May 19, he had entertained the notion of placing a portion of the army on what would amount to permanent leave. That day the president wrote Secretary of War William S. Fisher: "I have come to the conclusion as there is no prospect of an active campaign that one half to two thirds of the army may be furloughed for their time in service." Now that Huston and Johnston advanced the furlough idea themselves, Houston might release as many men as he wished and afterward allow that he had only acted upon his generals' proposal. The president authorized Fisher to grant leaves to as many of the troops as he deemed appropriate.[20]

When the secretary of war arrived in camp he was "assailed by crowds of applicants for furlough." The "tumultuario" seemed to have had enough of hunger, inactivity, and the rigors of camp life. Even before his arrival,

110   VAGABOND VOLUNTEERS

most of the troops were feeling footy. It was time to move on. Many of them were drifters anyway, gamblers, thimbleriggers, men on the make for the next big score. The majority, who had joined up anticipating a quick coup, now realized that military life offered nothing of what they craved. The vision of wealth, fame, and glory had proven a mirage. It was manifest: they would not fulfill their destiny in the Texas army.[21]

On May 24, Fisher wrote Houston asserting it "would be good policy to furlough all but military men and . . . new recruits. This would leave in the field a force of 600 men." The president immediately approved Fisher's proposition and in one stroke reduced the army to a manageable number. In time, those troops that remained served out their enlistments, received their furloughs, or deserted. Francis Lubbock, involved in Texas politics for more than sixty years, later stated the "furloughing of the army of the Republic in 1837 was one of the most marked evidences of statecraft" he had ever witnessed.[22]

President Houston's deft maneuver presented his riotous general with a fait accompli. When Huston wrote the president on June 3, he seemed a bit shell shocked: "Sir—Having received certain intelligence that the Honl. Secretary of War Wm. S. Fisher has furloughed and is engaged in furloughing a large part of the army indefinitely," he wrote, "I cannot, but think that such a decided step a rejection of the proposition made by Genl. A. Sidney Johnston and myself." The man's grasp of the obvious was profound.[23]

President Houston had resolved one crisis only to create another. Suddenly, hundreds of soldiers were free as the air and loose on the countryside. Since most were Americans, some booked passage back to the United States never to return. Many, however, had nothing waiting for them back home and cast their lot with Texas. Others had a jail sentence, or worse, awaiting them in the "old states" and had to remain. One fugitive admitted, "if there had been no such place as Texas I would have been hanged." Many could have said the same. For the most part the furloughed soldiers were young men, without money, skills, or connections. But following months of want and inactivity, they did have a thirst to quench, steam to blow off, and wild oats to sow. Houston sounded like their kind of town.[24]

The discharged warriors descended on the new capital like a plague of locusts. In most cases, however, it was they who found themselves stripped clean. Unscrupulous civilians were eager to exploit the desperation and gullibility of these young men. Many still had hay in their hair and cotton in their heads; suddenly they found themselves among hard-nosed hucksters with their feet on the ground and their hands in a rube's pocket. The volunteers were wholly out of their depth. A visitor noted that speculators found Houston a "fine field" for their "shrewdness and energies":

> Some were engaged in purchasing the discharges of the soldiers, each of whom is entitled, beyond his pay of eight dollars a month in government paper, to six hundred and forty acres of land for each six months' service and in proportion for a less period. For this he gets a certificate from the government. The discharged soldier comes to Houston, hungry and next to naked, with nothing but his claims upon the government, which his situation compels him to sell. If he gets ten per cent for his money script and fifty dollars for a six months' discharge, he receives quite as much as these claims were selling for during the summer. When the storm beaten soldier thus sees the reward of all his suffering reduced to a few dollars, he has too much reason to lament over the time which he has worse than thrown away and often in despair gives himself up to total abandonment.

The disgusted chronicler wanted to say more but as "Texas may have need for more soldiers, it is well that I should be silent."[25]

A masculine bonhomie prevailed in early Houston that Gustav Dresel found alluring. "At that time fifteen hundred to two thousand people, mostly men, were living in Houston in the most dissimilar manner," he recalled. "The President, the whole personnel of the government, many lawyers who found ample means of support in those regions, a large number of gamblers, tradesmen, artisans, former soldiers, adventurers, curious travelers from the United States, about a hundred Mexican prisoners who made suitable servants, daily new troops of Indians—all associated like chums on an equal footing." The young Rhinelander was a bit sanguine in his zeal. Former soldiers would not have believed that the pot-bellied merchants received them on an "equal footing."[26]

For all of its "common man" speechifying, the Age of Jackson remained extremely class conscious. Even in Texas, the social cream still rose to the top of the churn. Those who enjoyed a better education, dressed better, had a better grasp of society and its rules, clearly thought themselves, well, *better* than wayfaring rabble. Following John Hunter Herndon's encounter with some of the city's destitute, he exhibited a remarkable lack of concern. Then, perhaps it was not *that* remarkable; in a world filled with death and squalor, callous indifference was simply part of life. He did not consider such slovenly creatures worth more than a cursory mention: "Passed a Dutchman of thirty-five years who was, and had been for six months, living in a hogshead, another living in a house just six feet square and many others in like situation." When patricians had to hobnob with the hoi polloi, they frequently took pains to make them feel like pigs at a garden party.[27]

Such disdain, however, might easily get a fellow killed. Those on the bottom rungs of Houston's social ladder were quick to discern snub or slur. Texas settler Andrew Davis certainly considered himself a member of the "common man" fraternity. Indeed, he recalled that he was nine or ten years old before he wore a pair of shoes. Sprouting up along the Red River near Clarksville, he discovered that even the slave children boasted better clothing than his. "But if one of them showed that he felt himself above me," he crowed, "I lit on to him with a vengeance and never stopped until I whipped him." Expressing an attitude typical of his kin and culture, he explained: "I am more strongly tempted to fight if one shows he is above me than for almost any other offense." He concluded with a declaration that could have been the credo of any rowdy loafer: "I will allow a man to be greater than I, but not better."[28]

Southern fathers passed along their passion for liberty and contempt for privilege. Every man who took pride in that designation—and every boy who aspired to it—propagated and preserved the legacy of freedom. Independence was the birthright of every freeborn American, bought with the blood of patriots and secured through constant vigilance. One might humble himself before the Almighty, but before no other, no matter how affluent or highborn. To forge a life in a new land, their forefathers had defied tyrants. Here, none owed his livelihood to some preening aristocrat. Here, one scraped his living (or not) by the lights of his wits and energy.

Of course, not everyone shared the ebullience for social equality. English tourist Mrs. Frances Trollope numbered among its critics. A loyal subject of His Britannic Majesty and an adherent of a rigid class system, she found such beliefs repugnant:

> Their children inherit the independence; they inherit too the honour of being the sons of brave fathers; but this will not give them the reputation a which they aim, of being scholars and gentlemen, nor will it enable them

> to sit down for evermore to talk of their glory, while they drink mint julap
> and chew tobacco, swearing by the beard of Jupiter (or some other oath)
> that they are very graceful and agreeable, and, moreover, abusing every
> body who does not cry out Amen!

Yet, for all their bold talk, the loafers well knew that they would never be "scholars and gentlemen." The quality made sure they knew their place in the pecking order.[29]

When English visitor Nicholas Maillard arrived in the Texas Republic, he found "impenetrable lines of demarcation already established in society." He identified four "distinct classes." Topping the social ladder were planters, slaveholders, and officers of government, all of whom he scorned as "Despotic aristocratical Land-owners." Such men, according to Maillard, had not "the least spirit of accommodation in them, and the simplest act of civility may be considered as a very great condescension for them." Overseers, storekeepers, and master tradesmen occupied the second rung. Below them were the "contemptibles," that is "those who are obliged to labour hard to get their daily bread; these are also called 'white niggers.'" Nevertheless, Maillard reserved the bulk of his deprecation for the "Loafers," the dregs of Texian society. This bottom caste stumbled "about from one dram-shop to another for the purpose of gaming and sponging on their friends, and not unfrequently on strangers; but this latter practice is by far too common in Texas to be confined or strictly applied to any one branch of the community."[30]

Still, if misery loves company, the loafers at least enjoyed the companionship of those who shared their status. There was pleasure to be had as a young man in the company of other men, and a greater joy to stand aloof from laws and limits. One lively ditty suggests something of their joie de vivre:

Here we are met, we merry boys,

And merry boys I know are we

As ever tasted Bacchus' joys,

Or kicked up jolly rig or spree!

To boast and belch, to gather and palaver, to make noise with the boys: those are the pleasures of males in groups. Men occasionally yearn for these forms of camaraderie, and wise women give them leave. As a man matures, however, he learns to confine these diversions to sports bars, deer camps, and annual meetings of the Texas State Historical Association. Bureaucrats attempting to build a city where families may form and flourish typically strive to curtail such anarchic behavior.[31]

Moses Lapham, an earnest fellow, did not participate in, or approve of, such forms of male bonding. Bacchanals in Columbia, when it still served as the temporary capital, incited nothing more in him than repulsion:

The state of society here at present is truly wretched, and more especially here at the present capital; the town is filled with volunteers who have recently left the army having served six or three months. They were generally collected from the very dregs of cities and towns, where they had obtained a scanty living by pelf and petty gambling. They are the most miserable wretches that the word ever produced. On account of my business I am obliged to come here, once in a while; but I make my visits as short as possible, and not even curiosity induces me to go near the gambling and grog shops. It is most probably that these vagabond volunteers will soon leave this part of the country for they sell their discharges and bounty script for a very small sum, which they soon consume in revel and debauchery, and will be compelled to go somewhere where they can obtain the necessary food to sustain life.

When the seat of government moved to Houston, the "vagabond volunteers" tagged along.[32]

Furloughed soldiers swarmed on Houston like flies around the offal in its streets. Amid the fast-growing population of the poor were legions of "loafers," who had no regular occupation, no employer, and no fixed abode. As the Republic did not yet mint real currency, former soldiers flocked to the capital in an attempt to acquire their military script and bounty lands. "All is confusion hear," Kelsey H. Douglass wrote his wife. "Ev[er]y one [is] trying to get sum thing from this government." Even when able to secure clear title to Texas acres, veterans discovered themselves land rich but cash poor. The grants of land at first had appeared exceedingly generous. Yet, as Philadelphia editor and economist William M. Gouge told it, soldiers soon discovered the "cash value of the article bestowed was very small. Land, to him who has neither capital to stock it nor skill to cultivate it, is worth only what others are willing to pay for it." Following the San Jacinto battle, a 640-acre claim sold for as high as two or even three hundred dollars. Those values proved fleeting. By the time Fisher furloughed the army, claims sold "at a fraction more than one cent and a half an acre." While veterans fought through red tape and inefficiency, it increasingly became harder for them to keep body and soul together. The city's spiraling inflation soon munched through what little cash a man might have had. There were, of course, a number of enterprising Houstonians eager to barter rations for real estate.[33]

Some veterans became so desperate they squandered their script for drinks or a bit of tickletail. Gustav Dresel told how they "fully made up for the long-sustained privations by often patronizing Kessler's Round Tent." The proprietor of this notorious establishment, Henry Kessler, was keen to have "soldiers pawn their script certificates to him" in exchange for their libations. Kessler had himself arrived in Texas as a member of a

Kentucky volunteer company. The avaricious Silesian, however, suffered no pangs of conscience for fleecing his former comrades and "thus became a rich man in a very few years." Even so, Kessler, who died of natural causes on October 30, 1840, did not long enjoy his lucre.[34]

Veterans were not oblivious. They knew Houston merchants were exploiting them but, powerless, they accepted their fate. Even loafers had to eat, but the callousness of Houston residents stirred resentment and bitterness. American recruits believed that locals had lured them to Texas with honeyed words and fickle promises.

In a town growing as rapidly as Houston, one might expect that there would be an abundance of jobs for low-skilled laborers. Black slaves and Mexican prisoners taken at San Jacinto performed much of the dirty work and undercut poor whites. Houston's slave community worked as house servants or on the farms and plantations that lay just outside the city limits. Masters also rented the services of their slaves as cooks and waiters in the town's many hotels and boarding houses. Less fortunate were those whose masters hired them out to toil along various landings or in the town's many warehouses.[35]

Now that Texians no longer required U.S. volunteers, they had cast them out like a worn-out brogan. Veterans had answered the call; they had suffered privation and want. Now, all they had to show for their service were worthless parchment scraps. Discharged soldiers became estranged from (even hostile toward) the Texas establishment who, at least in their view, had bilked them. "The army was being furloughed in the winter of 1837 and 1838," Lubbock recounted, "and finally disbanded. This brought a large number of soldiers to the city, consequently there was much dissipation, gambling, and fighting." Once strutting soldiers now found themselves vilified as "loafers," and they bristled at the label. Dejection frequently gave way to "abandonment." Their behavior appalled

Congressman Douglass: "Drinking, fighting, and rangling is the order of the day at this place." By mid-1837, Houston City thronged with young men who were hungry, hopeless, and in a huff.[36]

Worse, almost all of them were armed. "It must be borne in mind," Francis Lubbock insisted, "the country was just emerging from a war that had been going on for a long while. Every man with but few exceptions had been in the army and bore arms, and the few civilians outside of the military were in the habit of going armed; so that people were ready to resent insult and wrong without waiting for the slow process of the law, hence many personal difficulties occurred." Unburdened with most of the world's goods, it was the rare loafer who did not retain at least one firearm. For Houston's discharged soldiers, weapons were the tools of their profession and they took pride in flaunting them.[37]

They were also expensive. A man's firearms might well be his most valuable possessions. One dared not leave them in his lodgings or, sure as clap in a cathouse, they would be missing when he returned. Prudent Houstonians kept a watchful eye on their weapons—and any items they valued. The town ran rampant with reprobates who did not think twice before filching the pennies off a dead man's eyes. As Colonel Stiff told it:

> Pick-pockets and every description of bad characters abound here and are in promiscuous confusion mingled with the virtuous part of the community; and so much is this the case, that a man can scarcely devine when or where he is safe from their depredations. The police of the City is entirely worthless, and the unfortunate wight [person] who suffers by the light fingered gentry must find out the rogue as best he can, and then take the law into his own hands or suffer in silence; a part which I not only learned by daily occurrences, but also by bitter experience, my own trunk

having been abstracted from my Hotel, and rifled of its most valuable contents, on the second night after my arrival in the City.[38]

No, safer for a man to go armed at all times: safer for the man and safer for the preservation of his weapons. Even the habit of securing weapons on one's person did not offer complete assurance. While Stiff slumbered, one nimble-fingered rascal lifted a Bowie knife "out of my bosom." Yet, not all of Houston's malefactors employed such craft. Armed robbers depended more on brute strength than skill and stealth.[39]

So ubiquitous was a particular weapon that it became an obligation of Houston City style. On any given day, one might see "parties of traders arriving and departing, composed too, of every variety of color, 'from snowy white to sooty,' and dressed in every variety of fashion, excepting the savage Bowie-knife, which as if by common consent, was a necessary appendage to all." One English tourist noted with considerable irony that Bowie's blade formed "a pretty ornament enough when peeping from under the corner of the waistcoat, or over the waistband of a pair of Texan trowsers." Still, such conditions were by no means singular to Houston. According to Matilda Houstoun most men she encountered in the Republic sported the blade: "The Texans, almost without exception, carry their national weapon, the Bowie knife, about them." Irish diplomat Francis C. Sheridan also corroborated that throughout the Texas Republic the "use of the Bowie Knife is in general among high & low."[40]

He avowed, however, that such was the case "more at Houston than anywhere else." Houstonians carried their blades "either in the sleeve, or within the back part of the coat collar. As to going about unarmed either with pistol or Bowie knife or dagger stick, it is a piece of neglect unheard of." Peddlers set up on the wharves to assist those fresh off the ships and

Bowie knives were "a regular article of commerce." These entrepreneurs always had a "goodly show of Bowie knives, pistols & rifles, & one with whom I was bargaining for a knife, told me I ought to let him have a dollar more than the price we agreed on, as he 'could warrant it had tasted blood.'"[41]

Numerous contemporary accounts mention the veterans' penchant for bearing arms. "It was very common to see men passing on the streets with from two to four pistols belted around them," Dr. Lockhart recollected, "with the addition of a large bowie knife." Sheridan left a vibrant description of the breed that most commonly involved themselves in these imbroglios. "The 'Rowdie' combines the qualities of a Loafer of the lowest cast with pugnacious propensities—as may be gleaned from the first syllable of his name—These gentlemen are generally cut off in early life either by the legal rope or Bowie Knife of an acquaintance."[42]

Gambling aggravated the violence. Most of Houston's gin joints also provided gaming tables. With few prospects on the horizon, a sense of hopelessness drove some to press their luck. Many wagered what little cash they had—and lost it all. Such habits sped their slide into "total abandonment." City officials attempted to curb vice and passed an anti-gambling ordinance in 1837. Residents openly mocked such decrees. District court records reveal several indictments for "dealing faro," for "permitting gambling," and "playing cards." The same records, however, indicate few convictions. Gambling was simply too ingrained in the Southern character, and few were willing to forgo this popular diversion. John Hunter Herndon noted how ineffectual anti-gambling edicts were. After securing lodgings at Floyd's Hotel, he visited the establishment's Billiard Rooms, where he wagered on his skill with a cue stick. The balls rolled his way, for he recorded that his game was "successful." Two days later, his diary reveals that he, "Took a game of billiards," and was "successful again." Other games of chance flourished openly. "In the same house are four Faro Banks in addition to which are a number of others in the place." Gambling may have been popular, but it was frequently dangerous as well. Many games erupted into violence when despairing men lost all they owned. At other times pistols flared and blades flashed amid charges of cheating.[43]

Racing combined the thrill of gambling with the passion for blooded horseflesh. Houstonians constructed a course at Post Oak that hosted mile and repeat races. By 1837, the Houston Jockey Club was open and flourishing. The "spirit of the people for racing" impressed one visitor from Natchez, Mississippi, where folks knew more than a little about the sport. In an article in the *American Turf Register and Sporting Magazine*, he insisted that in 1837 he had witnessed Texians making side bets of twenty-five hundred dollars—on one race. He was confident concerning the future of the activity in the new republic. "Texas is going to be one of the greatest racing countries in the world, to be racing and betting the way they do now."[44]

Houston's racetrack was the jauntiest, most waggish place in the town—mannish, and as genial as a garrulous barkeep. The swells went there to see and be seen, to move and shake. At the same time, it was also a popular loafer destination; it was a peculiar Southern boy who did not seek pleasure in a horse race. Yet, when plebians rubbed shoulders with patricians, the vast differences in education, breeding, and social standing most clearly manifested themselves. The running of fine horses was a gentleman's sport, and the gentry resented the presence of the lumpen on their turf. For their part, the loafers took umbrage at all the snooty airs. For David James Jones, this latent antagonism would have tragic repercussions.

The mood at the Houston racetrack, like that in the grog shops and gambling dens, could turn deadly in the time it took to cock a pistol—and for much the same reasons. Men at the track tended to imbibe too much, bet too much, boast too much. Notions of Southern honor coupled with the slip of an ill-considered word frequently culminated in mayhem, all of which left Francis Sheridan aghast. "It is reckoned unsafe to attend the races there," he cautioned, "or indeed to reside in the Town a week after them, so desperate is the Bowie-knifing & pistoling on these merry making occasions. At the last meeting of these 'gentlemen sportsmen,'" he further elucidated, "one man was shot dead, a lady in the stand narrowly escaped with her life, & a general stabbing concluded the day's diversion— besides which the feelings of some gentlemen had been so hurt, that they were seen for days afterwards bobbing round the corners of the streets, to avoid the shot of or gain a favourable opportunity of shooting an acquaintance."[45]

Notwithstanding the habitual "Bowie-knifing & pistoling," one American visitor expressed a charitable forbearance, although tinged with healthy skepticism.

> When it is remembered that the population of Houston is in a great measure composed of unfortunate and reckless characters who have hastily congregated, it is perhaps more to be wondered that things are not worse, that any surprise felt at what is every day to be seen. No man, certainly, of common understanding, would ever dream of finding in so newly settled country, and among such a heterogeneous mass, that high tone of moral feeling, or that respect and deference paid to the laws, or those clothed with authority, as ought, and generally does, exist in older communities; and however desirous may be many worthy individuals to introduce wholesome reforms, they cannot as yet exercise much influence, and the unfortunate, disappointed, and degenerate spend their time in folly, dissipation and vice without any salutary restraints.[46]

Some Houstonians, and not a few prospective immigrants, could not brook all the havoc and sought settings less bellicose. Local merchant Charles Hedenberg related an anecdote concerning one of his family members. After regaling a New Jersey uncle with the many opportunities the new capital offered, he had finally persuaded him to move to Houston and set up a carriage factory. Early one morning in November 1837, the uncle—laden with luggage—showed up at his nephew's place of business. Pressing obligations prevented Hedenberg from showing his relative about town, but the nephew invited him to stow his trunks in his office and explore on his own. As Congress was in session, Hedenberg suggested that his uncle visit the capitol. The New Jersey man took a seat in the Senate gallery and had just settled in when gunshots resounded through the hall. Clearing out alongside other occupants of the chamber, he arrived outside to glimpse men "bearing off Algernon Thompson, badly shot by one Brashear, both clerks in the senate." The New Jersey native, now badly stunned, hastened back to his nephew.[47]

Along the way, however, he observed more colorful Texian folkways. Nothing in this Yankee's experience had prepared him for what he saw next:

> He probably had never shot a pistol or seen the effects of a shot before, and immediately left the building, going down Main Street on the west side. After traveling very fast and walking several blocks, in passing the Round Tent Saloon a soldier who was shot by one Deevy nearly fell upon him. He at once with a double quick rushed across to the east side of the street, and just as he got over and directly in front of John Carlos' Saloon a party rushed out of the door, almost running against him, with his bowels protruding from an immense bowie knife wound inflicted by a discharged soldier.

Arriving at Hedenberg's office, the uncle inquired, "Charley, have you sent my trunks to the house?"

"No, uncle; not yet."

"Well, do not send them. Get me a dray so I can at once take them to the boat that leaves for Galveston this afternoon."

"Why, uncle what do you mean?" Hedenberg demanded. "Why, you have seen nothing; have not had time to look at the town."

"Charley," the older man snapped, "I have seen enough. I wish to return home immediately. I do not wish to see any more of Texas."

Francis Lubbock took particular notice of the incident. As he explained it, "Charley was a great friend of mine and brother to Maggie Hedenberg, who was then at our house, where she remained until she married C. K. Hall, both lifelong friends of ours." Thus, "on their account," Lubbock was "more than usually interested in the new immigrant, and though I have often laughed over it since that time, I sympathized deeply with him when Charley gave me a regretful and graphic description of his uncle's quick departure."[48]

In later years Lubbock may have found the incident amusing, but in the moment few town elders thought it a laughing matter. The loafers' wild behavior had chased away a valued craftsman, one who had wanted to establish an enterprise that would have benefited the budding community. Nor was it an isolated instance. Observing the brutality that constituted the town's daily life, hundreds of would-be Houstonians opted to settle elsewhere. Officials were willing to allow a degree of boisterous conduct so long as roisterers confined their shenanigans to prescribed areas. But that was the problem. Early Houston did not have a district set aside for gainful vice. It was, in every sense of the term, a "wide-open" town. "Pick-pockets and every description of bad characters abound here and are in promiscuous confusion mingled with the virtuous part of the community," Edward Stiff recalled. "So much is this the case, that a man can scarcely divine when or where he is safe from their depredations." As the Yankee carriage maker learned, there was simply no way for respectable folks to dodge the bloodshed that could erupt on any street corner, at any time.[49]

In Houston's first year, the toffs had no choice but to mix with the lowbrows. The awareness of social distance was powerful, but stronger still was the frontier convention that a man was free to shape his own destiny—without anybody's say so. Rowdies, gamblers, drunks, brawlers, and whores lived as they pleased. By the end of 1837, however, the violence, vice, and depravity had exhausted patrician patience. The old live-and-let-live rules were about to change.

Houston's nefarious reputation had injured the town financially and inhibited its growth. The reigning coterie was not about to stand by and watch that happen. Even in Galveston, which had more than its fair share of rousers and ragamuffins, citizens could boast that at least their town was not as bad as Houston. These divisions polarized Houston, the "rough characters" versus the men of "distinction and culture." It was about to become a struggle for the soul of the city. Each faction had its own interest to preserve and radically opposing visions for Houston's future. Loafers scorned the gentry as prissy popinjays who not only looked down their noses, but also stuck them where they did not belong. They soon discerned, however, that the quality held the land, drafted the laws, and administered justice. For their part, the elites regarded the loafers much as they did the rats that infested their city, a pestilence they would have to contain.[50]

That, or exterminate.

How Precious with Good Liquor in
Galveston: February 17, 1838

Like his new acquaintance John Hunter Herndon, physician Robert H. Watson is a professional man, a bon viveur, and an aficionado of human skulls. On this particular evening, he regales his companions following a wild night on the town. Charging the newest addition to his collection (one that has "yet brains in it"), he toasts his associates—and an inquisitive wharf rat—both of whom scrutinize his behavior with considerable bemusement:

> *This when living was not worth a pin,*
>
> *But now how precious with good liquor in.*

Dr. Watson is a gentleman and dresses to broadcast his status. He sports a "Wellington" beaver hat, the sartorial symbol of the stylish man. Earlier, fashion had demanded a black top hat. Yet, by the 1830s gray and even white headgear are in vogue. If a man can afford more than one, he wears lighter colored hats during the day and a black beaver at night. Watson dons a capped redingote against the winter chill; these normally come in broadcloth or other woolen fabrics. Beneath the top coat, he wears a tailcoat unbuttoned to better display his elegant waistcoat (vest). The good doctor has skillfully tied his cravat (or neckcloth), allowing starched collar tips to brush his fashionable side-whiskers. His tight-cut pantaloons (what modern readers would call trousers) feature straps that fasten under stockings or, as Watson prefers, under the shoe. Speaking of footwear, Watson's are three-eyelet, pegged-sole brogans.

While Watson's attire is au courant, harsh frontier conditions have left it worse for wear. Reputable tailors had little use for Houston. Consequently, most of the town's gentry had to abide apparel frayed at the collar and thin in the knees.

5
The Virtuous Part of the Community
Houston's Gentry

One might entertain the impression that every soul in early Houston was a shiftless, vicious, ne'er-do-well. Yet, one would be wrong. Truth was, many—indeed, most—of the city's residents were God fearing, hard working, and law abiding. "From the very first settlement of Houston," Francis Lubbock insisted, "we had good people, intelligent men, and elegant women—men and women of good breeding and fine culture." Despite that, the city faced a public relations nightmare. By the end of 1837, the mention of Houston evoked reports of riotous licentiousness. The town's reputable element resented the negative publicity. It was as if the loafers were sucking the air from the city. Citizens and visitors found it hard to smell the roses for the fertilizer. Daily, gentlefolk witnessed debauchery and bloodshed that sickened and alarmed them. Moreover, they thought it time to close the curtain on such activities. One man, however, pursued that objective with a zealotry few could equal.[1]

The early life of Dr. Francis Moore, Jr., revealed little of the witch hunter. The son of a physician, Francis Moore, he was born in Salem,

Massachusetts, in 1808. A boyhood accident (the exact circumstances remained murky) cost the younger Moore an arm. When he was twenty years of age, his family moved to Livingston County, New York, where, like his father, he studied medicine. By 1834, he was a practicing physician but also studying law and teaching school in Bath, New York. There, one long-time resident recalled him as an "accomplished scholar and gentleman." Yet, when he learned of the Texas rebellion, Moore and two friends, brothers Jacob W. and James F. Cruger, left Bath and set out to join the fray. Like many others, they arrived after the battle of San Jacinto. Nonetheless, Moore enlisted as a volunteer and assistant surgeon in Captain James L. Allen's Buckeye Rangers. He had missed the fighting, but as a member of that unit, he would see much action. It was not, however, against forces he had anticipated.[2]

During the summer of 1836, the Buckeye Rangers functioned as body-guards for David G. Burnet, protecting the ad interim president from mutinous elements within the Texian army that wished to bend the government to their will. In July, a few officers attempted to arrest Burnet and his Cabinet and arraign them before a drumhead court. The steadfastness of the Buckeye Rangers thwarted the plot. Moore came to admire Burnet's fortitude and resolve. In the years that followed, his regard never faded. Whatever the issue, he remained a staunch Burnet supporter. His loyalty earned Moore a new appointment; on September 2, he became warden of an army hospital in Velasco. His friend Jacob Cruger gained appointment as the army's assistant paymaster. This experience also guaranteed Moore's lasting contempt for military adventurers, who had created so much civil strife.[3]

When Fisher furloughed the army in 1837, Moore and the Cruger brothers ended their military careers but resolved to remain in Texas. Yet, the three New Yorkers had little devotion for the Texas Republic, desiring instead to add the Lone Star to the American firmament. Optimistic that the happy day would arrive soon, the Crugers opened a mercantile establishment in Houston.

Moore bought Thomas Borden's share of the *Telegraph and Texas Register*, a transaction that, while little noticed at the time, was to change the face of Texas journalism. Officials had just announced that the seat of government would move from Columbia to Houston. Gail Borden and his new partner decided the newspaper should move with it. The last issue of the paper printed and published in the old capital appeared on April 11, 1837. Shortly thereafter, the proprietors loaded their press aboard the steamboat *Yellow Stone*.

Notwithstanding an arduous journey up Buffalo Bayou, lack of suitable offices, and many other attendant difficulties, the first Houston edition of the *Telegraph* hit the muddy streets on May 2. Gail Borden, tired of the grind of running a newspaper, entrusted his partner with the editorial responsibilities. For his part, Moore was happy to accept. Under his direction, the *Telegraph* became a notably altered newspaper. Borden had been content to report the news, providing little editorial comment; Moore wanted to shape affairs. The new paper became an exceedingly personal enterprise. Modern journalistic standards, which stipulate at least the appearance of professional detachment, had no relevance for newspapermen of the 1830s. In the United States and the Republic of Texas, most were openly biased. Indeed, many newspapers were little more than organs of the various political parties. In his political leanings, Moore normally landed on the anti-Houston, pro-Burnet/ Lamar side of the fence. He made it clear, however, that he was in no man's pocket and no party's tool. Increasingly, the newspaper became a mouthpiece for his personal opinions, a vehicle to achieve his own aspirations.

In his first editorial outing, Moore stomped heavily on establishment toes. He condemned the practice of electing candidates in Texas who had criminal records in the United States. For a number of Houston's public men, this criticism landed too close to home. Expressing umbrage, many demanded to know who had presumed to air such opinions. "Those interested are hereby notified," Moore shot back, "that the author of that article is the editor of the Telegraph, who is not too stupid to discharge *unassisted* his editorial duties, nor too cowardly to persist in the path where those duties lead; if in that path even death be lurking, *he will walk onward.*"[4]

Moore made certain that Houston residents knew who was now in charge. The issue of May 30, 1837, ran a notice (dated March 9) in its advertising columns:

> The firm heretofore existing under the style of G. and T. H. Borden, is thi[s] day dissolved by mutual consent. The Telegraph and Texas Registe[r] will continue to be published by Borden and Moore. All persons indebted to the firm will make payment to G. Borden, Jr., or Francis Moore, Jr., now connected with this paper.

The announced partnership would be short. The younger Borden was ready to pursue other interests, accept new challenges. In June, he sold his interest to Moore's New York friend, the seventeen-year-old Jacob W. Cruger.[5]

The June 13, 1837, issue was the last to announce "PUBLISHED BY BORDEN & MOORE, PUBLIC PRINTERS." Moore proclaimed that his hand now directed the helm—and had been holding it steady for some time. The Bordens left enormous footprints and not all were confident that Moore could fill their boots. The tone of Moore's statement was, therefore, defiant but also somewhat defensive:

The notice in our advertising columns of dissolution of copartnership will show that the Bordens have no longer an interest in this establishment; except so far as every Texian has an interest in the welfare of a periodical which has been so closely identified with the most eventful and interesting period of [the] Texian story. We feel confident that this announcement will occasion no apprehension or dissatisfaction, when our patrons are appraised of the fact that since the first of March last this paper has been wholly conducted by the present editor; who now cheerfully renews his assurances that nothing shall be wanting on his part to furnish with each successive number of the Telegraph new proof that he *faithfully* LABORS FOR HIS COUNTRY.

In black, bold, type, the June 24, 1837, masthead informed readers that the paper was: "**PUBLISHED BY CRUGER & MOORE, PUBLIC PRINTERS.**" Moore wished all to understand that a new era had begun.[6]

Notwithstanding Cruger's tender years, Moore—who was eleven years older—could not have found a better business manager. Although Jacob Cruger had no personal knowledge of the newspaper business, his relative Daniel Cruger had achieved success as a printer back in the Empire State. Sitting around the family table, Jacob had absorbed considerable newspaper acumen. Moreover, at seventeen years of age, he had already been a partner in a mercantile store, Houston's postmaster, and assistant secretary of the Texas Senate.[7]

Two more disparate personalities could not have come together; oil and water, funny and foul, Cruger and Moore. The differences between them could have packed a hefty almanac. Moore craved acclaim; Cruger wilted in the limelight. Moore wanted to lead; Cruger worked best behind the scenes. Moore seemed to delight in offending; Cruger was outgoing and genial.

Moore appreciated how much of his success he owed to his associate, a debt which, years later, he acknowledged in an effusive tribute: "Mr. Cruger has been for more than eight years, my bosom friend and almost constant companion. We have, by turns, nursed and sustained each other in sickness, and cheered and defended each other amid privations and perils; in adversity and prosperity shared alike. We are connected by bonds of attachment more strong than those of fraternal love."[8]

Cruger was about the only person who won Moore's esteem. In his editorials, the former physician revealed himself a Massachusetts moralist. Unlike many Northerners who came to relish life in Texas, he behaved as if it was never entirely worthy of him. If that was the case of the republic in general, it was especially true of its capital. Moore found fault with almost everything and everybody. He did so in a condescending tone that suggested that he was but an altruist intent on helping these benighted Texians who, after all, did not enjoy the benefits of his education and breeding. If they would only heed his advice, he could lead them out of "barbarism"—one of his favorite words.

Moore nurtured an inflated sense of his own worth. He agreed with Voltaire who observed, "Opinion governs the world, and in the end the philosophes govern men's opinions." Moore was, of course, a newspaper editor, not a philosopher, but he never believed the two professions mutually exclusive. Indeed, he viewed himself as a philosopher-editor. Others thought him a pretentious ass. He explained his role:

Public journals are now considered as organs of PUBLIC OPINION: and public opinion is the great lever that moves the world. To editors, therefore, more than to any other class of society, is entrusted the guardianship of public and private morals. Their influence is more patent than even that of legislators upon the moral character of a state. They can bid tumult

TEXIAN MACABRE 135

and rapine stalk abroad over the land; or, with a breath exorcise the malignant spirits which are the bane of society, and bid virtue and peace exert a controlling power, diffusing on every side the blessings of genuine freedom.[9]

A prig of the first quality, Moore rubbed many Houstonians the wrong way. Edward Stiff, for one, loathed the man and recalled the editor's quizzical fashion sense. He daily wore the same clothes: "the same Kentucky jeans pants, the same pair of stitchdowns, the same long and flowing blue green robe, [and] the same redoubtable ancient drab beaver [hat]." Stiff described Moore as "tall and disproportioned," something of a disabled Ichabod Crane: a "long slabsided, knock-kneed, six-footer, and among other marks of vicissitude in life, sports but one arm; but how this important member was lost, history does not tell." Neither did Moore. At length, prose proved inadequate to convey Stiff's abhorrence:

> His ugly face has neither truth or art,
>
> To please the fancy, or to touch the heart;
>
> Dark and unskillful, dismal, but yet mean;
>
> With anxious bustle may every where be seen:
>
> Without a trace that's tender or profound,
>
> But spreads its cold unmeaning gloom around.[10]

Stiff was not alone in his scorn. William D. Redd, a friend of Vice President Lamar, called Moore the "one armed Proteus." President Houston, who suffered Moore's barbs on numerous occasions, was chief among his enemies. "The lying scribbler of the Telegraph is a one-armed man," he remarked. "You would forgive me for abusing a cripple, but I must confess that one arm can write more malicious falsehoods than any

136 THE VIRTUOUS PART OF THE COMMUNITY

man with two arms I ever saw. His one arm is more prolific for evil than the traditional bag that had seven cats and every cat had seven kits."[11]

Even so, a number of readers agreed with Moore on key issues, and he meant to convert them into constituents.

He had no faith in the Texas Republic and constantly beat the drum for joining the United States. As much as he supported annexation, he condemned dueling. In Moore's catalog of disdain, duelists took pride of place. But they enjoyed stiff competition. Among other Southerners the Yankee editor found odious were gamblers, idlers, brawlers, mountebanks, and drunkards. Small wonder he found Houston so distasteful. Nevertheless, editorial by editorial, Moore carefully shaped the image of a public-spirited civic leader.

Rare was the Texian who left his dwelling weaponless, a habit Moore deemed reprehensible. He reported a falling out of business partners L. Kelcy and Z. Hubbard, both Houston residents. When words failed, Kelcy drew his pistol and shot Hubbard in the knee. He should have aimed higher. The wounded associate "rushed upon him with a sword cane, and stabbed him in ten different places, killing him before assistance could be rendered." (One can only wonder what sort of "assistance" might have allayed the pernicious results of ten stab wounds.) Since everyone agreed that Hubbard had acted in self-defense, the jury rendered a verdict of justifiable homicide. Yet, as Moore viewed it, Kelcy was a "victim" of the "disgraceful custom of wearing deadly weapons. A custom which should be denounced and frowned down by every intelligent and respectable community." Perhaps, but Mr. Hubbard could have reminded the editor that Houston was still dangerous and his "custom of wearing deadly weapons" was the only reason he still counted himself among the living.[12]

If their owners had remained sober, weapons would not have been such an issue. With all the sanctimony of Cotton Mather—an earlier

Newspaper editor, Houston mayor, and demonstrable demagogue, Massachusetts native Francis Moore, Jr. achieved notoriety as the "one-armed Proteus." His obsession to see Jones and Quick hang subverted all conventional principles of justice. His brusque manner, eccentric habits, and barbed editorials earned him enemies among the high (President Sam Houston) and low (Constable Edward Stiff). Courtesy Houston Public Library, Houston Metropolitan Research Center.

resident of his hometown back in Massachusetts—Moore derided all who tippled the Devil's brew. In one editorial, Moore critiqued members of the new Congress:

> We are highly pleased with the appearance of the present members of congress. We notice among them a large proportion of grey heads, and men of tried abilities and integrity. We notice also but few red noses; this we consider an indication that this congress will afford but few, possibly none, of those most base, most groveling, and most despicable of *creeping things*, **DRUNKEN LEGISLATORS**.[13]

By October 1837, the new officials were sufficiently sober to discern the truth behind John K. Allen's honeyed assurances. Houston was so squalid that it was alienating talented men from public service. "We are Badly Situate[d] hear," Congressman Kelsey H. Douglass carped. "It is quite sickly and I never was so tiard of a place in my life." If living in a pigsty was a

138   THE VIRTUOUS PART OF THE COMMUNITY

requisite, "being a member of congress is not the thing." Never a fan of Houston, he reported, "*I have Sum hope* that the Seat of Goverment will be removed this session." When Congress began discussing the possibility of moving the capital to a less disagreeable locale, Moore came out swinging. "Most of the citizens who purchased lots in this city and erected buildings have considered the act 'locating temporarily the seat of government' a secure guarantee that their property here would continue to be valuable [for] at least three years," he harangued. "The stability of the contracts they have made was wholly based upon that law. We trust therefore that this congress will not be so unjust as rashly to deprive these citizens of what they may properly consider—vested rights." While the editorial won Moore few friends in Congress, it did gain him the esteem and support of Houston's business community.[14]

As owner and editor, Moore found the *Telegraph* a bully pulpit—and an exclusive one. From March 1836 until March 1837, it was the only newspaper in Texas. Throughout 1838, it remained the only paper of record. As long as he controlled what people read, he maintained a virtual stranglehold on public opinion. From the day Moore purchased an interest in the paper, it served as the handmaiden to his political ambitions.[15]

During the summer of 1837, Moore entered the race for mayor, an announcement that caught few Houstonians by surprise. On August 15, 1837, Houstonians went to the polls to cast their votes in the mayoral election. Moore won in a landslide; his opponents, Francis R. Lubbock and James S. Holman, received eleven and twelve votes, respectively. Small wonder, since Moore controlled the most important means through which candidates could address the public. Elected in August, Moore would not assume office until January 1, 1838. He did not, however, intend to squander the time in between. Now that his machinations had paved a path to office, he required a defining issue. Moore entered the race as a law-and-order, good government candidate. He was tough-minded, resolute, ambitious, and without scruple. In November, David James Jones would provide sensational copy and serve admirably as his scapegoat.[16]

Although Francis Moore, Jr., and John Hunter Herndon hailed from vastly different backgrounds, both were fair representatives of Houston's ruling class. As witness and chronicler, Herndon was essential to this story. His diary is one of the most remarkable (but also overlooked) documents in Texas history. Indeed, what James Boswell's journal is to 1760s London, Herndon's diary is to 1830s Houston. It is that rich in local color, period detail, and striking candor.[17]

Herndon was born on July 8, 1813, in Scott County, Kentucky. He received his education at Lexington's Transylvania College, where he earned degrees in art and law. In 1834, he was a member of the college's Whig Society. Shortly following graduation, he won admittance to the bar in Kentucky and practiced there long enough to build up a sizeable nest egg. His reasons for moving to Texas are obscure, but he made the journey as suited a gentleman of elegance and import. He traveled with "several thousand dollars and a substantial wardrobe of three pairs of silk and four pairs of yarn socks, three pairs of boots, one pair of pumps, and one pair of overshoes, five pair of drawers, six pairs of pants, four linen and seven cotton shirts, six bosoms, four stocks, four vests and coats, four linen-cotton and silk handkerchiefs, and three pairs of gloves." His journey was leisurely and he took in a number of sights. Along the way, he hunted, frolicked, dined lavishly, and attended a number of New Orleans theater productions.[18]

When Herndon arrived in Houston, he was still playing the tourist. He was in no hurry to reestablish his practice. Instead, the twenty-five-year-old attorney hunted, swam, played billiards, visited the grog shops, enjoyed mint juleps with his breakfast, charmed young ladies, helped organize the "Kentucky Wine Club," and kept his remarkably uninhibited diary.[19]

A well-educated professional, Herndon was just the sort of emigrant Texians were eager to attract. Tricked out in "Kentucky style," accomplished in his attainments, prideful in his bearing, and genteel in his manner, he had no trouble gaining access to the upper reaches of Houston society. Herndon was a nineteenth-century gentleman, with a patrician scorn for the vulgar herd. While many of his observations appear callous to modern readers, he only reflected the sensibilities of his time and place. He read novels, wrote articles for the *Telegraph*, and commented on social conditions. He had the cash, the connections, and the leisure to pursue a wide assortment of interests.[20]

Yet, one of Herndon's diversions was a tad peculiar. He accumulated skulls: human skulls. It was the Romantic Period when the gothic novel was all the rage. Many a literary gentleman owned a human skull as an intimation of mortality, but few maintained a collection. On February 11, 1838, Herndon enjoyed a day trip to the San Jacinto battleground. That evening he recorded the following: "Went to a most beautiful evergreen grove where a perfect summer scene was presented for contemplation." Incongruously, he also noted that he had, "obtained many sculls." Late in 1837, steamboat operators established a regular route from Houston to Galveston Island and other points on the bay. A few days after his San Jacinto picnic, Herndon took advantage of this service to visit Galveston City. While there, he enjoyed a bonanza: "Obtained a number of sculls (Mexican) which had been washed up by the high tide."[21]

During his Galveston trip Herndon made a new acquaintance, Dr. Robert H. Watson. The attorney discovered that the physician shared his enthusiasm for skulls. Watson, however, took his amusement to lengths that even Herndon found rather outré. Arriving on the island, the group took lodgings in a boarding house. Since the weather was freezing, Herndon warmed himself with the fiery rhetoric of Thomas Paine's *Age of Reason* while his companions went to "drink for self defence" against the chill. "Dr. W[atson] and Dr. Lewis went down to the city and returned very *amiable*," Herndon noted. "They amused the company very much after retiring. Dr. W[atson] drank whisky out of a scull that had yet brains in it." The incident stirred the inebriated physician to elegiac sublimity:

> *This when living was not worth a pin,*
> *But now how precious with good liquor in.*[22]

Gentlemen like Herndon enjoyed the company of those who shared an appreciation for learning and refinement. Early Houston provided little of both. Therefore, high-powered and well-heeled citizens formed associations that hived those of fellow feeling. On December 5, 1837, twenty-six gentlemen met in the capitol to organize the Philosophical Society of Texas—and what a remarkable assembly it was. These individuals were the republic's best and brightest. All were distinguished professional men: fourteen attorneys, four physicians, four planters, two soldiers, one clergyman, and one man of business. The last of these, Augustus C. Allen, the members prudently elected treasurer.

The officers were a virtual who's who of the republic's society. Mirabeau B. Lamar may have been vice president of the nation, but he was president of the Philosophical Society. The organization boasted five illustrious vice presidents: Surgeon General of the Army Ashbel Smith, Secretary of State Robert A. Irion, Congressman Anson Jones, Speaker of the House of Representatives Joseph Rowe, and Nacogdoches attorney David S. Kaufman. The recording secretary was clerk of the Supreme Court William Fairfax Gray. David G. Burnet, the former ad interim president

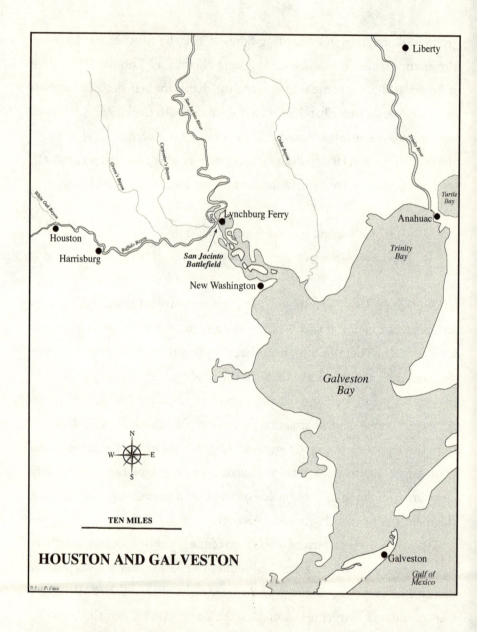

HOUSTON AND GALVESTON

of the republic, served as the Society's corresponding secretary, and John Birdsall, partner in the Houston law firm of Birdsall and Gazley, acted as librarian. Oddly, the preeminent member, Sam Houston, was not an officer. Fellow members understood that his public duties allowed him

Politician, poet, and philosopher, Mirabeau Buonaparte Lamar was among the most learned and accomplished men in the Texas Republic. Although winning laurels at San Jacinto, he was unable to win over the headstrong volunteers who rejected him as their commander in chief. During President Houston's first administration, Lamar served as vice president, at which time he was a founding member and president of the Philosophical Society of Texas. Succeeding Houston as president, he won the everlasting gratitude of some and the bitter enmity of others when he transferred the seat of government from Houston to Austin. In 1859. Lamar died at his Richmond plantation at the age of sixty-one years. *Courtesy Texas State Library and Archives Commission.*

little time to pursue private interests. Every chief executive officer of the Texas republic—Burnet, Houston, Lamar, and Jones—was a founding member of the Philosophical Society. As were two of the four vice presidents (Lamar and Burnet) and the first three commanding generals of the army (Houston, Rusk, and Lamar).

These men yearned for enrichment and sophistication, not only for themselves, but also for their nation's capital. They valued learning and order. They shared a common dream—that of a redeemed wilderness. Lamar declared the "single star of the West" should be "resplendent for all the acts that adorn civilized life." Dr. Ashbel Smith, a Phi Beta Kappa from Yale College, shared that optimism. "I feel a strong confidence," he wrote a friend in the states, "that our association will not only elevate Texas among civilized nations of the world, but in great probability extend the borders of Science." Members sought to promote the "collection and diffusion of correct information regarding the moral and social condition of our country, its finances, statistics, and political and military history, its climate, soil, and productions . . . animals . . . aboriginal tribes . . . natural curiosities ... mines . . . and the thousand other topics of interest which our new and rising republic unfolds to the philosopher, the scholar, and the man of the world." The Philosophical Society included men of conflicting political views. During the day, Burnet could lay into Houston with words that "disclosed a burning hatred towards the Chief Executive" yet meet with him the same evening to discuss the range of "natural curiosities."[23]

From the beginning, the Philosophical Society was elitist, distinguished as much by the persons excluded as those listed among its members. "It is decidedly exclusive," Dr. Smith bragged: "It is composed of the 1st men of the Republic." He knew more than a little about exclusivity, as he had won highest honors in Greek and Latin at Yale. Indeed, it was probably no accident that the members founded the Philosophical Society of Texas on December 5. Phi Beta Kappa celebrated its Founders' Day on the fifth day of the last month. The twenty-six founding members never questioned their own qualifications but established stringent requirements for all future applicants. Each would have to submit a written thesis that current members would then evaluate. Any three members might reject a candidate if they found his thesis—or his character—lacking in its content. Once rejected for membership, he could not reapply for six months.[24]

As an educated man, a veteran, a town leader, and a thriving businessman (although a journalist) Dr. Francis Moore, Jr., ranked among the local gentry. Even so, he never gained membership to the Philosophical Society. Perhaps he was so busy writing his scorching editorials that he did not have time to compose a learned disquisition. Alternatively, his acerbic editorials, his churlish manners, or his outlandish attire may have estranged existing members. With his almost constant invective

Doctor Ashbel Smith was thirty-two years of age when he arrived in Houston. This photograph captured him many years later when his fellow citizens revered him as the "father of Texas medicine" and "father of the University of Texas." During his time in the capital, he was one of the founding members of The Philosophical Society of Texas, a true friend to his roommate, Sam Houston, and a tireless defender of the much maligned republic. Courtesy *Texas State Library and Archives Commission.*

against "our leaders," it is difficult to imagine how he could have avoided insulting at least three of them.

The early records of the society are lost or incomplete so it is difficult to determine the efficacy of its application by thesis. Although it is certain few Houstonians had the education, the resources, or the leisure even to participate in the process. Indeed, the original members, burdened by their professional obligations, frequently had to beg out of scheduled presentations. In 1839, the society received a body blow when the capital moved to Austin. Meetings were to coincide with the annual sessions of Congress, which well suited the politicians. Even so, private businessmen who remained in Houston could no longer attend meetings, the chief reason that the society fell apart by 1841.[25]

Nevertheless, marvel not that such an organization was short lived, but rather that, in such a rancid setting, it ever existed. Stark was the contrast between the lofty ideals and the tawdry realities. Members found it jarring to discuss latest scientific and literary achievements over

146   THE VIRTUOUS PART OF THE COMMUNITY

sherry then walk down carcass-strewn streets. It also became increasingly evident that many in the community had no interest in participating in "all the acts that adorn civilized life." When the town was in its infancy, officials were more willing to tolerate the filth and vice; then, everyone was struggling to climb out of the muck. By the end of 1837, however, the disparity between gentlemen of "distinction and culture" and "rough characters" appeared in sharper focus. Thriving professional men like those represented by members of the Philosophical Society had (figuratively anyway) ascended out of the mud. To the full-fed men of the town, it seemed as though the loafers, like swine, were perfectly happy to wallow there.

This is not to suggest that all members of the upper crust were choir boys. When circumstance called for it, the quality could bust loose every bit as much as the common, ungilded folk. Still, how the gentry drank distinguished them from the loafers. The hard-core troublemakers got drunk and, for the most part, maintained that state on a daily basis. Conversely, men of eminence imbibed only on appropriate occasions: Christmas week, New Year's Eve, Battle of New Orleans Day, Washington's birthday, Texas Independence Day, the Fourth of July, and, of course, San Jacinto Day.

The notable exception was, of course, the president. It was an open secret that Sam Houston was an alcoholic. One of his friends warned that the president's "health and reputation would soon sink under the influence of liquor" and concluded, "May an alwise Providence chain you down to Sobriety and prudence." Houston's political enemies tried to make his drinking an issue, but it never seemed to register with the voters. Come Election Day, Texians excused his vices with a wink and a nod. Ultimately, who among his opponents had accomplished half as much sober as Houston drunk? It was as the anonymous sage observed: "The productive drunk is the bane of moralists."[26]

Speaking of moralists, the conduct of Texian elite on a spree horrified Methodist minister Littleton Fowler. He rebuked their behavior in a letter dated April 21, 1838: "Today is the second anniversary of the battle of San Jacinto, and a fine time for 'Big Bugs' to get drunk without reproach." Most Texians regarded sobriety on that day as downright unpatriotic. To celebrate the occasion, Fowler related that Houstonians held a "splendid ball." It was quite a set to. "About fifty ladies, and two hundred or three hundred gentlemen were in attendance. I enclose a ball invitation which may afford you some amusement to see how such things are done in the Capital of the Republic. Please do not infer from this that I am partial to such assemblies." Note Fowler underlined the word gentlemen. Everybody who was anybody received an invitation. Therefore, of Houston's total population, between two and three hundred might consider themselves "gentlemen." Shopkeepers, contemptibles, and loafers would have been conspicuously absent from the guest list. They celebrated the holiday in their own way, in the whorehouses, gambling dens, and bucket shops.[27]

Despite his self-deprecation, Preacher Fowler was himself something of a "big bug." Although his backcountry education was rudimentary, he made up the deficit through rigorous study. "All his life he was an ardent student," one of his associates recalled. "His style of speaking, both in the pulpit and in the social circle, was rigidly correct, and I was surprised to learn from his own lips that he had never had the benefits of scholastic training, but his attainments were almost entirely self-acquired." Upon his arrival in Houston in November 1837, those attainments were sufficiently impressive to convince the Texas Congress to elect Fowler its chaplain. Masonic brothers elected him the first Grand Chaplain of the

Grand Lodge of Texas, and he was present at its founding. Moreover, he was among the original twenty-six members of the Philosophical Society, the only clergyman so honored. Reverend Fowler, notwithstanding his calling, moved in high-powered circles. He counted himself among the "gentlemen" of the town and viewed its sots, gamblers, whores, bruisers, and loafers, not only with pious disapproval, but also through the lens of class.[28]

Nevertheless, the preacher was no hypocrite. He was not blind to the transgressions of the ruling class. The blasphemous behavior of President Houston and other of the Republic's politicos struck Fowler's constitution (which was never vigorous) a cruel blow. "So soon as I had recovered from my serious illness I took a trip to Galveston Island with the President and the members of Congress," he lamented, "and saw *great* men in *high life*. If what I saw and heard were a fair representation, may God keep me from such scenes in future." He commented favorably on the island and its inhabitants, recalling that they "hospitably entertained" his party. During the passage back to Houston, however, he learned how "great men" kept the Sabbath. "On our return on Sunday afternoon, about one-half on board got mildly drunk and stripped themselves to their linen and pantaloons."[29]

The role that fashion played in defining a nineteenth-century gentleman made their conduct even more scandalous. For men of the ruling class, one's attire had three tasks. The first was to clothe the man; the second was to distinguish his class; the third was to cow the lower orders. The mere suggestion that gentlemen would drink themselves to insensibility and then strip to their underwear was almost more than the good reverend could bear. He gasped, "Their Bacchanalian revels and bloodcurdling profanity made the pleasure boat a floating hell. The excursion to me was one of pain and not pleasure. I relapsed from this trip and was brought near to the valley of death." His standards, as a man of the cloth, may have been "rigidly correct." Nevertheless, if even a portion of what he reported was true, early Houston was a latter day Gomorrah.[30]

Class distinctions even affected the consumption of "ardent spirits." The beringed hands of the gentry likely hoisted as many drams as the work-roughened hands of the lowlifes. The difference was what, where, and with whom men of consequence sipped and staggered. A gentleman disdained drinking with inferiors—unless, of course, he was embroiled in a hard-fought political campaign. The electorate expected their candidates to buy and backslap. It remained distasteful, but everyone understood that a public man needed to rub shoulders with the ragtag and bobtails if he wanted their votes. A Texian woman described the process, remarking one of her boarders had declared for office because "on leaving this morning [he] gave the children cakes and apples, so I know he must be a candidate." Grown men, however, demanded stronger enticements. One recalled, "There was much recrimination and but little discrimination between the Candidates. One of them carried his best speech in his saddle bags in the shape of a bottle of whiskey which ever and anon we had recourse to, as it were to cheer us on our weary way. This speech though short made on *some* a very *visible impression*." Loafers normally drank to drown their troubles; the upper crust drank to prove their status. While the gentry might become royally snockered, they normally did so with other members of their class and beyond the prying eyes of the voters. Also—and this was a vital distinction—their drinking bouts rarely ended in murder and mayhem.[31]

Not all of the capital's violence, however, was the work of drunken street scavengers. Southern convention demanded that "gentlemen" settle their differences in strict accordance to the *code duello*. "I do not think I would be authorized to state that there were those in Houston who made dueling an occupation," one Ohio visitor jibed, "but I feel at liberty to say that there were some who seem to think that there was no better way to employ their time than to lecture upon the principals of honor, to lay down the laws of the pistol, and to let no occasion pass to encourage others to fight." To illustrate his point, he told of one "honorable" affair that deteriorated into farce.[32]

In the spring of 1837, even before carpenters had completed work on the house of Congress, a gaggle of blackguards, "in the spirit of polemics," began to convene in the unfinished edifice each night to thrash out the "heavy matters" of the day. Rotgut whiskey lightened their mood and loosened their tongues. The presence of these nocturnal squatters alarmed the contractor, Thomas William Ward. As well it should have. Until the Allen brothers took formal possession, he bore responsibility for the building and feared that celebrants "with their eloquence or something else" might set it ablaze. During the 1835 siege of Béxar, a Mexican cannonball took off Ward's leg—his companions found it practical to place the severed limb into Ben Milam's grave—but he was not a man to tolerate shenanigans on his job site. Late one evening "Peg Leg" Ward burst into the meeting "just at the time the whole was in full blast." The angry contractor snuffed out the candles and unleashed a torrent of invective upon the revelers.[33]

Ward's "abusive language" incensed one of the trespassers. He answered Peg Leg's order to leave with a smack on his face. Blind with rage, the contractor pulled a pistol, but bystanders prevented him from "doing mischief." The party broke up, and each went his own way. All understood, however, that the issue was far from resolved. A "humiliating blow" was an insult for which no gentleman could accept an apology. To endure such an affront would brand him as a "poltroon" in the eyes of his community. Nothing but blood could answer this offence.[34]

The following morning Ward sent a challenge, which his assailant promptly accepted. Both men agreed to meet at the outskirts of town on May 15. Word raced through town at the pace of a Post Oak thoroughbred. On the day, a large number of citizens gathered at the dueling grounds to witness, "what really appeared to them an amusing spectacle." What the participants believed a dignified private affair, their mobbish inferiors considered a guilty pleasure.[35]

Aided by their seconds, the principals took their marks. "Firing at a distance of ten paces," an observer recounted, "both parties missed." Ward announced that the first exchange had not satisfied honor, and his opponent consented to a second round. This time lead landed squarely on target. All right, not *squarely*, a smidgen lower.

The bullet had thwacked into Ward's peg leg—and spectators thought that priceless. What began as snickers climbed the scale to a crescendo of guffaws. The hilarity cut the tension and exposed the true nature of this lampoon. The aggrieved contractor conceded that a "bullet in a wooden leg was quite a sufficient apology for a slapped cheek and expressed his entire satisfaction."[36]

The following day, Dr. Moore reported the affair. Even he, who routinely editorialized against the code, seemed to have enjoyed the levity of this outing. "We had an affair of honor settled here yesterday, no blood shed however, all was amicably adjusted by merely shooting into wood."[37]

Not all encounters were so "amicably adjusted." Especially lamentable was the duel fought the following month between Dr. Chauncey Goodrich and Levi L. Laurens. A native of Philadelphia, Laurens arrived in Houston on May 31, 1837. He must have been a young man of remarkable achievement,

152   THE VIRTUOUS PART OF THE COMMUNITY

for that same day the members of the House of Representatives elected him reporter. In typical Houston fashion, Laurens shared a room with a number of acquaintances in Pamelia Mann's Mansion House. A roommate with whom he was not acquainted was Dr. Goodrich.[38]

And what a piece of work *he* was. A native of Vicksburg, Mississippi, the good doctor had stood trial in 1835 for nearly whipping a slave woman to death. Afterward, he threatened to shoot the man who had levied the complaint. Goodrich epitomized the Southern sociopath who kept a hair-trigger on both his pistol and his pride. His descendants continue to plague beer joints and honky-tonks throughout the region. Social critic Florence King illustrated the type:

> I know this man. I saw him many times during my roadhouse-crawling days in Mississippi and North Carolina, and he always looked the same: a round-faced, pink-cheeked gnome of a man, a mean good ole boy biding his time until somebody had the misfortune to make eye contact with him. That's *all* it takes.

He arrived in the republic on February 21, 1837, and became a surgeon in the Texas army. His tenure proved brief. Soon thereafter Secretary of War Fisher furloughed most of the doctor's potential patients. Goodrich appeared to have made his way to Houston along with hundreds of other discharged soldiers.[39]

So it was that he found himself bunking in the Mansion House when Laurens arrived. The next morning a thousand dollars turned up missing from Goodrich's pocketbook, a common occurrence in a city teeming with cutpurses and pickpockets. Without a scintilla of evidence, he accused Laurens of the crime. When friends called on Goodrich to explain his mingle-mangled logic, he could only tell them "men's suspicions were often involuntary." Perhaps, but it is more likely that bigotry propelled his accusation. Laurens was a stranger and a Jew.[40]

Friends explained to Laurens that he must issue a challenge. If he failed to demand satisfaction, "it would at least be presumptive evidence of the truth of the charge." Therefore, adhering to local custom, Laurens demanded a retraction. Goodrich refused, and the parties selected a date: June 25, 1837. The code duello decreed that the challenged party had the preference of weapons. Goodrich opted for rifles at twenty-five paces, which many at the time deemed unsporting. "The weapon was one with which Laurens was entirely unacquainted," a witness noted, "as was evident not only from his own admissions but from the awkward manner of his using it on the field, while it was familiar to his adversary, who on a former occasion had proved his skill in its use by killing his man." Even so, Laurens probably stood a better chance with a rifle than either dueling pistol or rapier. Both required months of practice to master.[41]

The day arrived and the antagonists met on the dueling ground at 6:00 A.M. Each took his shot. Predictably, Laurens's bullet strayed far from its mark; Goodrich's ripped through both thighs of his rival. Friends carried the wounded man to the home of Dr. Francis Moore, Jr., who employed all of his medical training to save the young man, but to no avail. Enduring "bodily suffering and mental anguish," for forty-seven hours, Laurens slipped away, another victim of Goodrich's malevolence.[42]

Even those who followed the code duello took umbrage at the way Goodrich had twisted its principles to force Laurens's challenge. A complete novice, he could never have met Goodrich on equal terms. Many influential citizens claimed that the duel had not satisfied the dictates of honor, but an unseemly lust for blood. These voices reached fever pitch when residents discovered that Cicero Marcus Stanley, the black sheep of a distinguished North Carolina family, had stolen the money.

154   THE VIRTUOUS PART OF THE COMMUNITY

Laurens, as he insisted, had been entirely innocent. Nevertheless, he remained entirely dead, and many believed that a pity. Facing community condemnation and fearing legal sanctions, Goodrich absconded in the dead of night.[43]

Ensconced in Fort Bend, he wrote fellow physician Ashbel Smith, threatening to whip Moore through the streets if the editor disparaged him in the pages of the *Telegraph*. Goodrich was a thug. Intimidation and carnage were his answers to all of life's problems. Moreover, the brute was too dull-witted to understand that the spectacle of him thrashing the disabled editor would not endear him to citizens, who already thought Goodrich a braggart and bully. Restraint was one of the traits that defined a gentleman; since his passions ruled Dr. Goodrich, many questioned his right to claim the label.[44]

Threats could not cow the feisty Moore. In a column trimmed in black, he unleashed all his eloquence to eulogize Laurens and denounce the practice of dueling, which he castigated as "one of the most fiendish, foulest practices that ever disgraced a civilized society." Then he took to task "our leaders" who did nothing to stop the pernicious practice.

> Let them answer for this to their God. From them we turn in shame, to the youth of Texas, and ask in the name of our beloved and deceased friend, in the name of suffering humanity and justice, in the name of our injured country, that they form an organized association to uphold the violated law, and to eradicate by every honorable means, a practice which, originated in barbarism, and is the foulest disgrace of an enlightened age.

By identifying a problem, scolding officials for neglecting it, and then offering a solution, Moore constructed an image as a public-spirited citizen—and a potential candidate.[45]

Moore's Massachusetts upbringing had shaped his views on dueling. Bay Staters reviled duelists and drafted draconian measures to dissuade residents from engaging in the odious practice. An 1784 law even required that for a person killed in a duel, his corpse be "buried without a coffin, [and] with a stake drove through" it. To most Texians duelists were pillars of society, men who upheld manly traditions of valor and honor; to Yankees they were as vampires, earning infamy and denunciation in this world and the next.[46]

Houstonians honored Laurens as a gentleman who had died in defense of his reputation. District Attorney Augustus M. Tomkins called on citizens to mourn the slain youth for thirty days by attaching crape to their left sleeves. He also appointed seven citizens to serve on a committee that would raise a monument to Laurens. To have been in Houston such a short time, he made a lasting and favorable impression. As had been the case in the Aaron Burr–Alexander Hamilton duel, the people praised the "loser" for his gallantry and damned the "victor" for his spite.[47]

But what of Goodrich? With his welcome worn out in Houston, the doctor wandered down to San Antonio de Béxar. Soon after his arrival in the Alamo City, he tangled with a gambler named Allen who, as it happened, was an even meaner son of a bitch than Goodrich was. Later that night, Allen slipped into Goodrich's room and, while he lay sleeping, pinned him to his mattress with a Bowie knife. Clearly, Mr. Allen was no disciple of the code duello. Moore likely experienced considerable gratification upon publishing this death notice:

> Dr. Chauncey Goodrich was recently killed at Bexar by a young man by the name of Allen. Goodrich in an affray had attempted to shoot Allen, and was found shortly after killed in his chamber. "WHOSO SHEDDETH MAN'S BLOOD, BY MAN SHALL HIS BLOOD BE SHED.[48]

Although Goodrich had met the fate he deserved, Moore was not about to give up a valuable campaign issue. While dueling was officially illegal, none of Houston's elected officials—aware of community standards and southern traditions—seemed eager to prosecute offenders. Moore, an outsider who neither shared nor understood such customs, found this unwillingness to enforce the law scandalous. "The law relating to dueling," he intoned, "is quite defective." Assuming the royal "we," he explained:

> We think it ought to be amended in such a manner that the punishment for the crime would be certain, even though the public officers should prove recreant in their duty. This could be easily affected, by modifying the law so as to "exclude from all *public offices,* from the right of suffrage, and from serving on juries, those who shall hereafter be convicted" of acting as principals or seconds in any duel. Let this law be once passed and we will warrant the abolition of the accursed practice. For the "thunders of the press" will be hurled at every duelists who offers himself as a candidate for any office, as they will be hurled at every *renegade felon.* Our virtuous judges of elections will shrink from the votes of duelists as they would shrink from pollution, and our counselors will strike their names from the list of jurors with the same abhorrence with which they would exclude a fratricide.[49]

Having watched Laurens suffer a needless and agonizing death, Moore had sufficient cause to despise dueling, but personal motives may have also been involved. Through his editorials, Moore seemed to go out of his way to offer insult, and it was remarkable that he never received a challenge: a one-armed man could still level a dueling pistol. Yet, who could expect Moore to participate in an activity he constantly denounced?

Ironically (or, perhaps, cleverly), his public opposition to the code also protected him from its perilous consequences.

Because Moore did not share Southerners' notions of honor, he misjudged their motives for dueling. For Houston's ruling coterie, dueling was not so much an expression of honor as it was a demonstration of caste. The aristocracy had embraced the cult of chivalry to stem violence, not promote it. Noble blood was simply too precious to spill promiscuously. As for the blood of commoners, who cared? It was cheaper than ditchwater. The elaborate rules and rituals of the code duello gave blue blood time to cool and frequently led to an accommodation that assuaged the wounded pride of all parties. Just as top hat, tailcoat, cane, and cravat marked a man of consequence, so too did his observation of the code and all its arcane procedures. The duel, then, became a way for the gentry to display their nobility and manhood. A gentleman, therefore, would only accept challenges from other gentlemen. No man at the top of the social ladder would debase himself, or risk his place in society, by exchanging shots with some soil-handed drudge. President Houston frequently declined invitations to the dueling grounds. Wounds received at Horseshoe Bend and San Jacinto were ample proof of his physical courage. As former governor of Tennessee, victor of San Jacinto, and now president, he had gained the summit of Texas society. Houston received challenges with commendable coolness. He once tossed a written challenge to his secretary, jibing: "This is number twenty-four. The angry gentleman must wait his turn." The president had nothing to prove and none could claim to be his social equal. He, therefore, routinely refused challenges of less accomplished men—or, as he quipped: "I never fought downhill."50

The code duello offered another advantage: its disciples almost never suffered legal prosecution—at least, not in Texas. The tenets of dueling

158 THE VIRTUOUS PART OF THE COMMUNITY

expressed an almost obsessive concern for fairness. Referees guaranteed the evenhandedness of a contest and seconds, with their own pistols primed and loaded, stood by to keep the combatants honest. A gentleman willingly participated in a duel and took the same chance as his rival. A man or his family, therefore, could not reasonably complain if the other fellow maimed or killed him. It was upon that principal that Houstonians censured the Goodrich–Laurens duel. Goodrich, a practiced duelist, had (in a manner unbecoming a gentleman) taken unfair advantage of a novice. Still, Laurens, no matter how much Goodrich had provoked him, had offered the challenge. The community, therefore, did not consider the victor's actions criminal, but something worse. They were unfitting.

Guttersnipes brawled; gentlemen dueled. Indeed, that was the chief reason the gentry denigrated the loafers. In their wrangles, they observed no sophisticated rituals, no subtlety, no grace. In brief, no breeding. It was, as David James Jones would discover, the difference between community approval and a short drop off the end of a horse cart.

Grave Robbers

Houston, March 28, 1838

Some of Houston's most esteemed gentlemen inspect their gristly handiwork. All are physicians except for John Hunter Herndon and Mr. Cavanaugh. Consequently, they draw the grubby assignment of disinterment.

Herndon is the dandy of the group. Not wishing to soil his clothing, Herndon has removed his top coat and rolled up his sleeves. Being a gentleman, he retains his "Wellington" top hat. His task successfully completed, he savors a cheroot.

Mr. Cavanaugh stands by, wary of his surroundings. The physicians have done this before. This is his first grave robbing, and apprehension reveals itself in his face. Despite his anxiety, he manages to illuminate the proceedings with a shaky candle lantern.

Dr. Watson makes a phrenological observation, employing his capital knife as a pointer. He and Dr. Snow have removed their tailcoats and donned leather surgical aprons. Leather did not allow blood to soak through to mar clothing, as a cloth apron would have done. While pondering the contours of Jones's head, Dr. Snow holds a capital saw, the better to cut through bone and ligament.

Dr. Price holds a sack open to receive Jones's head. Quick's head is already "in the bag." Careful observers might notice traces of blood seeping through the thin cotton fabric.

During the surgery, doctors Watson and Price have removed the nooses and nonchalantly tossed them on the ground. The remnant of the ropes dangles from the gallows. Jones's arm lolls out from his open grave, while bats flutter overhead.

6
An Excellent Sentence
The Reckoning

avid James Jones had to see a man about a horse. It was not a real job, just a chance to scrounge pocket change. But these were troublous times; a man had to make money whenever and however he could. A citizen owned a runner—a fast one. In a town as rife with thieves as Houston, only a fool would leave blooded horseflesh unattended. Consequently, on Sunday evening, November 11, 1837, he engaged Jones to watch his charger. Agreeing to terms, the mount's owner went about his business. He would return later to collect his animal.[1]

While running errands, the man came upon Mandred Wood, an old friend. The encounter was a surprise as Wood was not a local, but an out-of-town visitor. The conversation turned to sport, and Wood's friend mentioned that he had a game horse. When Wood expressed interest, his acquaintance invited him to take his animal for a test ride. He failed to mention, however, that Jones was guarding it, an oversight that set into motion a series of tragic events.[2]

164   AN EXCELLENT SENTENCE

Strolling a short distance, Wood located the horse and leapt into the saddle. While he was putting the beast through its paces, Jones saw an unfamiliar man astride the mount he had contracted to protect. Jones, naturally, called on the stranger to halt. Wood glanced toward his challenger. He would have determined from Jones's appearance that he was no gentleman. To Wood's view, Jones was just another loafer, of no more consequence than a cockroach, a louse, or a maggot. Thus, he took no notice of him and continued his ride. In Jones's eyes, what was Wood? A high hat, a puffed-up toad liable to burst under the weight of his own grandiosity. Jones became aggravated. He might need to slice open this supercilious bastard and let some of his pride spill out. Again, Jones called upon Wood to stop—this time using "insulting language."

Wood replied with some "harsh epithets" of his own. What had until then been a simple misunderstanding became a matter of honor. Like most loafers, Jones was quick to sense slight or insult. A ubiquitous, poorly controlled rage likely propelled Jones, a fury easily triggered by a lifetime of high steppers duping him, slighting him, or dismissing him. Wood's natty habiliments, his disdainful manner, this sweet-scented cockscomb's self-importance was as provocative as his language. Jones unsheathed his Bowie knife and, as Wood dismounted, plunged it into his belly.

As Wood collapsed, witnesses fell upon Jones. An ugly scene turned menacing. The mob tried to lynch Jones on the spot, and would have, had "influential persons not intervened." Constables arrested Jones and cast him in chains. Wood lingered for two days before succumbing to his wound.[3]

Homicides were practically daily occurrences in early Houston; loafers slaughtered each other with numbing regularity. Authorities never learned of many of these incidents and certainly the *Telegraph* failed to report most of them. Like other Texas editors, Moore believed it unpatriotic to print stories that tended to "hurt the country." If he could not gloss bad news with a sanguine varnish, he simply ignored it. Likewise, Houston officials ignored what they deemed casual killings. As long as the riffraff eradicated each other, the quality deemed it good riddance. Jones, however, had made a fatal error: he killed someone who mattered.[4]

A native of New York, Wood had been a man of consequence. During the Campaign of 1835, he served as commissary officer and quartermaster of Captain William Gordon Cooke's company of New Orleans Greys, a unit that had participated in much hard fighting during the siege and storming of Béxar. On February 1, 1836, Velasco settlers elected delegates to the Independence Convention. Wood served as a clerk of the election. More significantly, he was part of a prominent family. He was the brother of Fernando and Benjamin Wood. Fernando was a mayor of New York City and a representative from New York. Benjamin was later editor and publisher of the New York Daily News and, likewise, a state representative.[5]

Their brother's murder could have terrible repercussions. The Panic of 1837 had driven men of broken fortune to Texas, but it had also restricted the U.S. economy and curbed American investments. Might this incident lead to a New York boycott? It was within the realm of possibility. Northeastern abolitionists, like former president John Quincy Adams, already opposed Texas annexation. Newspapers in the United States painted Texians and their republic as penniless, lawless, and helpless to manage their affairs. Would the murder of Wood confirm such opinions, even place admittance to the Union at risk? Undoubtedly. Moore and other bureaucrats of the republic knew they would be unable to sweep this killing under the carpet.[6]

Influential Texians were aware of the bad press they were receiving in American newspapers. Typical was the article that appeared in a New Orleans daily:

166   AN EXCELLENT SENTENCE

> The city of Houston, it is said, is falling faster than it has risen—that goods
> are there selling at auction at any price they will bring, and that for lots
> there is *no* sale. . . . Such a result must have been expected by reflecting,
> intelligent men; that a place without scarce any natural advantages
> should suddenly rise to such importance and maintain it, is certainly not
> to be expected.

Emanating from New Orleans, such harangues were especially disquieting. The Crescent City acted as Houston's entrepôt to the rest of the United States. Such reports were not only humiliating, but also bad for business.[7]

Embarrassed officials recognized that public opinion in the "old states" threatened the future of the Texas Republic. Thus, they became both publicly optimistic and carefully defensive when writing associates in the United States. In a missive to a friend, Ashbel Smith protested:

> I have seen it stated in your newspapers that our Army is disaffected, our
> president insane, &c. There is not a shadow of truth in the statement.—
> We have in a good degree disbanded our Army, because it was not
> deemed necessary to keep it on foot.—Our President, so far from being
> a madman, is a gentleman of most excellent endorsements, and most
> princely and affable manners.

The good doctor was a tad disingenuous. True, Houston had disbanded the army, but had done so, in large measure, because it had been so "disaffected." Moreover, even his staunchest friends acknowledged that, when in the clutches of a bender, the president was neither "princely" nor "affable."[8]

Nevertheless, twelve days later, Smith reprised the same tune: "The accounts in the newspapers of the United States of dissensions in Texas, of the insanity of our chief magistrate, of the corrupture & frailty of our government &c &c, are *wholly and utterly false.*" Again, Smith was more ebullient than conditions in his nation's capital would have warranted.[9]

Houston was awash with violence—and city officials seemed unwilling to do anything about it. Constable Stiff noted the "impunity with which all order is set at defiance by disturbers of the peace, who frequently use bowie knives and other savage weapons with such effect, that if murder is not committed, the life of the victim is rendered a burden." Even when arrested, vicious loafers rarely received punishment commensurate with their crimes because their associates intimidated the judges. Houston's judiciary, Stiff alleged, dealt with offenders in "such a manner as to secure to the magistrate the greatest number of votes, regardless of every other consideration except alone that which may arise from an instinctive dread of reckless and intoxicated men."[10]

Gustav Dresel also lamented the impotence of Houston's law enforcement. "The police in those days tried to maintain peace and avert disaster," he explained, "but it rarely happened that anyone was arrested." City ordinances forbidding games of hazard notwithstanding, the gamblers hove around the green tables day and night. "What is more," continued Dresel, "these blacklegs even formed a regular guild, against which any opposition was a risky matter." Yet, some Houstonians stood ready to hazard the wrath of gamblers, boozers, and brawlers. "The resident citizens . . . who were intent on the peace and good reputation of their new dwelling place, checked with all their might the nuisance that had gained ground."[11]

Authorities had placed Jones under arrest, but incarcerating him proved a challenge. Houston did not yet have a jailhouse. On November 14, Sheriff Moore hauled Jones to Liberty, where he remained until December 5. Liberty, an older, more established community, presumably had facilities where Jones could stay until Houston officials made other arrangements. Andrew Lawson (also spelled Larson) presented the Republic a bill for housing Jones from December to March. It remains unclear what kind of facility it was, but, like most Houston dwellings, it was makeshift. Jones was not alone. Lawson also oversaw the housing of numerous prisoners—but not that well. A document recording the disposition of the prisoners between November 1837 through June 1838, showed that six were free on security, seven escaped, eight won acquittal, the county discharged three, one gained executive clemency, and one died in prison.[12]

There was no more devoted guardian of Houston's reputation than Francis Moore, Jr. To him, and increasingly other civic-minded Houstonians, the rowdy loafers were low-life scum, blights on the community. They were responsible for most of the crime and bad press. Honest citizens needed to wean the undesirables of their pernicious habits, or else induce them to practice them elsewhere. Houston's ruling class would have to place rowdies on notice—and provide an example of what would befall them if they did not heed it.

Nothing but a complete housecleaning would suffice. Gambling promoted drinking; drinking promoted arguments. Add the habit of carrying weapons to the mix, and arguments turned deadly. The city had laws on the books against these offenses, but few of the officers of justice seemed willing to risk community disapproval by enforcing them. That malfeasance drove Moore apoplectic. He transformed his newspaper into a sounding board for all those who shared his opinions. An open letter on the issue, addressed to "Mr. Editor," appeared in October 1837:

> The sheriff of this county is requested to attempt his duty in carrying into full effect the law relating to gambling. The owners of several houses

in town have already made themselves liable to heavy penalties. Those officers who faithfully discharge their duties will be supported by

MANY CITIZENS

The "one-armed Proteus," was certainly protean in his views of discharged volunteers. One of their number, Moore was at first an advocate. In August 1837, he reported that most of the furloughed troops "still remain in the country and are engaged in useful occupations. They all hold themselves in readiness to rally again to the Texian standard, at the call of their commander." By February 1838, however, few "useful occupations" remained open to them. Public opinion toward the loafers had shifted. Moore made sure he kept pace:

> We notice a great many young men loitering idly about our streets, apparently wanting for employment. We advise them to go immediately into the country and commence farming; the fertility of the soil will amply reward their industry. A young man who commenced farming on the Trinity last spring has raised twenty bales of cotton upon fifteen acres of land. Let the idlers of our city "go and do likewise" and they may well enjoy a competence. Should they however neglect this advice, indolence may soon lead them to the GROG SHOPS, which in the low country of Texas take but the portals to the grave.[13]

On the surface, Moore's advice appeared sound. The editor, however, failed to consider harsh realities. Because of the disorder that prevailed in the government, many volunteers had yet to receive title to their promised acres. Others who did have clear title did not have cash in hand to procure stock or seed. Those who had planned to turn a quick profit by selling

170 AN EXCELLENT SENTENCE

their land discovered that it was practically worthless. When the bottom dropped out of the land market, all Houstonians suffered. As Mary Austin Holley told it:

> Every body has land for sale, but they keep up their prices, & purchasers— the few who have money (& there is no use in selling on credit) are waiting for a fall. The greatest part of the emigration consists of small farmers who come in by land & settle above, where land is cheaper, & they get small tracts, in healthy situations. The capitalists come by sea, travel every where & remain undecided—not knowing where to choose—& as I said, waiting until the still greater embarrassments of the proprietors shall compel them to sacrifice their estates.

Worse, for many of the loafers, hard times had already forced them to "sacrifice their estates" for booze or legal services.[14]

On December 21, 1837, Congress passed an act that bestowed donation certificates of 640 acres each to all veterans of San Jacinto, to those wounded in the skirmishing on April 20, and to those who guarded the baggage at the camp below Harrisburg. The same law granted bounty warrants to veterans of the siege and storming of Béxar, the Goliad campaigns of 1835 and 1836, and to heirs of the Alamo slain. As a participant in the Goliad campaign and the battle of San Jacinto, Jones was entitled to two 640-acre grants, which he would have found encouraging had he not been incarcerated and awaiting trial for murder.

On January 1, 1838, Francis Moore, Jr., took the oath of office as mayor, and he lost no time placing his fiery oratory into action. His first undertaking was to expand the city limits. At that juncture, the bayou provided the town's northern boundary, Walker Street the southern, Carolina the eastern, and Bagby Street the western. Moore inflated the limits to embrace an area of nine square miles. Several settlers had constructed their residences just beyond the old city lines to avoid paying city taxes. Closing this loophole, Mayor Moore increased the taxable area, the municipal coffers, and the number of people who hated his guts.[15]

Later that month, as if on cue, another high-profile murder roiled Houston. Pennsylvania native and San Jacinto veteran, Moses W. Brigham, had gone to the Houston House, a notorious taproom and gambling den. Another revolutionary veteran, John Christopher Columbus Quick, joined Brigham at the emerald board for a friendly game of chance. Friendly, that is, until one of them lost more than he could pay. In the brawl that ensued, Quick pulled a dirk and gutted Brigham. He lingered in agony for days, but finally slipped away. Houstonians placed the dead man in the ground and his killer behind locked doors. Witnesses came forward charging that Brigham had not been his only victim; Quick, splashed the *Telegraph*, had actually "committed five murders!"[16]

Moore lost no time in exploiting another murder for political advantage. The same issue of the *Telegraph* that reported Brigham's death also ran a letter from "L," an outraged Houston citizen:

> Sir:—A murder has been committed—a deliberate, wanton *murder*. Of the parties, we have no knowledge, but the fact is fully attested.
>
> In the practice of every nation, civilized or barbarous; exacted by justice and sanctioned by custom; by express laws or tacit consent, the assassin must atone for the crime with his blood—otherwise life is insecure, and society unsettled. Shall Texas alone be excepted!
>
> Her enemies abroad, (and they are not few,) have enumerated with a degree of malignant satisfaction, crimes committed with impunity; laws made, violated and unpunished: they have represented her inhabitants lawless and inadequate to the task of government; as incapable of

172   AN EXCELLENT SENTENCE

> obedience and incompetent to rule; and have hence deduced not only a recklessness of personal character, but also as an obvious result, the instability of our institutions. Our pretensions to a national existence they have met with the smile of derision; and remarking with the insolence of gratified malice, (yet not without justice,) that imbecility aiming at importance is ever ridiculous, and would be contemptible, could it merit contempt. It is time for Texas to speak—to annihilate their hopes and rebuke their craven spirits, by exacting judicious compliance with the law, and enforcing its entire execution.

This letter did such an outstanding job of expressing Moore's opinion that he could have written it himself—and may have. The letter's proselytizing style certainly parroted Moore's.[17]

Mayor Moore linked Quick and Jones in his mind and in his newspaper. He opined that Quick was a "fit companion for Jones, with whom he is now imprisoned, and who has been charged with three murders! *Par nobile fratrum* [a noble pair of brothers]." He could not resist taking a swipe at anti-Texas newspapers back in the states. "Doubtless, these miscreants, confiding in the statements of certain *learned* editors, have supposed that Texas would prove a safe asylum for murderers." There was but one way to correct this false supposition. "A couple of halters," Moore predicted, "may ere long cause them to entertain more *elevated* notions of our fellow citizens."[18]

Nor could Moore pass up an opportunity to rebuke the sin of gambling and the officials who ignored it. "This disgraceful transaction may possibly convince certain officers of justice that gambling may be productive of evil. Would that they could be as thoroughly convinced on the awful truth that the blood of this victim is upon their hands."[19]

TEXIAN MACABRE

What should one make of this? The "enemies abroad" mentioned in L's letter were not the Mexicans, as one might have expected. Rather they were opponents of Texas in the American congress and press. Scoundrels like Jones and Quick made Texas look bad. If they found justice at the end of a rope, perhaps Americans might come to believe that Texians were as enlightened and law abiding as they were. Moore's message was a variation on that theme. In his view, American newspapermen who reported Texas mayhem had to share a portion of the guilt. Linking the cases of Jones and Quick, he found both guilty by association. Remarkably, the editor called for the death penalty before the prosecuting attorney did. Moore tried and convicted Jones and Quick in the pages of the *Telegraph*. Doubtless, Moore believed that he was performing his role as guardian of "public and private morals." Who, indeed, was better qualified? This was an occasion when a committed editor could "exorcise the malignant spirits which are the bane of society." Neither defendant, of course, could have received a fair trial after Moore poisoned the jury pool. Mind, both L's letter and Moore's editorial appeared before either Jones or Quick had stood trial. So much for the presumption of innocence.[20]

As Moore, Smith, and other boosters told it, "enemies" unjustly sullied the character of Houston and its citizens. Yet, it would have been difficult to exaggerate the number of offences. Herndon's observations of a four-month period in 1838 demonstrated that murder and mayhem were commonplace in the Bayou City:

Tuesday, January 30: "Several rows in town, man killed."

Monday, March 5: "A day of rioting. Several fights."

Sunday, March 11: "Arkansas set in town. Several old men knocked down by them."

Thursday, March 15: "An affray in town with Bowie knives and pistols, but no serious injury."

Sunday, March 18: "Many Indians in town who made much noise. A squaw drunk, the first I ever saw."

Tuesday, March 20: "A man arrested for passing counterfeit money."

Saturday, April 14: "I am just informed all the justices in town are now employed in the investigation of crime: One for Murder, another for Counterfeiting and others for petit larceny. What a den of villains must there not be here?"

But the law—or what passed for it in Houston—was about to dispense with one of those villains. Indicted on March 19, David James Jones stood trial on March 22, 1838. Most Houstonians believed it a waste of time and taxpayer money. Nonetheless, it was important to show critics that Houstonians, no less than anyone, observed the legal niceties. Adopting an obsequious tone, Moore drove the point:

The proceedings of the District Court held in this City, during the present week, have been beheld by our citizens with exultation and pride.

The remarkable decorum which has continually prevailed; the cordiality, and even officiousness, which have been everywhere shows us sustaining the officers of justice in the discharge of their duties; the intelligence and respectability of the jurors, the decorous and gentlemanly deportment of the several attorneys engaged; and the ability, integrity, and decision of the presiding judge, have combined to render this court one of the most august and interesting spectacles which our city has ever afforded.[21]

Moore surely admired the roster of participants at Jones's trial. Archibald Wynns, William Lawrence, and Clement N. Bassett represented the defendant. Judge James W. Robinson, former acting governor and San Jacinto veteran, presided. The judge probably remembered the defendant; he had fought stirrup-to-stirrup with Jones in the cavalry skirmish on April 20, 1836. After San Jacinto, Robinson returned to his family and resumed the practice of law. On December 16, 1836, the Republic's Congress named him Judge of the Fourth Judicial District, which also made him a justice of the Supreme Court. If sitting in judgment of a war hero and a former companion-in-arms created any ambivalence in Judge Robinson, he never let it show.[22]

Few envied the officers of the court. This was an open-and-shut case. It seemed that half of Houston had witnessed the accused kill Wood, a fact Jones never denied. The trial was sure to end with the desired results. Or, at least those desired by Moore and his henchmen. Herndon viewed the proceedings with a professional eye: "Counsel attempt to take advantage of legal technicalities and imperfections in pleadings." These arguments hauled little freight with the jury members, who required only an hour before returning a guilty verdict. They agreed with Herndon that "a plainer case" had "seldom been submitted to a Jury." At the time of his conviction, Jones was virtually penniless for on March 24, Judge Robinson certified that the defendant had shown his "inability to pay the cost of suit," which amounted to $19.38. Jones had entered Houston with considerably more than three thousand dollars in his pocket. Now he was indigent.[23]

The following day Quick received his portion of Houston justice. Again, Judge Robinson presided, and again the trial was pro forma. J. C. Watrous, a newcomer to the city, represented Quick. The attorney delivered a rigorous defense based upon "objections founded in rules of law." Francis Lubbock, the jury foreman, recalled that Watrous sought a new trial and employed every legal maneuver to delay a death sentence. Yet, as Moore explained it, he was "laboring against a sweeping tide of public indignation, which was strong against both culprits." After all of his prejudicial editorials, small wonder that. The fix was in. Under enormous pressure to deliver a guilty verdict, Judge Robinson made sure that Quick would not walk on a technicality and overruled every defense motion. Incensed at this hijacking of the legal process, Watrous issued a charge for which the judge could have found him in contempt of court. The attorney contended that if Robinson delivered a death sentence it would be "judicial murder." Tempers flared, but Robinson maintained order in his court.[24]

The jury wasted no time before returning the expected verdict. "After retiring about twenty minutes," Moore trumpeted, "they returned with a verdict of **GUILTY**." The finding surprised no one; even Quick accepted the decision with stoic equanimity. Herndon thought the defendant a "savage bloodthirsty, malicious looking devil" but noted he "changed not a feature or mussel of his face upon the verdict being announced." Robinson tried to salve Watrous's wounded pride. He told Quick that he had no reason to protest. He had received "benefit of counsel who evinced talents which greatly ornamented the profession—who threw around him the best defense which ingenuity could suggest, and of which the highest legal attainments were capable."[25]

The defendant remained unimpressed. Quick did not see that he had any reason to appreciate his lawyer's abilities. In lieu of a regular fee, Quick had agreed to assign Watrous a thousand acres near the town of Texana. When the jury declared against him, however, Quick defiantly refused to transfer the title. It was a bad deal for all concerned: the client lost his case; the lawyer lost his fee. Still, the court could exert little leverage upon

Quick. What could it do, hang him twice? Like Jones, Quick could not pay the court cost; the taxpayers would have to pick up the tab, which came to twenty-seven dollars. But what else could one expect of rowdy loafers?[26]

Although Jones and Quick had received guilty verdicts, Judge Robinson had yet to deliver his sentence. On Saturday, March 24, he met community expectations (and delighted Moore) when he condemned both men to hang and ordered Sheriff John W. Moore to execute the judgment the following Wednesday between the hours of 9:00 A.M. and 4:00 P.M. In Herndon's professional opinion, it was an "excellent sentence." He commended Judge Robinson's ruling as "brief and comprehensive and pregnant with salutary advice and heavenly commendation."[27]

The severity of Judge Robinson's sentence had an immediate effect. The following day, Herndon chronicled: "Fair fine morning, all peacable, a decided reformation in the morals of Houston." Three days before, citizens had witnessed "Four criminals whipped at the post." That, and the impending fate of Jones and Quick, cast a pall over the gambling dens, grog shops, and whorehouses. Somber and sullen, the loafers were, at least for a while, no longer rowdy. They finally realized that, even in Houston, their actions had consequences. And murderous actions carried fatal consequences. For the length of that "peacable" Sunday, the "merry boys" walked the straight and narrow. That night Herndon noted: "No affray this day." Along with the stink of unwashed bodies, stale tobacco, and cheap whiskey, Houston's underclass now reeked of fear.[28]

The tranquility would not last. On Monday, March 26, rumors of an unpleasant episode shook the town. Street-corner gossips spread the word that Jones, while confined, had attempted suicide. It was no idle blather. The condemned man had tried to shoot himself but flinched as he squeezed the trigger and hurled the ball over, not through, his head.[29]

This incident raised a number of questions—not the least of which was how a condemned murderer awaiting execution could have gained access to a loaded pistol. On January 18, 1838, Chief Justice of Harrisburg Andrew Briscoe testified that contractor Maurice L. Birdsall had agreed to erect a jail for the fee of $4,750.00 and a courthouse for $3,800.00. Yet, an April 7 report indicated the jail was still under construction. Jones and Quick would not have had the opportunity to enjoy the new facility. They had to make do with Andrew Lawson's hospitality. As indicated by the number of prisoners that escaped, security was inadequate. It would have been easy enough for one of Jones's friends, not wishing him to suffer a shameful death on the gallows, to supply him an alternative.

Another possibility is more intriguing. Might someone have slipped Jones the pistol with the full knowledge and blessing of the city fathers? Many citizens were aware of Jones's service to Texas. Mayor Moore and other municipal officers found themselves in the awkward position of having to hang a certifiable hero. If, however, Jones were to take his own life, a single pull of the trigger might untangle several knotty political difficulties. A suicide could serve the demands of justice without forcing politicians to carry out what might well prove an unpopular sentence. Who knew how loafers would react to seeing one of their own swing? Might they attempt a rescue? Could they riot? All those questions remained unanswered. But a suicide would mollify public opinion and get Moore and the others off the hook. If such were the scheme it was a clever one, but a trembling hand dashed all their hopes. They would have to conduct the execution as scheduled.

Tuesday, March 27, dawned "cloudy and warm." Herndon took advantage of the balmy weather to breakfast with his friend John Woodruff. Considerations other than friendship and appetite motivated the young attorney. Woodruff, who lived on the outskirts of town, possessed a well with some of the sweetest water in the region. While he was there, Herndon "took a wash." There was a ball that evening and someone of his breeding would never have attended without first taking a proper bath, even if it meant riding a bit out of his way.[30]

Clean and spruce, Herndon left Woodruff's and made his way back into town. Along the way he passed a slaughterhouse where the sight of two hundred severed cows' heads repulsed him. He, nevertheless, was a resilient fellow, for a "little further and I saw a pretty girl—how great the contrast?" Pondering the vagaries of life in Houston, he returned to Floyd's boarding house, where he made ready for that evening's revelries.[31]

That day marked the second anniversary of the Goliad Massacre. Houston's gentry took notice of the date with a notable lack of discernment. "This is the anniversary of the Massacre of Fannin's Company," Herndon noted, "and it is celebrated with a Ball!" The exclamation mark said it all. One might *observe* or *commemorate* such a day, but Herndon thought it peculiar that Texians "celebrated" such a woeful loss of life. It, nevertheless, provided an opportunity to meet young ladies. He would attend.[32]

He was not disappointed. Beginning at nine o'clock, the dance displayed the cream of Houston society. Forty gentlemen "and as many ladies" appeared in full frippery. Stylish was each man, and stunning each woman. Herndon was in his element: "Had a fine set, supper, good wines and interesting ladies." He declared that, "all in all," these festivities were equal "to a Kentucky Ball." High praise, indeed. A gaffe occurred when a "very pretty lady" lost her balance and "fell flat on the floor." She should not have been self-conscious, for later a "gentleman also came to his marrow bones." Herndon was too refined to mention it aloud, but he noticed something odd about Houston women. "The ladies have rather large feet, owing perhaps to their having gone barefooted a little too long." After a wonderful evening, Herndon stumbled back to Floyd's Hotel around 4:00 A.M. Houston's patricians apparently saw nothing contradictory in celebrating the heroic sacrifice of Fannin's garrison that evening, while preparing to hang one of its members the following day.[33]

Wednesday, March 28, continued the stretch of good weather that Houstonians had enjoyed for more than a week. "A delightful day," a bleary-eyed Herndon observed, one "worthy of other deeds." The entire city was abuzz, for on this day Jones and Quick were to hang. Early that morning crowds assembled although the execution was not scheduled until two o'clock that afternoon. Judge Robinson's order stipulated that Sheriff Moore had to carry out the sentence between the hours of 9:00 A.M. and 4:00 P.M. He could have carried out the executions that morning and spared Jones and Quick hours of mental anguish. Why did he delay? Many folks were traveling from out of town to view the hanging, so he may have pushed back the proceeding in deference to them. Also, the city's leading citizens had attended the Fannin Massacre Ball and had been up until the wee hours. A two o'clock drop time allowed them to sleep in that morning, enjoy a hearty lunch, and be bright-eyed for the big show.

Houston's "tarnation tall men" wanted as many people as possible to witness the execution. That was the entire point behind public hangings. On the most elemental level, they were cynical applications of social control. Officials also considered them useful civics lessons; citizens who witnessed them could ponder the wages of sin. Frequently, the prisoner's final words warned against gambling, drinking, jealousy, or running with wicked companions. A "good" hanging was a ritual, with all parties playing hackneyed roles. If the prisoner was popular, the crowd would cheer him and boo the hangman. If, on the other hand, the condemned

TEXIAN MACABRE 181

was, say, a child murderer, the mob would jeer, hiss, and pelt him with rotten vegetables. The mob appreciated it when the victim "died game." If he had not lived well, he might at least die well. Conversely, a sniffling demise earned the player harsh reviews.

Civil authorities urged parents to take their children to hangings so they might learn the "lessons of the gallows." One English schoolmaster took his charges to observe "improving scenes" at the gallows. In 1824, the headmaster declared a school holiday so his students could observe a girl hanged at Horsham. But executions did not always constitute a carefree day out. Strict fathers escorted their progeny to hangings and flogged them afterward so they "might remember the example they had seen." It was much the same in the United States—and the Republic of Texas. One Houstonian certainly found the executions of Jones and Quick an opportunity for edification: "Their fate suggests many solemn and awful reflections to the passionate and vicious."[34]

It was important, therefore, that Houston's officials carry out the sentence with proper gravitas and decorum. Sheriff John W. Moore, especially, was under enormous pressure to assure the hangings proceed without embarrassment. He dipped into his own pocket to assure the executions would bring credit on the town. Neither Jones nor Quick owned a pair of decent socks, so Moore shelled out two dollars for "2 pair of Socks," to assure the prisoners made a favorable impression on the gallows. He also paid $23.87 to a local carpenter to build two coffins, $6.00 for digging two graves, $9.63 for eleven yards of cambric "for Shrouds," and another $6.00 to a tailor for "making ditto." Moore charged the Republic $15.00 for "hauling Jones & Quick to [the] place of Execution," which seemed excessive. Still, a gratuity for the militiamen who served as escort for the condemned men may have accounted for the high expense. Sheriff Moore dutifully kept an account of his

182　AN EXCELLENT SENTENCE

expenses and later filed a claim for reimbursement that District Judge Robert "Three-legged Willie" Williamson certified.[35]

The mob grew impatient, but the program finally opened with all the principals playing their parts. Fearing a rescue attempt, authorities called out "several" of the city's militia companies. But none of the rowdy loafers appeared willing to risk the effort—or for that matter, even express compassion—for the condemned men: "A concourse of from 2000 to 3000 persons on the ground and among the whole not a single sympathetic tear was dropped." When the prisoners arrived at the gallows, the executioner placed them on the cart's tailgate and fastened the ropes. Then came the most poignant portion of the performance.

Spectators hushed one another to silence, as they strained to hear the condemned's last words. Mayor Moore approved of Quick's address—as he should have since it echoed most of his talking points. "At the gallows Quick made a long and somewhat impressive speech, in which he expiated upon the dangerous influence of gambling and the practice of wearing concealed weapons." Moore conceded that Quick "met his fate with great firmness and resignation." Herndon agreed: "Quick addressed the crowd in a stern, composed and hardened manner." To Herndon's eye, the proceedings left Quick "entirely unmoved." Jones's behavior, on the other hand, let down the prickly editor. "Jones maintained to the last a sullen silence; he appeared to be completely stupefied with fear or shame, and manifested the utmost indifference to what was passing around him." Jones also may have been drunk out of his mind, as many prisoners were on their way to the gallows. To Herndon, "Jones seemed frightened altho' as hardened in crime as Quick." In the end, his performance failed to meet expectations. Jones seemed not to fully appreciate the magnitude of the occasion.

Sheriff Moore kept a sharp eye on his timepiece. He knew he would pay hell if the executions did not come off on schedule. At exactly two o'clock—both Moore and Herndon marked the time—he signaled the hangman, who thrashed the horse. The cart heaved forward. Toes of brogans tripped across the tailgate before toppling off. Unusually, neither Jones nor Quick "danced the hempen jig." Herndon verified that the duo slipped into oblivion without the "slightest struggle." He seemed crestfallen. After the bodies of Jones and Quick had hung limp for thirty-five minutes, the sheriff cut them down. According to Moore, the remains "were immediately buried beneath the fatal trees which had upheld them for destruction." The deed was done; spectators began the walk back to Houston. No mourners lingered.[36]

As falling night cast its shadows across the grove, five of Houston's most respectable gentlemen returned to the hanging ground. Three were physicians and brought their medical bags. Two others carried shovels. They quickly removed the soil covering the bodies; the graves would not have been deep. Posterity knows about their excursion only because one of them, John Hunter Herndon, recorded it in his diary. "Dr.s Price and Watson, Snow, Cavanaugh and self went out to the graves and cut off the heads of Quick and Jones and brought them in for dissection." Herndon's tone was so nonchalant, one might think he was acquiring a new handkerchief. This was no hack-and-chop job. The medical men, desiring useful specimens, took their time and carefully employed their surgical instruments to remove the heads. Shining in the moonlight, the polished blades of knife and saw lost their luster as blood veiled their sheen. The operation finished, the associates bagged their prizes and returned to the city. Later that evening, Herndon enjoyed a "good supper." The sight of severed cows' heads may have disturbed his refined

184   AN EXCELLENT SENTENCE

sensibilities, but decapitating members of his own species bothered him not a whit.[37]

In 1838, however, Herndon's indifference would not have seemed peculiar since dismemberment of executed criminals was a time-honored custom. As early as 1504, Scotland's James I recognized the need for cadavers in medical training. Consequently, he granted the Edinburgh Guild of Surgeons and Barbers the remains of specified felons for dissection. In England, medicine engaged the interest of Henry VIII, who was the first of his country's kings to sanction anatomization—an older word for dissection—of human remains. In 1541, the king and Parliament granted four prisoners a year to the College of Physicians and Surgeons. By 1663, the need had grown so much that Charles II increased Henry's original grant to six convicted felons.

In the early eighteenth century, some judicial critics argued that hanging alone was insufficient deterrent, or, as the title of a 1701 pamphlet intoned: *Hanging Not Punishment Enough*. In 1752, an act of Parliament made despoliation of the corpse part of the prescribed punishment. The legislation denied condemned murderers Christian burial. Their bodies would undergo dissection. That, or hang in chains until they rotted. It was the judge's call.[38]

This act abandoned the pretext that anatomization advanced the cause of medical science. Instead, it admitted explicitly that Parliament intended to intimidate potential murderers and further defame those who had done the deed. The legislation was titled "An Act for better preventing the horrid Crime of Murder," and its preamble was especially revealing:

> Whereas the horrid Crime of Murder has of late been more frequently perpetrated than formerly and particularly in and near the Metropolis

of this Kingdom, contrary to known Humanity and natural Genius of the British Nation: And whereas it is thereby become necessary, that some further Terror and Peculiar Mark of Infamy be added to the Punishment of Death, now by Law inflicted on such as shall be guilty of the said heinous Offense . . . .

Under no circumstance would the remains of a convicted murderer receive burial unless it had first suffered the disgrace of dissection. Thus, surgeons and anatomy students, no less than the hangman, found themselves executors of the court's sentence.[39]

Surgeons, branding murderers with the "Peculiar Mark of Infamy," frequently anatomized their bodies before the public. During the eighteenth century, the dismemberment of felons became something of an event, attracting stylish gentlemen of scientific pretensions. The practice survived well into the nineteenth century. Following his execution in 1828, the body of murderer William Corder lay on exhibit in the shire hall. As spectators gawked, the surgeon exposed the cadaver's internal organs. Yet, the desecration of Corder's remains had only started:

The bones of Corder having been cleared of the flesh, have been reunited by Mr. S. Dalton, and the skeleton is now placed in the Suffolk General Hospital. A great portion of the skin has been tanned, and a gentleman connected with the hospital intends to have the Trial and Memoirs of Corder bound in it. The heart has been preserved in spirits.

After the 1831 hanging of John Holloway, twenty-three thousand spectators filed into Lewes town hall to view the disfigured body. Ghoulish individuals were as keen to examine the anatomized carcasses as they

186   AN EXCELLENT SENTENCE

were to view their owners hanged. Even after dissection, the remains did not receive a proper burial; for years thereafter the Sussex county hospital displayed Holloway's skeleton.[40]

While dissection fascinated most of the British public, it enraged a vocal minority. These Englishmen resisted dismemberment of human remains even in the cause of science. Christians believed that mutilation of the body interfered with God's plan for resurrection, when He would gather the departed faithful—in the flesh—around His celestial throne. Destruction of the corpse might easily cause the loss of the soul's identity. Many predicted that on Judgment Day dissected corpses would stumble through the streets of Heaven in a futile search for their missing parts. The public understood the necessity of sentencing sinners in this life, yet who but God had the right to condemn a soul for all eternity? On several occasions, brawls erupted around the gallows when family and friends of hanged criminals fought to defend their bodies from the surgeon's knife.

Like other elements of English Common Law, anatomization traveled across the Atlantic to colonial courts. In March 1733, Massachusetts surgeons performed the first documented American dissection on the remains of "Julian," an Indian. A Boston judge sentenced Julian, who had murdered a man the previous year, to hang and his remains bestowed to medical students. A local newspaper reported details of the post mortem:

> The body of Julian the Indian man, who was executed here last week, having been granted several young students in physick, surgery, and etc. at their request; the same has for several days past been dissecting in their presence, in a most accurate manner; and it is hoped their critical inspection, will prove of singular advantage. The bones are preserved, in order to be framed into a skeleton.

In the American colonies, as in the mother country, hanged criminals appear to have been the principal source of anatomical specimens.[41]

The early nineteenth century witnessed the proliferation of medical schools in Europe and the United States. With more eager students than ever before, the supply hangmen provided no longer met demand. This disparity created opportunities for an abhorrent breed of scumbag: the body snatchers. Variously described as "fishermen," "grabs," "grave robbers," "resurrectionists," "snatches," or "sack-'em-up-men," these rogues provided cadavers to those physicians unconcerned about the source. Potter's Fields and Black cemeteries were especially susceptible to late night raids. Even if caught in the act, grabs knew poor folks did not have the money, contacts, or status to seek legal remedy. The dissection table was the only place in antebellum America were people of color enjoyed absolute equality. The odious trade became so prevalent that the affluent engaged "grave watchers" to protect resting places of departed family members. These guardians of the dead minded the burial spot until its inhabitant had gone moldy: anatomists required fresh specimens. Yet, not even guards guaranteed that the dead rested in peace. Expert sack-'em-up-men took professional pride in thwarting the grave watchers.[42]

When American medical students required cadavers to complete their schooling, they frequently traded their scalpels for shovels. For the young surgeon-in-training, the robbing of his first grave marked a significant rite of passage. This explains the entry in The Devil's Dictionary, a volume penned by American satirist Ambrose Bierce: "Grave, n. A place in which the dead are laid to await the coming of the medical student." That Dr. Frankenstein robbed graves to supply his experiments did not shock the first readers of Mary Shelley's novel; it was something they expected of medical practitioners. Indeed, when physicians Price, Snow, and Watson

188   AN EXCELLENT SENTENCE

pulled Jones and Quick from their shallow pits, it was probably not their first body snatch.[43]

The nineteenth-century study of phrenology motivated the actions of Houston's grave robbers. The 1828 Webster's dictionary defines the practice as: "The science of the human mind and its various properties. Phrenology is now applied to the science of the mind as connected with the supposed organs of thought and passion in the brain, broached by Gall." The idiosyncratic Viennese physician Franz Joseph Gall (1758–1828), recognized by contemporaries as the founder of the discipline, included these basic tenets in his system:

1. The brain is the organ of the mind.
2. The mind is composed of multiple distinct, intrinsic traits.
3. Because they are distinctive, each trait must have a separate base or "organ" in the brain.
4. The development of the various organs determines the shape of the brain.
5. All other factors being equal, the size of an organ is the gauge of its power.
6. Since the brain determines the conformation of the skull, a trained Phrenologist can interpret its surface as an indicator of psychological abilities and predispositions.[44]

Phrenologists ran their fingertips or palms over the subject's skull to locate any bumps or dimples. Frequently, they employed measuring tapes and calipers to better plot the surface of the skull. Serious practitioners memorized phrenological charts that delineated the head's cartography. They were also conversant with the characteristics of the thirty-five or so (the number kept changing) "organs" of the brain.[45]

With the heads of Jones and Quick back in Houston, the grave robbers could scrutinize them at their leisure. The day following the hangings, they "commenced dissecting and examining the heads." A recreational phrenologist, Herndon had, nonetheless, mastered the jargon and took pains to record the proceedings in the scientific vernacular.

> Phrenologically, Jones had a very bad head, all moral power very deficient, the bumps of disructiveness and firmness remarkably large. No reverence, Veneration, and but little perception, with no comparison or ideality. His animal organs well developed.

Just as he favored Quick's behavior under the gallows, he now preferred the shape of his noggin. "Quick had a much better head. His moral powers pretty well developed and intellectual tolerably well, but distructiveness and combativeness very large. His animal powers also strongly developed."[46]

Even the most persevering phrenologist conceded that there were limits to the information one could assemble by examining the skull's surface. Therefore, two days after the hanging, the physicians broke out their surgical saws. After carefully removing the skullcap, they scooped out the brains. "Finished the dissection of Quick's and Jones' heads," Herndon entered that evening. Desiring a keepsake of the procedure, he "preserved the brains of Jones."

But Herndon was an active man about town. He could ill afford to spend his entire day pickling brains. Later, he penned an article for the *Telegraph*, visited a Misses Humphreys, and "wrote a piece of Poetry to _____." It is illustrative of the nineteenth-century sensibility that the same fellow who, with no hint of embarrassment, described robbing graves, dissecting heads, and preserving brains refrained from divulging the name of a sweetheart—even in the privacy of his diary.[47]

190   AN EXCELLENT SENTENCE

Saturday, March 31, was eventful. As he did every night before retiring, Herndon registered the day's activities:

> Lovely weather. Called on Esquire Waters and Dr. Shepherd. Spent the remainder of the morning in reading Vattels *Law of Nations*. In the afternoon Dr. Price and self took a ride to the country. Went to Holland's where we spent an hour with Misses Holland and Bond. Thence to Judge Smith's where we had the pleasure of seeing Miss Smith, an interesting young lady. Thence over the prairie beautifully clad with grass and wild flowers by M. Baker's to Mrs. Smith's where we had an excellent supper and fine society. Invited to board. Miss Smith walked me out into the garden to behold the beautiful results of her industry. Returned to town at 8 O'clock. Had several calls. Buried the remains of Quick's and Jones' heads.[48]

Judging from Herndon's entry, dumping the heads was his final task before turning in that night. It had been three days since the decapitations; the heads would have been turning ripe. Why else would he not have waited until morning? Given the time of night, the distance to the graves, and the offhand way he chronicled their disposal, it is a sure bet that Herndon did not reunite the heads with the rest of Quick and Jones. Most likely, he traipsed out behind Floyd's Hotel, dug a hole, and plunked them in. In morose moments, one wonders if their skulls are still there, forlorn, forgotten, shrouded under the blacktop of a frenzied, modern city.

Nothing indicated that dissection was part of Judge Robinson's sentence. That Herndon and the others returned to the gallows that night—after the crowd had dispersed—suggested that the disinterments and dissections were extra-legal. Most citizens would have reviled their furtive experiments: What better reason to conceal them? Houston's resurrectionists might have justified their actions had they filched cadavers to supply anatomy students. But they took the heads and left the bodies to rot. The only reason for this desecration was the satisfaction of a perverse curiosity: rich boys playing at their hobbies.

Caste shaped their callousness. What harm, after all, had been done? If they had not harvested the heads, they would have simply rotted anyway. What did it matter? Herndon and his associates told themselves that hanged culprits were human offal, savage brutes with nary a glimmer of the divine spark. The "up-street men" disparaged loafers for their denunciation of good breeding, good manners, good order, good sense, why, even goodness itself. If they behaved no better than swine, why treat their carcasses with any more regard than those at the slaughterhouse?

Twenty-first-century readers experience difficultly accepting such elitist opinions. Social anthropologists have advanced numerous theories to describe the various ramifications of class distinctions. This case, however, requires none of them. The explanation is deceptively simple. Why did Herndon and his partners treat the bodies of Jones and Quick with such scornful disregard?

Because they could.

Epilogue
Vengeance of the Public Hatred
Legacy

In the days and weeks that followed, Houstonians struggled to come to terms with the hanging. The next Saturday, the Telegraph and Texas Register ran a lengthy article extolling it. The author employed the nom de plume of "A CITIZEN," but his copy read suspiciously like that of Editor Moore. One passage seemed to have been included more for U.S. readers than local subscribers:

> I congratulate the good people of the republic of Texas that Law and Justice have been for on[c]e, with an energy and pro[m]ptitude of judicial sanction hitherto unparalleled, enforced against the boldest and most reckless offenders. It had been for a long time a proverbial opinion, out of Texas, that capital offences, that cold-blooded, malicious murder, might be perpetrated here without the fear of a condemnation of the law or public feeling. And yet, have two of the heroes of the war been prosecuted with the most terrible rigors of criminal justice, condemned, and executed in the short space of four days after the pronunciation of the sentence! Let not calumny repeat the slander, that this is a lawless community; that here a delinquent may despise or escape the penalties

due to crime. He Cannot. The terrors of retributive justice—the vengeance of the public hatred—the scorn of unsympathizing community, are sure here, in all time to come, to prosecute to the tomb, those who shall be bold enough to stalk forth, in defiance of the wise provisions of human, and the denunciations of the Divine law, to perpetrate deeds of Hell.[1]

"Citizen" conceded irregularities that appalled readers who valued an equitable legal process. The court, he admitted, had prosecuted the defendants "with an energy and pro[m]ptitude of judicial sanction hitherto unparalleled." To enforce the crackdown on rowdy loafers, Robinson judged them by harsher measures than any Houston court had ever exercised. "Citizen" further acknowledged that "the vengeance of the public hatred" colored the verdict, which should never have entered into it.[2]

A blindfolded woman brandishing scales and a sword is the allegorical symbol of Justice. The scales weigh the evidence; the sword punishes the guilty. The blindfold demonstrates her impartiality. She does not favor friends over strangers, or the high born over the humble, because she does not see them. Yet, she is not deaf, for she listens to all the evidence submitted to her. Such is the ideal.

But during the trials of Jones and Quick, Houston's "Big Bugs" pushed Lady Justice off her pedestal. Even before their hearings began, she peeked under her blindfold to gauge which direction political winds were blowing. In the Bayou City, she wielded her sword, not in the name of the law, but in the service of interest. Moreover, in Quick's case when Judge Robinson denied every defense motion, he rendered her deaf. Under pressure from influential politicos, he perverted the legal process to secure convictions. His conduct was all too human, certainly explicable, but never admirable. Finally, by sowing the seeds of odium and discrimination, Francis Moore,

Jr., destroyed any chance for the defendants to receive a fair trial. At every step, he had his thumb on Lady Justice's scales.

Some veterans grumbled that Robinson should have considered the defendants' military service and shown leniency. "Citizen" heard these rumblings and addressed them. "Both Quick and Jones were engaged in the battles of the republic. The latter was in the affair of San Jacinto, after having escaped the massacre at Goliad. The high merit of such service being utterly unable to shield them." By twisting logic like a pig's tail, "Citizen" transformed Jones's execution into a civic virtue. If Houstonians had dispatched one of their most esteemed heroes, who could deny that they were serious about law and order. It also put rowdy loafers on notice: If we hanged Jones when he stepped out of line, imagine what we will do to you. As he normally did, Francis Moore, Jr., made certain that he, or at least a "Citizen" who acted as his mouthpiece, had the last word:

> The result [of the hanging] will doubtless prove of the utmost advantage to the public peace. It will long stand as an impressive admonition to bad men, that they may not expect, with the blackness of guilt upon their hands and consciences, to elude the severities of justice in the courts of law in this republic.[3]

In time, Houstonians got on with their lives. Politicians grappled with concerns regarding Mexican invasion, worthless currency, and possible annexation. Merchants hawked their wares and counted their profits. Whores attracted new clients and dreaded the approach of another birthday. Rowdy loafers begged for drinks, wandered off, or died of yellow fever. Jones and Quick faded from memory. Moore had hoped that the loafers would learn the lessons of the gallows, but their subsequent behavior left him disillusioned. On May 11, 1839, a reporter for the *Morning Star* protested: "Loafers have increased, and are increasing, and ought to be diminished. District Court in session—crimes and criminals are undergoing its scrutiny—hope it will have some effect on the loafers." In the end, the example of Jones and Quick made little or no impression on Houston's criminal underclass.[4]

In 1899, Francis Lubbock wrote that Houstonians still called the spot where the two men died "hangmen's grove." The concrete tsunami of urban sprawl eventually obliterated the "beautiful islet of timber." No bronze plaque marks the spot. Between 1936 and 1939, the state erected a 570-foot monument to "commemorate the heroes of the battle of San Jacinto." Officials charged Louis Wiltz Kemp, the author of *The Heroes of San Jacinto* (1932), to compile the official list of the veterans. He overlooked Jones. Consequently, his name does not appear on the honor roll. One might suspect that Kemp purposely excluded Jones, but it was an honest mistake. He continued to conduct research on the San Jacinto veterans. Before his death in 1956, Kemp admitted his gaffe: "The compiler is responsible for omitting the name of *David J. Jones* from the plaque in the San Jacinto memorial monument on which are inscribed the names of the Texans who participated in the battle of San Jacinto. The name should be added to the list." Despite Kemp's recommendation, Jones's name remains conspicuously absent.[5]

In subsequent years, most (but not all) of the actors in this gaudy melodrama enjoyed active and productive lives—excluding, of course, Quick and Jones.

JOHN HUNTER HERNDON

A week after he reburied the heads of Quick and Jones, he encountered another one of Houston's "Merry Boys": "I . . . took [an] agreeable siester [siesta] and went bathing which proved very comfortable. Saw a gentleman Loafer without a Stitch to his back."[6]

Herndon's star rose like a rocket. On April 12, he won election as clerk of the Republic's House of Representatives. By year's end, he abandoned Houston in favor of Richmond, Texas. A young lady prompted his decision. On November 23, it was in his new hometown that the Texas bar admitted him as a member. Herndon often joked about marrying a rich widow but did even better. On August 27, 1839, he wed Barbara Makall Wilkinson Calvit. The bride was the only daughter of Alexander Calvit and heir to a Brazoria County sugar plantation. Miss Calvit was a lucrative catch, but it seemed a genuine love match. Herndon sired four sons and two daughters.[7]

Herndon, already a man of style, became a man of substance. He operated stock ranches in Guadalupe, Matagorda, and Medina counties. He dabbled in real estate and kept his hand in several thriving enterprises. A pillar of Richmond society, he was director of the local Masonic Hall and trustee of the Brazoria Male and Female Academy.

Fortune smiled on the Kentucky immigrant. In 1842, he served as a member of the Somervell Expedition. Prudently, he refused to join the Mier Expedition and thus evaded the Black Bean Episode. By 1850, he wa worth $100,000; by 1860, he had acquired $1,605,000 in real estate, $106,050 in personal property, and forty slaves. That year, John Hunter Herndon was the richest man in Texas.

Then the war came. A militia colonel in the home guard, he never saw combat. Instead, from 1862 to 1865, he headed the Buffalo Bayou, Brazos and Colorado Railway Company. Defeat and Reconstruction swept away his fortune.

198   VENGEANCE OF THE PUBLIC HATRED

Following the war, he tried to recoup his losses—and failed. In 1875, a hurricane smashed his Velasco mansion. He abandoned it and moved to Hempstead. His efforts there came to naught, and he moved again, this time to Boerne, where he died at the age of sixty-five in 1878.[8]

In Hempstead, his remains lie undisturbed.

EDWARD STIFF

His tenure as a Houston constable was brief. Twice dismissed from the post for drunkenness, he held Mayor Moore responsible and plotted revenge. He abandoned the Texas Republic and retired to Cincinnati, Ohio. There he published *The Texan Emigrant: Being a Narrative of the Adventures of the Author in Texas, and a Description of the Soil, Climate, Productions, Minerals, Towns, Bays, Harbors, Rivers, Institutions, and Manners and Customs of the Inhabitants of That Country; Together With the Principle Incidents of Fifteen Years Revolution in Mexico: And Embracing a Condensed Statement of Interesting Events in Texas, From the First European Settlement in 1692, Down to the Year 1840.* He intended the volume to be inclusive. The title page reveals that, while he had never served a day in the military, he had promoted himself to colonel.[9]

Never one to forgive or forget, Stiff excoriate the one-armed editor in the pages of *The Texan Emigrant:* Never one to shrug off criticism, Moore's review of the book drips vituperation.

> To those Texian emigrants who like *Col.* Stiff emigrated *from* the Republic because they were too vicious and too shiftless to conduct any honest business there, and who derived no benefit in visiting the country than a *stolen title*, the book may be useful; but to all persons desiring to acquire accurate information relative to the country or its inhabitants it is . . . useless. . . . Indeed, the copy now before us was handed to us

by an emigrant, who said he "bought it at an auction for a bit, and got *bit* at that."[10]

The image people had of him never matches that which Stiff nurtured in his imagination. He later published *A New History of Texas* (1847) and ran a newspaper in Cedar Bluff, Alabama. Still, no matter where he went, locals were slow to recognize his talents—military or literary—and his fortunes plummeted. He shot and killed a man in Ashville, Alabama, and found himself behind bars. Horrified and humiliated, he closed the curtain on his dreams, schemes, and himself with an overdose of laudanum. His corpse occupies an unmarked grave.[11]

Dr. Moore was not surprised.

GUSTAV DRESEL

From 1838 to 1841, he traveled between Texas, Louisiana, and Mississippi, finally investing in a New Orleans cotton-export business. In 1842, he returned to Germany to help with the family wine business.

But Texas beckoned. In 1846, Dresel left the old country for good. Settling in Galveston, then the state's largest city, he became business manager for the Adelsverein—a society designed to promote and assist German immigration to Texas.

By 1847, the Adelsverein was on the verge of bankruptcy. Dresel worked tirelessly to save the agency, but he collapsed before it did. On September 14, 1848, yellow fever finally accomplished what Houston's climate, squealing hogs, rowdy loafers, and ravenous rats could not.[12]

FELIX HUSTON

He finally got his war, but not against an enemy he desired. In the summer of 1840, more than six hundred warriors swept across the Republic during the Great Comanche Raid. On August 11, General Huston arrived at Plum Creek near Lockhart and, as the ranking officer on the field, took command. As an Indian fighter, he was an amateur. The approach of the enemy horde unmanned him, and he offered tactical command to ranger captains Edward Burleson and Matthew "Old Paint" Caldwell. Settler James Wilson Nichols—never a great speller—recorded the general's excuse: "Gentlemen, those are the first wild Indians I evar saw and not being accustom[ed] to savage ware fare and both of you are, I think it would be doing you and your men especially great injustice for me to ta[ke the] command." Attempting to salvage a remnant of his pride, Huston added, "Now give me a disciplined civ[iliz]ed command and a deciplined enemy to fight [and] I would redily take command." Sadly for the fastidious General Huston, Texas was experiencing a genuine dearth of "deciplined" Comanches that summer. The grizzled veterans thanked the general for his confidence, but declined his offer.[13]

Huston opted for a defensive formation, even dismounting the ranger companies. This played to Comanche strength and the tribesmen employed their splendid mobility to ride rings around the anchored Texians. A sharp-eyed rifleman brought down a war chief, which temporarily demoralized his braves. The ranger captains saw an opportunity. Almost apoplectic with rage, Caldwell shouted into Huston's face: "Now, General, is your time to charge them! They are whipped!"[14]

Without waiting for Huston's reply, Caldwell, Burleson, and Ben McCulloch led their companies in a spirited rush. Astride their mustangs, rangers could now match Comanche mobility and bring their superior firepower to bear. In a sprawling melee like this, the official chain of command was less important than the initiative of each ranger and the proven leadership of each troop captain. "Our boys charged with a yell and did not fire until they got close to the enemy," participant Robert Hall remembered. "The Indians were panic stricken, and fled at once. The Texans followed them over the prairies for fifteen or twenty miles." Huston claimed victory, but veterans of the battle knew how little he did to achieve it.[15]

His military prospects dimmed after the Plum Creek fight, and he began to look elsewhere to fulfill his destiny. During the autumn of 1840, Huston quit the Republic and became a partner in a New Orleans law firm. Nevertheless, Texas was not entirely behind him; four years later, he was a staunch advocate of its annexation to the United States. As the states grew further apart, he emerged as a fire-eating secessionist. A civil war might have satisfied his martial ambitions, but he never found out. Huston died in Natchez in 1857.[16]

That is the story of his life. Felix Huston, for all his strut and swagger, always botched his quest for fame and glory.

SUSANNA DICKINSON WILLIAMS

On March 24, 1838—the same day that Judge Robinson condemned Jones and Quick to the gallows—he granted Susanna Dickinson Williams a divorce from her husband. Recall she had married John Williams the previous November. But the marriage was a catastrophe; Williams was abusive. She petitioned in Harrisburg (later Harris) County for a divorce. The petition alleged that Williams had thrashed her "to such a degree as to produce or cause an abortion." The document further avowed, "He also abused and beat the child of your petitioner beyond endurance." The court granted the divorce, one of the first in the county.[17]

In Houston, an unclaimed woman did not stay long on the market. On December 20, she wed Francis P. Herring in Houston. Herring died in 1843 of what the *Telegraph* reported as "digestive fever." The reporter employed a gentle euphemism; one of Herring's relatives claimed that he "died of drink, not water."[18]

In 1847, Susanna married drayman Peter Bellows—and abandoned him in 1854. He finally filed for divorce in 1857 and, if one believes the petition, his estranged wife returned to the one vocation that had proven consistently profitable. Bellows alleged that she "was guilty of adulting with several persons, whose names to your petitioner is unknown." He also asserted that "on or about the 1st day of October A.D. 1854, she took up her residence in a house of ill fame, in the City of Houston, and remained therein, as one of its inmates for the accom[m]odation of the public, and whilst in said house, great numbers of men were in the habit of visiting said house." He concluded with the charge that in that bordello "she was in the constant habit of committing adultery with various persons." On July 15, 1857, a jury found Mrs. Dickinson-Williams-Herring-Bellows guilty of adultery and the judge granted Mr. Bellows a divorce on those grounds.[19]

By then, Susanna had moved on, from both Bellows and the Bayou City. In Lockhart later that year, she met and marries William Hannig, a native of Germany and twenty years her junior. The fifth time was a charm. The couple moved to Austin and lived in happiness and prosperity.[20]

Now comfortable in her domestic and business life, Susanna suffered another misfortune. Her daughter, Angelina—the "Babe of the Alamo"— grew into a troubled woman. In 1851, she married farmer John Maynard Griffith, and the union produced three children. When the marriage ended in divorce, Angelina left two of her offspring with Susanna and palmed the other off on an uncle. She then wandered to New Orleans, where she made her living as a lady of pleasure. She married Oscar Holmes in 1864 and gave birth to his child in 1865. But that marriage failed as well, and Angelina drifts to Galveston, where she continued her trade as a harlot. In 1869, Susanna heard that her daughter had died of a uterine hemorrhage, probably the result of a botched abortion. Mrs. Hannig faced this heartbreak as she had so many others. She endured.[21]

Her remaining years in Austin were happy ones. When she died on October 7, 1883, the community mourned her as a respected businesswoman and frontier heroine. Hannig laid her to rest in Oakwood Cemetery. He married again, but stipulated that upon his passing he was to rest beside his first wife.[22]

Now in death, as in life, Susanna and her beloved Hannig lie together.

MARY AUSTIN HOLLEY

Following her Houston visit, Widow Holley returned to New England, the place of her birth. In 1840, she returned to Galveston, but was soon off again to Lexington, Kentucky. In 1843, during her final Texas stay, she interviewed old colonists and gathered material for a planned Stephen F. Austin biography.[23]

In 1845, she returned to a previously held position as governess to the Hermogene Labranche family in Louisiana. In 1837, Mrs. Holley had declared Buffalo Bayou "unhealthy," but the swamps that surrounded New Orleans were hardly more salutary. On August 2, 1846, she died of yellow fever, and her friends laid her to rest in St. Louis Cemetery.[24]

KELSEY HARRIS DOUGLASS

Not content to "liv like hogs," Representative Douglass rejoiced when the capital moved to Austin.

In the Redlands of East Texas, Douglass was a "tarnation tall man." In 1839, when Texian forces took the field against the Cherokees, he was one of the commanders at the battle of the Neches on July 15 and 16. An active Mason, he was a charter member of the Grand Lodge of Texas.

On October 4, 1840, he died suddenly in Nacogdoches. His friend and Masonic brother, Adolphus Sterne recorded the activities surrounding Douglass's passing:

> Last night at 12 oclock General Kelsey H. Douglass died—was called by a Servant to go to the House, got there a little after his demise, helped to lay him out, Gen. D. Died of Consumption, his death was unexpected, in him this County has lost one of its best citizens, he was a good man, honest, liberal, & brave, he was a good Father, a good husband, a good neighbor, and a friend *in need*—Douglass, my best friend, rest in peace— . . . at 4 1/2 P.M. interred Douglass with all requisite Masonic Honours, the longest, largest funeral seen here this Summer.

The grieving community buried him in Oak Grove Cemetery.

Notwithstanding the number of mourners at his funeral, Douglass's friends and neighbors reneged on the debt they owed his memory. He died with a sixty-thousand-dollar estate, but his wife went bankrupt paying his debts.

At least he did not die in Houston.[25]

FRANCIS RICHARD LUBBOCK

In 1837, he and his Creole bride arrived in Houston to open a general store. Lubbock sold the first barrel of flour and the first bag of coffee in the new capital. He kept a foot in the business world, but while living in the Bayou City politics got into his blood. President Sam Houston appointed him comptroller of the Republic of Texas. He later won election as clerk of Harris county district court and served in that post from 1841 to 1857. He subsequently won election as lieutenant governor in 1857, but in 1859 lost his bid for reelection.

A southern Democrat, he supported secession. In 1860, he traveled to Charleston, South Carolina, where he was a Texas delegate to the national Democratic convention. He was among those Southerners who walked out of the convention to protest the party's platform and Stephen A. Douglas's nomination. He walked out again with disgruntled delegates in Baltimore. At their own convention at Richmond, Virginia, the southern Democrats nominated John C. Breckinridge, split the Democratic voting block, and virtually guaranteed the election of the "black Republican," Abraham Lincoln. Lubbock chaired the Richmond Convention.

In 1861, he returned to Texas to win the governorship. While in that office, he steadfastly supported the Confederacy and defended Texas from Federal invasion. He resigned to don the gray and served on the staff of Major General John Bankhead Magruder. In 1864, Lubbock traveled to Richmond to serve as aide-de-camp to Confederate President Jefferson Davis. He never waivered in his admiration of Davis, later lauding him as, "preeminently fitted for the high position to which he had been elevated." Following Appomattox, he fled Richmond with Davis, but Union troops captured them in Georgia. Yankees imprisoned Lubbock in Fort Delaware, where he endured eight months of solitary confinement.[26]

Eventually paroled, he returned to Texas. He tried his hand at ranching, found that he was ill suited for it, and returned to Houston to enter business. Nevertheless, politics was never far from his mind. He became the state treasurer and served in that post from 1878 to 1891. Retiring from public life at the age of seventy-six, he spent his final years writing his memoirs. On June 22, 1905, at the age of ninety, he died peacefully in Austin.[27]

Reviewing his active years, the former governor recalled his days in early Houston as the happiest of his life:

206   VENGEANCE OF THE PUBLIC HATRED

I had a comfortably fitted up little house, a lovely wife, and for servants two Mexican prisoners. I could entertain my friends in a quiet way, among them the President, Mosely Baker, Dr. Ashbel Smith (Surgeon-General of the army), the Allens and others, men of distinction and culture, as well as many a jolly good fellow that laughed at the difficulties of life. In truth, society in Houston at that early day, mixed though it was with some rough characters, and without the sheen of later day finery, was just glorious; and I was young. I wonder if I am yet old.[28]

ASHBEL SMITH

Arriving in Houston in 1837, he found himself bunking with an illustrious roommate, President Sam Houston. Houston recognized his ability and appointed him surgeon general of the Republic's army. In that capacity, Smith established the first hospital in the city. No Texas physician knew more about epidemic diseases. Few comprehended the mosquito's role in transmitting the yellow fever (also called the "black vomit") virus. Many maintained that infected persons transmitted the disease. Smith knew better and argued against needless quarantines. Many ignorant quacks and superstitious citizens resisted his reasoning. During an 1839 yellow fever outbreak in Galveston, Dr. Smith made his point and silenced his critics when he collected "black vomit" from his patients and publicly ... ATE it. He did not contract the malady and thus won the debate. He authored a treatise on the epidemic entitled *An Account of the Yellow Fever Which Appeared in the City of Galveston, Republic of Texas, In the Autumn of 1839*. In 1853, he was a founding member of the Texas Medical Association, chairing the committee that drafted its constitution and bylaws.[29]

Although normally a man of serenity and dignity, Smith was also a man of honor. In 1839, he horsewhipped senator and fellow physician

Stephen H. Everitt who publicly called him a liar. The resulting scandal drove Smith to resign his post as surgeon general to spare President Lamar further discomfiture.[30]

Smith was also a clever diplomat. In 1838, Houston dispatched him to parley with the Comanche tribe. From 1842 to 1844, Smith served as the Republic's chargé d'affaires to England and France. "No one," bibliophile John H. Jenkins asserted, "with the exception of Sam Houston and Anson Jones, was more intimately involved in the process of acquiring international recognition of the Republic of Texas and bringing about annexation than Dr. Ashbel Smith." Following statehood, he served three terms in the Texas legislature as a Harris County representative.[31]

When war came, Smith laid down his scalpel and took up the sword. He raised and led a company of Texas infantry, the Bayland Guards. He drilled his men incessantly. "In ancient Greece and in ancient Rome," he wrote his old Houston neighbor, Governor Francis R. Lubbock, "their citizens were both men of thought and action. Their statesmen were soldiers, scholars, and philosophers." Serving under another Houston friend, General Albert Sidney Johnston, Captain Smith led his men at the battle of Shiloh, where half his unit became casualties. When a Yankee Minié ball ripped through his arm, Smith cried out, "God damn it!" He quickly recovered himself and, while Union bullets buzzed around him, prayed, "Lord, forgive me." Two months passed before he could use the shattered arm, and it troubled him for years afterward. He won promotion to colonel and commanded the Second Texas Infantry, which saw hard fighting at Vicksburg. Toward the end of the war, Colonel Smith oversaw the defense of Galveston Island.[32]

Dr. Smith never married. As a callow youth, he impregnated a North Carolina lass and confided in his journal: "I made a compromise with Peter

T———- for a release from all responsibility on account of his daughter's bastard, by giving him two notes for $30 each." His "sin of passion" shamed him. He admitted to his brother, "I see clearly the dark and rotten parts of my conduct." This tawdry affair seemed to cloud his future relations with eligible women, many of whom had their eye on the doctor. Sam Houston ribbed his younger friend: "I wish you luck in marrying. If you can marry a fine woman, and she should have a *large fortune*, do not let it be a reason for breaking off the match!!!"[33]

A life-long advocate of public education, he worked tirelessly to improve Texas schools. In the 1880s, he was the president of the University of Texas Board of Regents and recruited distinguished faculty members and established a curriculum consistent with a first-class university. So critical were his achievements that many hail him as the "father of the University of Texas."[34]

On January 21, 1886, he died at eighty-one years of age. In recognition of his many achievements, his remains lie in the Texas State Cemetery surrounded by other, "individuals who have made a significant contribution to Texas." [35]

Dr. Smith would appreciate its exclusivity.

JUDGE JAMES W. ROBINSON

He continued to involve himself in the affairs of the Texas Republic. On March 19, 1840, he was visiting in San Antonio when the infamous Council House Fight ensued, and he was wounded by a Comanche arrow. He recovered, but was in the wrong place again on September 12, 1842, when Mexican General Adrian Woll surprised and captured the town. Robinson was among those Texas officials that Woll hauled back to Mexico in chains. Robinson took advantage of his position as a high-level official of the Texas government, to open a furtive correspondence with Santa Anna. At length, Robinson even visited the butcher of Goliad at his home. Santa Anna released Robinson from prison to be his courier to Sam Houston. Robinson reached Galveston on March 27, 1843 and immediately rode to the Town of Washington, then the capital of the Republic, to deliver Santa Anna's proposal and confer with President Houston. Houston rejected Santa Anna's proposition out of hand, but Robinson may have been instrumental in effecting an armistice of several months duration between the two nations. Nevertheless, some suggest that Robinson had acted as Santa Anna's errand boy simply to secure his freedom.

In 1850, Robinson moved his family to San Diego, California. There, as in Texas, he became embroiled in public matters. From 1852 to 1855, he served as district attorney and, in 1854, added school commissioner to his list of responsibilities. He joined a group of promoters attempting to build a railroad from El Paso to southern California. Finally, he speculated in real estate, securing large tracts across the bay from San Diego. In October 1857, Robinson died in San Diego.

In his will, he requested that his heirs settle his estate out of court. Perhaps he had participated in too many backroom deals to have any confidence in the legal system.[36]

FRANCIS MOORE, JR.

Upon becoming mayor early in 1838, he did not surrender the editor's chair at the *Telegraph and Texas Register*. Consequently, he promoted the executions of Quick and Jones as editor, supervised their hanging as mayor, then, as editor, endorsed his actions as mayor. Modern readers might call this a "conflict of interest," but that expression had little currency in 1838. Moore did not feel at all conflicted about pressing his advantage. It was simply an instance of one hand washing the other. Still, he may have experienced a twinge of embarrassment, which likely caused him to adopt the "Citizen" pen name.

Moore kept his campaign promise to be an active and aggressive mayor. He hired the town's first police officers. One of these constables was Edward Stiff, but their association was short lived and tumultuous. He passed a town charter and purchased a fire engine—a prudent precaution in a city constructed entirely of wood. As mayor and editor, he worked to improve Houston's sanitation. In the summer of 1839, he resigned the office and travels to New York where he rekindled his relationship with Elizabeth Mofat Wood. They wed in 1840, returned to Houston, and their union produced nine offspring.

Moore enjoyed being mayor. In 1843, he won the office again and oversaw the building of the first bridge across Buffalo Bayou. He served successive terms from 1849 through 1852 during which he improved city roads.

Moore also involved himself with a number of profitable enterprises. He was the director of the Harrisburg Town Company and sat on the board of directors of the Harrisburg Rail Road and Trading Company.

His political ambitions outgrew Houston. From November 1839 to February 1842, Moore was a member of the Texas Senate's fourth, fifth, and sixth congresses as the representative from Harris, Liberty, and Galveston counties. From the first time he set foot on Texas soil, he championed annexation to the United States and voted for it as Harris County's representative during the 1845 Convention.

Certain it is that politics make strange bedfellows, but few anticipated the rapprochement between the "one-armed Proteus" and the "Sword of San Jacinto." As the nation marched blindly toward civil war, Moore and Houston aligned themselves with the Unionist cause. After becoming governor in 1860, Houston appointed Moore state geologist. Moore had long possessed an interest in the discipline, but it did not translate to ability. Most saw the post for what it was: blatant patronage. One critic lambasted Moore as "superficial in a high degree, and largely uninformed in geology, and utterly unfit for the office of State Geologist." Ignoring such misgivings and his lack of formal training, Moore set off in the winter of 1860-1861 on an expedition of the Trans-Pecos region. There, he gathered samples and came to believe the area rich in mineral resources. When he returned to Austin, however, he discovered that the state legislature had deposed Houston as governor, abolished the office of State Geologist, and joined the Confederacy.

With that, Moore severed his ties to Texas. He moved his family to Brooklyn, New York. In August 1863, he traveled to Minnesota. Still fancying himself a geologist, he was in the employ of a copper mining company. On September 1, 1864, he died in Duluth, Minnesota, of what was likely appendicitis. Pioneer historian, fellow newspaper editor, and contemporary John Henry Brown eulogized Moore as a "fine orator, a sincere Presbyterian, and one of the purest men in the country, in whose nature patriotism was a passion." Moore's remains rest at Green-Wood Cemetery in Brooklyn.[37]

Doubtless a person of his purity and passion was more comfortable there. A Yankee bluenose to the last, he would not have wanted to lie forever under benighted Texas soil.

HOUSTON, TEXAS

No less than its residents, the City of Houston is a major—probably the major—character in this story. Conditions in this rough-and-tumble frontier capital shaped the fate of everyone who lived there. Chances are if David James Jones had been elsewhere, he would never have committed

212   VENGEANCE OF THE PUBLIC HATRED

murder. Yet, vice, violence, and degradation drove many men, and not a few women, to acts of hopeless desperation.

The acronym for the Republic of Texas is ROT, and as long as Houston served as its capital, many believed it was wholly fitting. Putrefaction epitomized the city: physical decay, political decay, social decay, moral decay. Kelsey H. Douglass represented many Republic officials who were eager to transfer the seat of government to a less sordid locale and scrape Houston's mud off their boots forever.

When Mirabeau B. Lamar became the Republic's president in 1839, he immediately launched plans to transfer the capital. His first Congress created a commission to supersede those of his predecessor. On April 13, 1839, the commissioners submitted their recommendation: move the capital. The suggested site was the village of Waterloo on the east bank of the Colorado River. Having already inspected the spot, Lamar declares it would serve as his "seat of Empire." To honor the "Father of Texas," Congressmen agreed to name the new capital, Austin.

A member of the Lamar camp, Mayor Moore nonetheless railed against removal:

> In the report of the Commissioners appointed to locate the Seat of Government, it will be seen that the location has been made at Waterloo, an inconsiderable hamlet . . . on the extreme verge of the northern frontier. The country around this point is represented to be exceedingly fertile and beautiful, and the climate remarkably healthy. It is, however, almost entirely uninhabited, and what is worse probably, more exposed than any other point on the frontier to the depredations of the hostile Indians. Indeed within a few months past, parties of Indians have ventured many miles below it. As it will not therefore afford those conven-

> iences of life and the security requisite for the purposes intended, we can hardly believe that the offices of Government will be removed during the present year.[38]

Moore's incredulity notwithstanding, Lamar's government did move the capital "during the present year." In 1839, Millie Gray logged in her diary that yellow fever infected one-third of Houston's citizens. The epidemic killed as much as twelve percent of the municipal population. Moore and other boosters found it embarrassing to sing the city's praises while it had become a yawning graveyard. By the end of October, Republic officials shifted the archives and other papers to Austin. Sam Houston's namesake city continued to thrive as a mercantile center but, to his dismay, it ceased to function as the political hub.[39]

Republic officials left; the loafers, gamblers, and prostitutes remained. They soon forgot the "lessons of the gallows" and disproved "A Citizen's" prediction that the executions of Quick and Jones would promote "the public peace." For the next several years, Houston's criminal underclass cultivated a general mood of lawlessness. In 1839, as the government prepared to abandon the city, a gang of armed rowdies shut down a theatrical performance, assaulted the house manager, molested unarmed patrons of the Exchange Hotel bar, and crashed a posh dance upstairs. City officials called out the Milam Guards who, amid "horrid yells and curses," finally quelled the deviltry. A few days later, the self-styled "Callithumpian Society" took to the streets for nocturnal carousels fired by fiddle and fife. They (for reasons no one could quite fathom) halted their shenanigans periodically to raise three cheers. Citizens abed did not share their enthusiasm. Even someone as publicly optimistic as Ashbel Smith doubted privately that Houstonians possessed a "sufficient regard

214   VENGEANCE OF THE PUBLIC HATRED

for virtue in which religion and a well-based morality can take root and attain a permanent stand." [40]

Throughout the remainder of the nineteenth century, commerce and cotton were the mainstays of the Houston economy. Merchants acquired trade goods from Galveston, marked them up, and then sold them to eager customers throughout the state. Even so, yellow fever continued to blight the city, with epidemics in 1844, 1847, 1848, 1854, 1858, 1859, 1862, and 1867.[41]

Houston's big break came in 1900, when a hurricane devastated Galveston. With their chief rival in ruins, Houstonians leapt into the breach. They understand, however, that Houston could never profit from Galveston's calamity unless and until ocean-going ships could dock in their city. To accommodate these mammoth vessels, citizens lobbied the federal government to dredge and widen Buffalo Bayou. In 1914, the Houston Ship Channel opened, making the city a deepwater port. Houston became the state's gateway to the world, and the world's gateway to Texas. Bayou City businessmen stood poised to accept the toll. Their municipality quickly supplanted Galveston as the state's most prosperous city. Houstonians took the lead and never looked back.[42]

Twentieth-century Houston continued the dichotomy of class and crass begun by its first citizens. The city became home to excellent museums, superb restaurants, exceptional universities, and the internationally renowned Texas Medical Center, containing the world's largest concentration of research and healthcare facilities. Space Center Houston opened as the visitor center of NASA's Lyndon B. Johnson Space Center. The Globalization and World Cities Group and Network designated Houston a "world-class city." Mirabeau Lamar, Ashbel Smith, and the other founding members of the Philosophical Society of Texas would be proud.[43]

By the twenty-first century, however, they would also recognize some of the city's seedier aspects that they had deplored in 1838. The stench of rotting animals no longer wafted the streets, but the odor of oil refineries and exhaust fumes continued to assault Houston noses. Likewise, whores still strutted their wares in Houston "grog-houses," while murder and other serious crimes persistently threatened the security and good name of the city. The paved streets and speeding cars would astound David James Jones, John C. C. Quick, and the other rowdy loafers of 1838 but, other than that, they would feel oddly at home.

Like individuals, a city frequently finds it difficult to overcome its heritage.

Readers, and above all, writers of history need guard against what the late Grady McWhiney termed "present mindedness": the pernicious practice of judging long dead people by current trends. It disregards professional methodology, is arrogant, and, ultimately, dishonest. The historian's responsibility is to understand and explain the past, not condemn those who lived it. How can a tub-bellied academic, hunched over a keyboard, ensconced in a climate-controlled office, presume to criticize people who had to endure the misery of life in early Houston?

This is not to say, however, that the living should view the past only as mute observers. Even by 1830's standards, Francis Moore, Jr., was a sanctimonious prig, Chauncey Goodrich was a cheap thug, and John Kirby Allen was a snake oil salesman. Moreover, any historian would have to be pitifully mealy-mouthed not to say so.

It is tempting to view Jones as a victim. Any modern lawyer worth his fee would have secured a change of venue. How could Jones—indeed, any rowdy loafer—receive a fair trial in Mayor Moore's Houston? A psychiatrist would lecture the jury concerning Jones's anger management issues. Today's attorneys would attempt to arouse pity in the jury. After all, they might argue, didn't Jones have a right to be angry? Hadn't Texians lured him and the other American volunteers with false promises? After all his meritorious service, didn't the people of Texas owe him something more than their sullen contempt?

In 1838, no one would have thought in those terms—certainly not in Houston. Jones was no victim. Valor in battle should earn a man the respect of his community, but it does not mitigate murder. Furthermore, people expect their officials to create environments where families can grow and prosper in peace and security. No matter how much one's heart might bleed for Jones and his cronies, few readers would tolerate gangs of rowdy loafers terrorizing their neighborhoods.

By the custom of his time and place, Jones received the proper sentence, but the motives of the men who delivered it were reprehensible. Blinded by anger, he killed an unarmed man and never denied his guilt. No civilization can condone such behavior. He deserved a guilty verdict; he probably even deserved the death penalty. Jones did the crime, but many people did crimes in Houston who did not hang for them. His timing was far worse than his offence. He killed Wood during a period when the public had finally agreed to support Moore's crackdown on rowdy loafers. That, and his choice of victim, was unfortunate; had Wood been one of Houston's inferior sorts, the gentry likely would not have noticed. Ultimately, Houston's elite hanged Jones more for who he was and what he represented than the crime he committed. Jones may have been a murderer but was he a worse menace than, say, Chauncey Goodrich?

Jones may have earned his fate, but he did not deserve to have the Houston establishment turn his case into a show trial. He did not deserve to be a scapegoat for the aspirations of a mayoral candidate. He did not deserve to hang as a deterrent to other rowdy loafers. Certainly, his transgressions did not merit the despoliation of his corpse at the hands of ghoulish dilettantes. At last, T.S. Eliot might have written David James Jones's epitaph:

> The last temptation is the greatest treason:
> To do the right deed for the wrong reason.[44]

Notes

INTRODUCTION

1. Frederic Remington, *Men With the Bark On* (New York: Harper & Brothers Publishers, 1900).
2. John Graves, "Foreword," in Harry Huntt Ransom, *The Other Texas Frontier* (Austin: The University of Texas Press, 1984), 8.
3. John Emerich Edward Dalberg, Lord Acton, "Historical Essays and Studies," in *The English Historical Review*, (1888) III: 808.
4. Bob Dylan, *Chronicles* (New York: Simon & Schuster, 2004), 51; David McCullough, "The Course of Human Events" a lecture presented before the National Endowment for the Humanities, Washington, D.C., 2003, full text at *www.neh.gov/about/awards /jefferson-lecture/david-mccullough-lecture*.
5. State House Press website, *www.tfhcc.com/press/*.

PROLOGUE

1. Witnesses could not agree on the exact numbers gathered to view the executions. The *Telegraph and Texas Register* cited the total as "2000 and upwards." John Hunter Herndon noted in his diary that the assembled throng numbered "from 2000 to 3000 persons." *Telegraph and Texas Register* (Houston), March 31, 1838. John Hunter Herndon Papers, 1814–1872, Center for American History, University of Texas at Austin, Diary, 1837–1838, March 28, 1838. [Hereinafter cited as Herndon Diary.] A remarkably well edited and annotated transcription of the Herndon diary may

220   NOTES

be found in Andrew Forest Muir, (ed.), "Diary of a Young Man in Houston, 1838," *Southwestern Historical Quarterly*, 53 (January, 1950), 276–308.

The crowd, while impressive by Republic of Texas standards, would have left British visitors questioning the reason for all the fuss. In 1807, some 45,000 London spectators assembled to watch the hanging of murderers Holloway and Haggerty. Reporters estimated the mob that witnessed the 1820 executions and decapitations of the Cato Street conspirators reached 100,000. In 1824, as many people gathered to view the hanging of forger Fountleroy and again in 1828 when another forger, Hunton, met his Maker. These numbers proved problematic for London officials as well as dangerous for those caught in the throng. At the 1807 execution of Holloway and Haggerty, thirty people died when the crowd collapsed. Thereafter, city officials placed warning signs in streets that led to the gallows: "Beware of entering the Crowd!—Remember Thirty Poor Creatures were pressed to death when Haggerty and Holloway were executed." For more on the English gallows crowd, see V. A. C. Gatrell, *The Hanging Tree: Execution and the English People, 1770–1868* (Oxford: Oxford University Press, 1994), 56–89.

[2] Again witnesses to the same event could not agree on details. A reporter on the scene recalled that Quick and Jones "were conducted to the place of execution under an escort of one hundred soldiers." *Telegraph and Texas Register* (Houston), March 31, 1838. John Hunter Herndon, on the other hand, recorded that "one hundred forty men [were] ordered out to guard the criminals to the gallows." Herndon Diary, March 28, 1838. The "pomp of pow'r" reference is from the ninth stanza of Thomas Gray's "Elegy Written in a Country Churchyard":

> The boasts of heraldry, the pomp of pow'r,
> And all that beauty, all that wealth e'er gave,
> Await alike the inevitable hour:
> The paths of glory lead but to the grave.

[3] *Telegraph and Texas Register* (Houston), March 31, 1838. While no observers explicitly described the gallows, two uprights and crossbeam was the convention in horse-and-cart hangings and when the executioner had to accommodate multiple clients. See "The history of judicial hanging in Britain," online at www.richard.clark32 .btinternet.co.uk/hanging1.html [accessed December 20, 2005]. Assuming that

NOTES 221

the unidentified reporter's placement was precise, the gallows stood near the intersection of modern Webster and Main streets.

4 Gatrell, *The Hanging Tree*, 51.

5 While death may *appear* instantaneous, the long drop requires three to twenty-five minutes to kill. The fracture or dislocation of the neck causes death by comatose asphyxia. While prisoners may register vital signs, to all outward appearances they seem dead. The victim is severely unconscious, a result of the dislocation of the cervical vertebrae and the separation of the spinal cord. The author employs the present tense because, as the book goes to press, long drop hanging remains a legally sanctioned form of execution in the states of Delaware and Washington.

Hackneyed folklore suggests that nooses employed in executions contained thirteen coils, denoting misfortune. Yet, so many coils produce an elongated knot that, at the vital moment, twists and bends in on itself. It appears, therefore, that outside pulp westerns and horror movies, no self-respecting hangman employed the thirteen-coil noose. The seven- or eight-coiled hangman's noose was, and remains, the standard. For the origins of the idiom "to come to the end of one's rope," see Charles Earle Funk, *A Hog on Ice and Other Curious Expressions* (New York: Harper & Row, Publishers, 1948), 119–20.

6 "The history of judicial hanging in Britain."

7 Jean Kellaway, *The History of Torture & Execution* (London: Mercury Books, 2005), 48–49; Gatrell, *The Hanging Tree*, 46.

8 Nigel Cawthorne, *Public Executions* (London: Arcturus Publishing Limited, 2006; rpt. ed., Edison, New Jersey: Chartwell Books, Inc., a Division of Book Sales, Inc., 2006), 76.

9 See mention of the euphemism in Brian Bailey, *Hangmen of England: A History of Execution from Jack Ketch to Albert Pierrepoint* (New York: Barnes & Noble Books, 1989), 22.

10 "The history of judicial hanging in Britain." Admittedly, under those unfortunate circumstances, fifteen seconds would have seemed an eternity.

11 *Telegraph and Texas Register* (Houston), March 31, 1838; Herndon diary, Wednesday, March 28, 1838. The Houston hangman did not observe strict protocol. Normally, professionals allowed bodies to hang a full hour to ensure that the condemned were well and truly dead. As the following chapters will reveal, Texians were far handier with pistols and Bowie knives than dictionaries and style manuals. The

222   NOTES

standard [sic] after every misspelling and grammatical error would clutter the text with little benefit. Throughout the book, therefore, the author presents quotations as originally written.

[12] Ibid; for scriptural reference see Deuteronomy 21:22–23.

CHAPTER ONE

[1] For a learned examination of the role of Texas in the American imagination, see William C. Davis, Lone Star Rising: The Revolutionary Birth of the Texas Republic (New York: Free Press, 2004), 5–25; dated in its scholarship, but still a rollicking good read is John Edward Weems, Men Without Countries: Three Adventurers of the Early Southwest (Boston: Houghton Mifflin Company, 1969); more than sixty years after its publication, the best study of the ill-fated Gutiérrez-Magee Expedition remains Julia Kathryn Garrett, Green Flag Over Texas: A Story of the Last Years of Spain in Texas (New York: The Cordova Press, Inc. 1939; rpt. ed, Austin: The Pemberton Press, [1969]). In this definition of the word, filibusters were adventurers who engaged in private and unsanctioned military expeditions in foreign countries.

[2] For Austin's contributions, see Gregg Cantrell, Stephen F. Austin: Empresario of Texas (New Haven: Yale University Press, 1999); Stephen F. Austin to James F. Perry, December 31, 1829, in Eugene C. Barker, ed., The Austin Papers, 2 vols. (Washington, DC: Government Printing Office, 1924, 1928; 3rd vol. (Austin: University of Texas, 1927), 2:307–309.

[3] For an excellent history of Texas land policy, see Joe B. Frantz and Mike Cox, Lure of the Land: Texas County Maps and the History of Settlement (College Station: Texas A&M University Press, 1988); for a detailed account of the Spanish, Mexican, and American land usage in Texas, see Dudley Wooten, Comprehensive History of Texas, 1685–1897, 2 vols. (Dallas: William G. Scarff, 1898; rpt. ed, Austin: Texas State Historical Association, 1986), 1:325–31, 784–811.

[4] Stuart Reid, The Secret War for Texas (College Station: Texas A&M University Press, 2007), 7.

[5] Manuel de Mier y Terán to Guadalupe Victoria, June 30, 1828, quoted in Alleine Howren, "Causes and Origin of the Decree of April 6, 1830," Southwestern Historical Quarterly, 16 (April 1913), 395–398; Manuel de Mier y Terán, Texas by Terán: The Diary Kept by General Manuel de Mier y Terán on his 1828 Inspection of Texas, edited by Jack Jackson (Austin: University of Texas Press, 200), 81; the final quotation is from

Constantino de Tarnava to the Minister of War and Navy, Mexico, January 6, 1830, but he was voicing Terán's opinion. Tarnava quoted in David J. Weber, *The Mexican Frontier, 1821–1846: The American Southwest Under Mexico* (Albuquerque: University of New Mexico Press, 1982), 170.

6   Andrés Tijerina, *Tejanos & Texas Under the Mexican Flag, 1821–1836* (College Station: Texas A&M University Press, 1994), 127; Alamán quoted in David J. Weber, *Myth and the History of the Hispanic Southwest* (Albuquerque: University of New Mexico Press, 1988), 145.

7   Paul D. Lack, *The Texas Revolutionary Experience: A Political and Social History* (College Station: Texas A&M University Press, 1992), 11–24.

8   Randy Roberts and James S. Olson, *A Line in the Sand: The Alamo in Blood and Memory* (New York: The Free Press, 2001), 14–15.

9   Stephen F. Austin to Columbia Committee, September 19, 1835, in Barker, ed., *Austin Papers*, 3:128–29.

10   The author examines the Gonzales fight in greater detail in *Texian Iliad: A Military History of the Texas Revolution, 1835–1836* (Austin: University of Texas Press, 1994), 7–13; for a superb study of the siege and storming of Béxar, see Alwyn Barr, *Texans in Revolt: The Battle for San Antonio, 1835* (Austin: University of Texas Press, 1990).

11   Miguel Barragán, dispatch sent to all Governors and Military Commanders, no date, quoted in General Miguel A. Sanchez Lamego, *The Siege & Taking of the Alamo* (Santa Fe: Printed by The Blue Feather Press, Santa Fe, New Mexico, for The Press of the Territorian, 1968), 14.

12   *Red River Herald* (Natchitoches) reprinted in *New Orleans Bee*, October 14, 1835.

13   Henry Smith to the Legislative Council of Texas, November 16, 1835, in John H. Jenkins, ed., *The Papers of the Texas Revolution*, 10 vols. (Austin: Presidial Press, 1973), 2:439; Abishai M. Dickson to Ann M. Dickson, December 29, 1835, in Dickson Family Papers, Doc. 5180, Daughters of the Republic of Texas Library at the Alamo, San Antonio, Texas; James Butler Bonham to Sam Houston, December 1, 1835, in Jenkins, ed., *Papers of the Texas Revolution*, 3:61; David G. Burnet to James Morgan, May 28, 1836, in Ibid. 6:393; for a knowledgeable discussion of the relationship between the Texians and the U.S. Volunteers, see Lack, *Texas Revolutionary Experience*, 122, 124, 139, 141.

14   Title Bond, David J. Jones to David Ayres, BEX–2–213, Original Land Grant Collection, Texas General Land Office, Austin; David J. Jones, Bounty Certificate,

224 NOTES

BEX–B–432, Original Land Grant Collection, Texas General Land Office, Austin; Thomas Lloyd Miller, *Bounty and Donation Land Grants of Texas, 1835–1888* (Austin: University of Texas Press, 1967), 24.

[15] D. C. Barrett to James W. Robinson, February 9, 1836, in Jenkins, ed. *Papers of the Texas Revolution*, 4:292.

[16] "JAMES W. ROBINSON," Handbook of Texas Online, www.tsha.utexas.edu /handbook/online/articles/RR/fro37.html [accessed February 16, 2007].

[17] Wooten, *Comprehensive History of Texas*, 1:190.

[18] For a more expansive discussion of this debacle, see Roy W. Smith, "The Quarrel between Governor Smith and the Council of the Provisional Government," *Quarterly of the Texas State Historical Association*, 5 (April 1902), 270–346; Lack, *Texas Revolutionary Experience*, 53–74.

[19] Stanley Siegel, *A Political History of the Texas Republic, 1836–1845* (Austin: University of Texas Press, 1956), 26–31.

[20] Houston to Henry Smith, January 6, 1836, in Jenkins, ed., *Papers of the Texas Revolution*, 3:425–26.

[21] Henry Smith to General Council, January 9, 1836, in ibid., 3:458–60; see also Reid, *Secret War for Texas*, 84–88.

[22] General Council to the People of Texas, January 11, 1836, in Jenkins, ed., *Papers of the Texas Revolution*, 3:470–75.

[23] Siegel, *Political History*, 28–29; Henry Smith to James W. Robinson, January 18, 1836, in Jenkins, ed., *Papers of the Texas Revolution*, 4:68–69.

[24] D. C. Barrett et al. to James W. Robinson, February 9, 1836, in Jenkins, ed., *Papers of the Texas Revolution*, 4:292.

[25] Note to document 2048 in ibid., 4:527.

[26] James F. Pittman's name appears on Colonel James W. Fannin's record of the sale of his rifle to Private James S. Batts of Captain Burr H. Duval's Kentucky "Mustangs," which he dated February 24, 1836. If Pittman had arrived in Goliad by that date, one may conclude that the rest of Acting Lieutenant Samuel Sprague's squad had as well.

[27] Harbert Davenport, "Notes from an Unfinished Study of Fannin and his Men, with biographical sketches," online at www.tsha.utexas.edu/supsites/fannin/hd -home.html [accessed May 20, 2007]. The study may be "Unfinished," but it is the most comprehensive work of its kind currently available. No person ever knew more about Fannin's command or the Goliad Campaign of 1836 than

Harbert Davenport did. Students of the Texas Revolution had long consulted Davenport's manuscript at the University of Texas's Center for American History, but in 2002 H. David Maxey won the undying appreciation of Texas historians by placing this remarkable study online.

28   Ibid. The roster of the San Antonio Greys is listed below:

OFFICERS AND NCOS

Cooke, William	*Resigned as Captain, 15 February 1836*
Pettus, Samuel O.	*Captain—after 15 February 1836*
Grace, John C.	*First Lieutenant*
Heath, Ebenezer Smith	*First Sergeant*
Hunter, William L.	*Second Sergeant*
James, [first name unknown]	*Third Sergeant*
Riddle, Samuel	*Fourth Sergeant*

ENLISTED

Brenan, William
Bynum, Alfred
Carbajal, Mariano
Carrer, Charles J.
Cass, James M.
Dickinson, Noah
Escott, [first name unknown]
Gilland, George M.
Gould, [first name unknown]
Gray, Francis H.
Green, George
Griffin, Peter
Harper, William
Hill, Stuart
Hodge, Nathan
Holland, Benjamin H.
Irish, Milton
Johnson, William P.
Jones, David James

226   NOTES

Kenny, David J.

Logan, John C.

Mahoney, Dennis

Moody, Edward

Noland, James

Perkins, [first name unknown]

Phillips, Charles

Preusch, William G.

Rees, John

Riddle, Joseph P.

Sargent, Charles

Scott, R. J.

Vose, George

Wallace, [A. J.]

West, James

Wood, John

[29] J. C. Logan to Friend, February 24, 1836, Sons of Dewitt Colony Texas website, www. tamu.edu/ccbn/dewitt/goliadletters2.htm [accessed May 26, 2007].

[30] Fannin to Robinson, February 21, 1836, and Fannin to Robinson, February 22, 1836, in Jenkins, ed., Papers of the Texas Revolution, 4:391–92, 398–401.

[31] Travis and Bowie to Fannin, February 23, 1836, in Jenkins, ed., Papers of the Texas Revolution, 4:419; for a masterful examination of the Alamo siege, see Alan C. Huffines, Blood of Noble Men: The Alamo Siege & Battle, An Illustrated Chronology (Austin: Eakin Press, 1999). The "Foreword" is especially worthwhile.

[32] José Urrea, "Diary of the Military Operations of the Division Which Under the Command of General José Urrea Campaigned in Texas," in Carlos E. Castañeda, ed., The Mexican Side of the Texan Revolution (Dallas: P. L. Turner Company, Publishers, [1928]; rpt. ed., Austin: Graphic Ideas, 1970), 219.

[33] Traditional accounts maintain that Dr. James Grant was out on an expedition to capture wild mustangs, but Stuart Reid argues, that "the secret expedition" was not to be a mere horse-gathering foray, let alone a "mustanging" expedition, but was rather a last attempt to link up with his federalist friends, with or without the aid of the Texians." For his version of events, see The Secret War for Texas, 129–47.

[34] Urrea, "Diary," in Castañeda, ed., Mexican Side of the Texan Revolution, 233.

35 Ibid.

36 In 1836, Texians called Washington-on-the-Brazos the "Town of Washington." The designation Washington-on-the-Brazos came later. Ellen N. Murry, *Notes On The Republic: An Anthology of Essays from the Star of the Republic Museum's Quarterly Journal, the Notes* (Washington, Tex.: Star of the Republic Museum, 1991), 9. For information about Houston and the convention see Davis, *Lone Star Rising*, 233.

37 Craig H. Roell, *Remember Goliad!* (Austin: Texas State Historical Association, 1994), 49.

38 Ruby Cumby Smith, "James Walker Fannin, Jr., in the Texas Revolution," *Southwestern Historical Quarterly*, 23 (January 1920), 200; Hardin, *Texian Iliad*, 135.

39 J. G. Ferguson to A. J. Ferguson, March 2, 1836, in Kathryn Stoner O'Connor, *The Presidio La Bahía del Espiritu Santo de Zuniga, 1721–1846* (Austin: Von Boeckmann–Jones Co., 1966), 163–614; B. H. Duval to William P. Duval, March 9, 1836, in Jenkins, ed., *Papers of the Texas Revolution*, 5:33–35.; William Corner, "John Crittenden Duval: The Last Survivor of the Goliad Massacre," *Quarterly of the Texas State Historical Association*, I (July 1897), 49.

40 Jane M. Robertson, "Captain Amon B. King," *Southwestern Historical Quarterly*, 29 (October 1925), 147–50; Roell, *Remember Goliad!*, 52–53.

41 Richard G. Santos, *Santa Anna's Campaign Against Texas, 1835–1836: Featuring the Field Commands Issued to Major General Vicente Filisola* (Waco: Texian Press, 1968), 87.

42 Houston to Fannin, March 11, 1836, in Jenkins, ed., *Papers of the Texas Revolution*, 5:51–54.

43 Stephen L. Hardin, *The Alamo 1836: Santa Anna's Texas Campaign* (Oxford: Osprey Publishing Ltd., 2001), 61.

44 John Shackelford, "Some Few Notes upon a Part of the Texas War," in Henry Stuart Foote, *Texas and the Texans; or, Advance of the Anglo-Americans to the Southwest Including a History of Leading Events in Mexico, From the Conquest of Fernando Cortes to the Termination of the Texas Revolution*, 2 vols. (Philadelphia: Thomas, Cowperthwait & Co 1841; rpt. ed., Austin: The Steck Company, 1935), 2:231.

45 Santos, *Santa Anna's Campaign Against Texas*, 88.

46 Hardin, *The Alamo 1836*, 61–62.

47 Herman Ehrenberg, *With Milam and Fannin: Adventures of a German Boy in Texas' Revolution* (Dallas: Tardy Publishing Company, Inc., 1935), 172.

48 Roell, *Remember Goliad!*, 61.

49 Hardin, *Texian Iliad*, 169.

228   NOTES

50   Hardin, *The Alamo 1836*, 65.

51   Able Morgan, "An Account of the Battle of Goliad and Fanning's [sic] Massacre: And the Capture and Imprisonment of Able Morgan, Written by Himself," in O'Connor, *The Presidio La Bahía*, 86.

52   Urrea, "Diary," in Castañeda, ed., *Mexican Side of the Texan Revolution*, 234–35.

53   Roell, *Remember Goliad!*, 64–66.

54   Joseph H. Barnard, *Dr. J. H. Barnard's Journal, December 1835–June 1836*, edited and annotated by Hobart Huson (n.p.: Goliad Bicentennial Edition, 1949), 28.

55   Ibid. 29; John C. Duval, *Early Times in Texas, or the Adventures of Jack Dobell* (Austin: H. P. N. Gammell & Co., Publishers, 1892; rpt. ed., Lincoln: University of Nebraska Press, 1986), 85–86.

56   Duval, *Early Times in Texas*, 88–89.

57   Charles B. Shain, "Narrative of C. B. Shain of Louisville, A Volunteer in the Cause of Texas," *The Louisville Kentucky Journal*, June 30, 1836, reprinted on Sons of Dewitt Colony Texas website, www.tamu.edu/ccbn/dewitt/goliadshain.htm [accessed June 10, 2007]; Abishai M. Dickson to Ann M. Dickson, December 29, 1835; Roell, *Remember Goliad!*, 70–71; Hardin, *Texian Iliad*, 173; William Herman Oberste, *Remember Goliad* (Austin: Von Boeckman–Jones Co., 1949), 61.

CHAPTER TWO

1   For the effects of gun smoke in battle, see Brent Nosworthy, *With Musket, Cannon and Sword: Battle Tactics of Napoleon and His Enemies* (New York: Sarpedon, 1996), 5, 14, 32, 192, 210, 355–56, 396; see also John Keegan, *The Face of Battle* (New York: The Viking Press, 1976), 131, 139–40, 316.

2   Quoted in René Chartrand, *Santa Anna's Mexican Army, 1821–48* (Oxford: Osprey Publishing Ltd., 2004), 4.

3   A list of Fannin's men who escaped the Goliad Massacre follows:

BULLOCK'S COMPANY

Brown, Samuel T.

DUVAL'S COMPANY

Allen, Thomas G.

Holliday, John

Mason, William

Shain, Charles B.

Sharpe, V.

WYATT'S COMPANY

Butler, Bennett

BURKE'S COMPANY

Devenny, N. J.

Ehrenberg, Hermann

Kemp, Thomas

PETTUS'S COMPANY

Hunter, William L.

Brenan, William

Holland, Benjamin H.

Irish, Milton

Jones, David James

Rees, John

SHACKELFORD'S COMPANY

Brooks, Zachariah S.

Cooper, Dillard

Hamilton, Isaac D.

Simpson, Wilson

HORTON'S COMPANY

Hadden, William

Martindale, Daniel

SPRAGUE'S SQUAD

Hazen, Nathaniel

Murphy, Daniel

---

[4]   Charles B. Shain, "Narrative of C. B. Shain of Louisville, A Volunteer in the Cause of Texas," *The Louisville Kentucky Journal*, June 30, 1836, reprinted on Sons of Dewitt

230 NOTES

Colony Texas website, www.tamu.edu/ccbn/dewitt/goliadshain.htm [accessed June 10, 2007], hereinafter, Shain, "Narrative"; Charles B. Shain to Father, April 11, 1836, in John H. Jenkins, ed., *The Papers of the Texas Revolution*, 10 vols. (Austin: Presidial Press, 1973), 5:440–41.

5 Shain, "Narrative."

6 Ibid.

7 Ibid.

8 Ibid.

9 William B. Travis, *The Diary of William Barret Travis, August 30, 1833–June 26, 1834*, edited by Robert E. Davis (Waco: Texian Press, 1966), 17, 100.

10 Shain, "Narrative;" Stephen L. Moore, *Eighteen Minutes: The Battle of San Jacinto and the Texas Independence Campaign* (Dallas: Republic of Texas Press, 2004), 194.

11 N. D. Labadie, "San Jacinto Campaign," in James M. Day, comp., *The Texas Almanac, 1857–1873: A Compendium of Texas History* (Waco: Texian Press, 1967), 148; [Robert M. Coleman], *Houston Displayed, or Who Won the Battle of Jacinto? By a Farmer in the Army* (Velasco: Printed by the Velasco Herald, 1837; rpt. ed., Austin: The Brick Row Book Shop, 1964), 13.

12 Moore, *Eighteen Minutes*, 436.

13 Shain, "Narrative;" Shain to Father, April 11, 1836, in Jenkins, ed., *Papers of the Texas Revolution*, 5:440–41; Moore, *Eighteen Minutes*, 194–95.

14 Jesse Billingsley, "Account of San Jacinto campaign from the *Galveston News*, September, 15, 1857, on Sons of Dewitt Colony Texas website, www.tamu.edu/ccbn /dewitt/miscmemoirs7.htm [accessed September 30, 2007] ; Jonathan Hampton Kuykendall, "J. H. Kuykendall's Recollections of the [San Jacinto] Campaign," *Quarterly of the Texas State Historical Association*, 4 (April 1901): 302; for an erudite discussion of Houston, the army, and the controversy surrounding the "forks of the road," see William C. Davis, *Lone Star Rising: The Revolutionary Birth of the Texas Republic* (New York: Free Press, 2004), 263–64, 330.

15 Moore, *Eighteen Minutes*, 242–47; Kuykendall, "Recollections."

16 Muster Roll of Major McNutt's Command, Texas General Land Office, Austin.

17 James W. Pohl, *The Battle of San Jacinto* (Austin: Texas State Historical Association, 1989), 29–30; Moore, *Eighteen Minutes*, 272; Lysander Wells quoted in Henry Stuart Foote, *Texas and the Texans; or, Advance of the Anglo-Americans to the Southwest Including a History of Leading Events in Mexico, From the Conquest of Fernando Cortes to the Termination*

of the *Texas Revolution*, 2 vols. (Philadelphia: Thomas, Cowperthwait & Co., 1841; rpt. ed., Austin: The Steck Company, 1935), 2:301–302. Foote mistakenly identified Wells as "Major Wills."

[18] Wells quoted in Foote, *Texas and the Texans*, 2:302; Moore, *Eighteen Minutes*, 276.

[19] Moore, *Eighteen Minutes*, 443–44; Col. John M. Swisher, *The Swisher Memoirs*, edited by Rena Maverick Green (San Antonio: The Sigmund Press, Inc., 1932), 44–45.

[20] Archie P. McDonald, *The Trail to San Jacinto* (Boston: The American Press, 1982), 38; Shain to Father, April 11, 1836, in Jenkins, ed., *Papers of the Texas Revolution*, 5:440–41.

[21] Joseph Milton Nance, *After San Jacinto: The Texas-Mexican Frontier, 1836–1841* (Austin: University of Texas Press, 1963), 10–11.

[22] Kathryn Stoner O'Connor, *The Presidio La Bahía del Espiritu Santo de Zuniga, 1721–1846* (Austin: Von Boeckmann–Jones Co., 1966), 157.

[23] [Rusk Order], June 2, 1836, in Jenkins, ed., *Papers of the Texas Revolution*, 6:501; text of Rusk's June 3 address in D. W. C. Baker, *A Texas Scrap Book, Made Up of the History, Biography and Miscellany of Texas and Its People* (New York: A. S. Barnes & Company, [1875]; rpt. ed., Austin: The Steck Company, 1935), 156–57; Mary Whatley Clarke, *Thomas J. Rusk: Soldier, Statesman, Jurist* (Austin: Jenkins Publishing Company, 1971), 77; Jones's discharge certificate indicates that he had served in the army from December 21, 1835, until October 3, 1836. Therefore, he must have been present for the memorial for his fallen Goliad comrades. David James Jones, Bounty Certificate, BEX–B–432, Original Land Grant Collection, Texas General Land Office, Austin.

[24] Gerald S. Pierce, *Texas Under Arms: The Camps, Posts, Forts, & Military Towns of the Republic of Texas, 1836–1846* (Austin: The Encino Press, 1969), 167–74.

[25] Robert Hall, *Life of Robert Hall* (Austin: Ben C. Jones & Co., 1898; rpt. ed., Austin: State House Press, 1992), 22.

[26] Daughters of the Republic of Texas, *Muster Rolls of the Texas Revolution* (Lubbock: Printed by Craftsman Printers, Inc, 1986), 87–88; Thomas Lloyd Miller, *Bounty and Donation Land Grants of Texas, 1835–1888* (Austin: University of Texas Press,1967), 26.

[27] David J. Jones, Bounty Certificate, BEX–B–432, Original Land Grant Collection, Texas General Land Office, Austin.

[28] Miller, *Bounty and Donation Land Grants of Texas*, 24–26.

[29] George B. Erath, *The Memoirs of Major George B. Erath, 1813–1891: As Dictated to Lucy A. Erath* (Waco: The Heritage Society of Waco, 1956), 54, 56.

232   NOTES

[30] Title Bond, David J. Jones to David Ayres, BEX–2–213, Original Land Grant Collection, Texas General Land Office, Austin; William Barret Travis, *Diary of William Barret Travis, August 30, 1833–June 26, 1834*, edited by Robert E. Davis (Waco: Texian Press, 1966), 114; William Barret Travis to David Ayres(?), March 3(?), 1836, in Todd Hansen, ed., *The Alamo Reader: A Study in History* (Mechanicsburg, Penn.: Stackpole Books, 2003), 38. Since the original letter appears to have disappeared, one cannot determine the addressee with certainty. Nevertheless, since Charles was boarding with Ayres at the time, it is unlikely that he would have dispatched it to anyone else.

[31] "AYRES, DAVID," Handbook of Texas Online, www.tsha.utexas.edu/handbook /online/articles/AA/fay5.html [accessed June 10, 2007].

[32] Ibid. David Ayres to David G. Burnet, June 18, 1836, in Jenkins, ed., *Papers of the Texas Revolution*, 7:189; Title Bond, David J. Jones to David Ayres, BEX–2–213, Original Land Grant Collection, Texas General Land Office, Austin.

[33] David J. Jones, Bounty Certificate, BEX–B–432, Original Land Grant Collection, Texas General Land Office, Austin; "MORGAN, JAMES," Handbook of Texas Online, www.tsha.utexas.edu/handbook/online/articles/MM/fmo50.html [accessed June 10, 2007]; for a well reasoned examination of the tizzy surrounding Emily D. West (misidentified by earlier writers as Emily Morgan), see Jeff Dunn, "One more Piece of the Puzzle: Emily West in Special Collections," *The Compass Rose*, 19 (Spring 2005), online at http://libraries.uta.edu./SpecColl/crose)5/West.htm [accessed August 21, 2007] and his "Emily West de Zavala and Emily D. West: Two Women or One?," *The Compass Rose*, 20 (Spring 2006) online at http://libraries .uta.edu/SpecColl/crose06/CR-Spr2006.pdf [accessed August 21, 2007]. Less definitive, but perhaps more accessible to the general reader, is James E. Crisp's "Afterword: The Silence of the Yellow Rose," in *Sleuthing the Alamo: Davy Crockett's Last Stand and Other Mysteries of the Texas Revolution* (New York: Oxford University Press, 2005) 179–98,

CHAPTER THREE

[1] *Telegraph and Texas Register* (Houston), August 30, 1836.

[2] Ibid. Joe B Franz, ed., "Moses Lapham: His Life and Some Selected Correspondence," *Southwestern Historical Quarterly*, 54 (January 1951): 326–27 and (April 1951): 468–69; Surveying the Houston town site was only one of Lapham's claims to fame. He was one of the volunteers who helped Erastus "Deaf" Smith

destroy Vince's bridge before the battle at San Jacinto. He died in a fight with Comanches on October 20, 1838. Sam Houston Dixon and Louis Wiltz Kemp, *The Heroes of San Jacinto* (Houston: The Anson Jones Press, 1932), 195; David G. McComb, *Houston: A History* (Austin: University of Texas Press, 1969), 14.

3 Jonathan W. Jordan, *Lone Star Navy: Texas, the Fight for the Gulf of Mexico, and the Shaping of the American West* (Washington, DC: Potomac Books, Inc., 2006), 40–41; John Allen quoted in James E. Buchanan, ed., *Houston: A Chronological & Documentary History, 1519–1970* (Dobbs Ferry, NY: Oceana Publications, 1975), 70–71; David Nevin, *The Texans* (New York: Time-Life Books, 1975), 184.

4 Nevin, *The Texans*, 184; Dudley G. Wooten, ed., *A Comprehensive History of Texas*, 2 vols. (Dallas: William G. Scarff, 1898), 2:370.

5 Francis R. Lubbock, *Six Decades in Texas; Or, Memoirs of Francis Richard Lubbock, Governor of Texas in War Time, 1861–63. A Personal Experience in Business, War, and Politics* (Austin: Ben C. Jones and Co., 1900), 45; Edward Stiff, *The Texan Emigrant: Being a Narration of the Adventures of the Author in Texas, and a Description of the Soil, Climate, Productions, Minerals, Towns, Bays, Harbors, Rivers, Institutions, and Manners and Customs of the Inhabitants of That Country; Together with the Principal Incidents of Fifteen Years Revolution in Mexico: and Embracing a Condensed Statement of Interesting Events in Texas, From the First European Settlement in 1692, Down to the Year 1840* (Cincinnati: Published by George Conclin, 1840; rpt. ed., Waco: Texian Press, 1968), 79; *Journal of the House of Representatives, Republic of Texas, First Congress, First Session* (Columbia: n.p., 1836), 213. Among the other settlements in contention for the seat of government were: Matagorda, Washington, Velasco, Quintana, Nacogdoches, Hidalgo, Refugio, Fort Bend, Goliad, Groce's Retreat, Béxar, Columbia, San Patricio, Brazoria, and Orozimbo. Ernest William Winkler, "The Seat of Government of Texas," *Quarterly of the Texas State Historical Association*, 10 (October 1906): 165. Anson Jones, *Memoranda and Official Correspondence Relating to the Republic of Texas* (New York: D. Appleton & Company, Inc., 1859), 18–19. John K. Allen served in the House as Nacogdoches's representative. Since Nacogdoches was among the towns in contention for the site of a permanent capital, his constituents probably wished that Allen had employed his "enterprise and influence" on their behalf. See Stanley Siegel, *A Political History of the Texas Republic, 1836–1845* (Austin: University of Texas Press, 1956), 57.

6 Lubbock, *Six Decades in Texas*, 46. Lubbock was the "young merchant in fine clothes."

7 *Telegraph and Texas Register* (Houston), May 2, 1837. Here Dr. Moore is gently mocking the Allen brothers and their August 30, 1836, advertisement. The ad

234   NOTES

began: "Situated at the *head of navigation*, on the West bank of Buffalo Bayou, is now for the first time brought to public because, until now, the proprietors were not ready to offer it to the public, with the advantages of capital and improvements" [italics added]. For a history of the vessel, see Donald Jackson, *Voyages of the Steamboat Yellow Stone* (New York: Ticknor & Fields, 1985).

[8] Jonnie Lockhart Wallis and Laurance L. Hill, eds., *Sixty Years on the Brazos: The Life and Letters of Dr. John Washington Lockhart, 1824–1900* (Los Angles: Privately Printed, 1930), 78–79.

[9] *Telegraph and Texas Register* (Columbia), August 30, 1836.

[10] Noah Webster's *An American Dictionary of the English Language* (1828) defines "yawl" as: "A small ship's boat usually rowed by four to six oars." Lubbock, *Six Decades in Texas*, 46.

[11] Ibid., 46–47.

[12] Robert Boyce quoted in Marguerite Johnson, *Houston: The Unknown City, 1836–1946* (College Station: Texas A&M University Press, 1991), 11.

[13] Andrew Forest Muir, ed., *Texas in 1837: An Anonymous, Contemporary Narrative* (Austin: University of Texas Press, 1958), 34.

[14] James O. Breeden, ed., *A Long Ride in Texas: The Explorations of John Leonard Riddell* (College Station: Texas A&M University Press, 1994), 44; Mary Austin Holley, *The Texas Diary, 1835–1838*, ed. and intro. by J. P. Bryan (Austin: Humanities Research Center, University of Texas, 1965), 38.

[15] "Reminiscences of Mrs. Dilue Harris," *Quarterly of the Texas State Historical Association*, 4 (October 1900): 186–87; Adele B. Looscan, "Harris County, 1822–1845," *Southwestern Historical Quarterly*, 18 (April 1915): 406. A native of Pennsylvania, John W. Moore (ca. 1797–1846) immigrated to Texas in 1830. He was a friend of William Barret Travis and accompanied him during the Anahuac Disturbance of 1835. He served as a delegate from Harrisburg to the Consultation. On November 18, 1835, the General Council named him contractor for the Texian army. One of three Harrisburg representatives, Moore attended the 1836 Convention and signed the Texas Declaration of Independence. On October 3, he joined the House of the First Congress of the Republic of Texas as a member from Harrisburg County. Yet, Jesse H. Cartwright contested the election and eventually replaced Moore in the seat. In January 1837, the troops of the Second Militia District elected him captain. At the same time, he became sheriff of Harrisburg County—a thankless job since his jurisdiction included the raucous town of Houston.

NOTES   235

[16] James L. Haley, *Sam Houston* (Norman: University of Oklahoma Press, 2002), 186; Sam Houston to Robert A. Irion, April 28, 1837, in Amelia W. Williams and Eugene C. Barker, eds., *The Writings of Sam Houston, 1813–1863*, 8 vols. (Austin: University of Texas Press, 1938–1943), 4:29. As he frequently did, President Houston may have engaged in hyperbole. Francis R. Lubbock arrived in Houston "about the first of January, 1837" and found the place abuzz with activity. "Several small houses were," he recalled, "in the course of erection. Logs were hauled in from the forest for a hotel to be erected . . . by Col. Benjamin Fort Smith, who was the inspector-general at the battle of San Jacinto. A small number of workmen were preparing to build cabins, business houses, and this hotel." It is odd, therefore, that some twenty days later Houston claimed there was but a single "small log cabin" in the entire community. Conditions in early Houston were certainly austere, but perhaps not as bleak as Houston suggested. Lubbock, *Six Decades in Texas*, 46–47; Dora Fowler Arthur, ed., "Jottings from the Old Journal of Littleton Fowler," *Quarterly of the Texas State Historical Association*, 2 (July 1898): 80.

[17] A. Pat Daniels, *Texas Avenue at Main Street: The Chronological Story of a City Block in Houston, The Most Significant Block in the History of Texas. An informal but factual history of the block now occupied by the Rice Hotel, site of the Capitol Building of the Republic of Texas when Sam Houston was President* (Houston: Allen Press, 2803 Fannin, a Division of Allen Printing and Letter Service, Publishers, 1964), 4.

[18] Muir, ed., *Texas in 1837*, 29; Mattie Austin Hatcher, ed., *Letters of an Early American Traveller: Mary Austin Holley, Her Life and Her Works, 1784–1846* (Dallas: Southwest Press, 1933), 74.

[19] Johnson, *Houston: The Unknown City*, 16; Adele B. Looscan, "Harris County, 1822–1845, *Southwestern Historical Quarterly* 19 (July 1915): 41; Daniels, *Texas Avenue at Main Street*, [6–7]; E. K. Lindley, comp., *Biographical Directory of the Texan Conventions and Congresses* (Huntsville: printed by order of the House of Representatives, 1941), 43.

[20] Joe B. Frantz, *Gail Borden: Dairyman to a Nation* (Norman: University of Oklahoma Press, 1951), 125; *Telegraph and Texas Register* (Houston), May 16, 1837.

[21] Ashbel Smith to Henry Barnard, Houston, July 8, 1837, Ashbel Smith Papers, Center for American History, University of Texas at Austin; Hatcher, ed., *Letters of an Early American Traveller*, 70.

[22] Kenneth W. Wheeler, *To Wear a City's Crown: the Beginnings of Urban Growth in Texas, 1836–1865* (Cambridge: Harvard University Press, 1968), 51; *Telegraph and Texas Register* (Houston), January 30, 1839; Lubbock, *Six Decades In Texas*, 54; Rena Maverick

236   NOTES

Green, ed., *Samuel Maverick, Texan: 1803–1870, A Collection of Letters, Journals and Memoirs* (San Antonio, Privately Printed, 1952), 82; [Millie Gray], *The Diary of Millie Gray, 1832–1840 (nee Mildred Richards Stone, Wife of Wm. Fairfax Gray) Recording her Family Life Before, During and After Col. Wm. F. Gray's Journey to Texas in 1835, and the Small Journal Giving Particulars of All That Occurred During the Family's Voyage to Texas in 1838* (Houston: The Fletcher Young Publishing Company, 1967), 152; Wallis and Hill, eds., *Sixty Years on the Brazos*, 80; Samuel A. Maverick to Mary A. Maverick, Houston, December 29, 1838, in Green, ed., *Samuel Maverick, Texan*, 80–82; Holley, *The Texas Diary*, 38; Ashbel Smith to [?], August 16, 1837, Ashbel Smith Papers, Center for American History; Kelsey H. Douglass to Minerva Douglass, Houston, [October?] 27, 1837, Kelsey H. Douglass Papers, Center for American History.

23   Dr. O. F. Allen, *The City of Houston From Wilderness to Wonder* (n.p.: privately printed, n.d.), 1–2. The Texians held some 730 Mexicans prisoners from the battle of San Jacinto. Since the Republic of Texas and Mexico were still officially at war, and Texian officials were expecting General José Urrea to launch another offensive, they were loath to release their captives. Hostages would have been the more appropriate term. Officials made the prisoners available to prominent Houstonians as "servants." Francis Lubbock, for example, recalled having two. The city leaders relegated prisoners of war—slaves in all but name—the most unpleasant and dangerous tasks, as Dr. Allen confirmed. For more on the wretched POWs, see Margaret Swett Henson, "Politics and the Treatment of the Mexican Prisoners After the Battle of San Jacinto, *Southwestern Historical Quarterly* 94 (October 1990): 189–230.

24   Frantz, *Gail Borden*, 123; Gustav Dresel, *Gustav Dresel's Houston Journal: Adventures in North America and Texas, 1837–1841*, trans. and ed. by Max Freund (Austin: University of Texas Press, 1954), 32.

25   Wallis and Hill, eds., *Sixty Years on the Brazos*, 80.

26   *Telegraph and Texas Register* (Houston), July 31, 1839. Although the article appeared in 1839, the editor was recalling events that occurred in 1837.

27   Quoted in William Ransom Hogan, *The Texas Republic: A Social and Economic History* (Norman: University of Oklahoma Press, 1946), 231; Kelsey Douglass to Minerva Douglass, Houston, [October?] 27, 1837, Kelsey H. Douglass Papers, Center for American History.

28   Hogan, *Texas Republic*, 31.

29 C. C. Cox, "Reminiscences of C.C. Cox," *Southwestern Historical Quarterly*, vol. 6 (October 1902): 118.

30 Muir, ed., *Texas in 1837*, 58; Stiff, *Texan Emigrant*, 78; Matilda Charlotte (Jesse) Fraser Houstoun, *Texas and the Gulf of Mexico; or, Yachting in the New World*, edited by Marilyn McAdams Sibley (London: John Murray, Albemarle Street, 1844; rpt. ed., Austin: W. Thomas Taylor, 1991), 151; Lubbock, *Six Decades in Texas*, 44.

31 Dresel, *Houston Journal*, 102–103, Cox, "Reminiscences," 118.

32 McComb, *Houston: A History*, 5; *Morning Star* (Houston), May 11, 1839; Stiff, *Texan Emigrant*, 77–78; Sam Houston to Anson Jones, June 12, 1838, in Anson Jones, *Memoranda and Official Correspondence Relating to the Republic of Texas, its History and Annexation. Including a Brief Autobiography of the Author* (New York: D. Appleton and Company, 1859), 132–33; quoted in Llerena Friend, *Sam Houston: The Great Designer* (Austin: University of Texas Press, 1954), 88.

33 Ashbel Smith to Copes, June 25, 1838, Ashbel Smith Papers, Letter Book, Center for American History; *Morning Star* (Houston), September 23, 1839.

34 Stiff, *Texan Emigrant*, 81; A. B. Lawrence, *Texas In 1840: Or the Emigrant's Guide to the New Republic* (New York: n.p., 1840), 28.

35 Wallis and Hill, eds., *Sixty Years on the Brazos*, 325; *Telegraph and Texas Register* (Houston), March 17, 1838; Dresel, *Houston Journal*, 36; Lubbock, *Six Decades in Texas*, 54, 66; Kelsey H. Douglass to Minerva Douglass, Houston, December 10, 1837, Kelsey H. Douglass Papers, Center for American History; John Hunter Herndon Papers, 1814–1872, Center for American History, University of Texas at Austin, Diary, 1837–1838, January 29 and February 4, 1838. Hereinafter, Herndon Diary.

36 Hatcher, ed., *Letters of an Early American Traveller*, 72; Holley, *The Texas Diary*, 58.

37 Herndon Diary, January 23, 1838; Ashbel Smith to cousin, Houston, November 8, 1837, Letter Book, Ashbel Smith Papers, Center for American History; John Henry Brown, *Indian Wars and Pioneers of Texas* (Austin: L. E. Daniell, Publisher, [1892–1893]; rpt. ed., Austin: State House Press, 1988), 59.

38 Ashbel Smith to cousin, Houston, November 8, 1837, Letter Book, Ashbel Smith Papers, Center for American History.

39 Lubbock, *Six Decades in Texas*, 47, 53, 66; Holley, *The Texas Diary, 1835–1838*, 38; Audubon quoted in Friend, *Sam Houston*, 87.

40 *Telegraph and Texas Register* (Houston), May 2, 1836.

238 NOTES

41 Ibid., May 16, 1837. In nineteenth-century printer's jargon, pi was a word meaning jumbled print, while the "devil" was a printer's apprentice.

42 Dresel, Houston Journal, 31–32.

43 Hogan, The Texas Republic, 106–107; Kelsey Douglass to Minerva Douglass, Houston, September 4, 1839, Kelsey Douglass Papers, Center for American History; Dresel, Houston Journal, 32; Cox, "Reminiscences," Southwestern Historical Quarterly, 118; Herndon Diary, January 24, 1838.

44 Houstoun, Texas and the Gulf of Mexico, 177–78. Mrs. Houstoun indicated that her landlord at the Houston House was a "Captain or Colonel Baldwin." Since the title was purely honorific, the author has taken the liberty of promoting him to colonel. As Mrs. Houstoun observed, "Military titles are taken and given here with as little ceremony as the title of Count on the Continent: Mr. Houstoun sprang into a General at once" (p. 176).

45 Z. N. Morrell, Fruits of Flowers from the Wilderness (Boston: Gould and Lincoln, 1872), 66; Stiff, Texan Emigrant, 80–81; Ashbel Smith to George, August 17, 1837, Letter Book, Ashbel Smith Papers, Center for American History.

46 Wheeler, To Wear a City's Crown, 49; Dresel, Houston Journal, 32, 131.

47 Telegraph and Texas Register (Houston), February 20, 1839; Muir, ed., Texas in 1837, 34; Dresel, Houston Journal, 33.

48 S. W. Geiser, "Naturalists of the Frontier," Southwest Review 16 (Autumn 1930): 126; Nicholas Doran P. Maillard, History of the Republic of Texas, From the Discovery of the Country to the Present Time; and the Cause of Her Separation from the Republic of Mexico (London: Smith, Elder, and Co., 1842), 103; Dresel, Houston Journal, 36; Herndon Diary, January 24, 1838; Erasmus Manford, Twenty-five Years in the West (Chicago: E. Manford Publisher, 1867), 53.

49 Maillard, The History of the Republic of Texas, 213.

50 Morning Star (Houston), March 6, July 1, 1841.

51 Sam S. Smith Affidavit, Valentine O. King Collection, Box 2–23/920, Texas State Library, Austin. The author is indebted to Professor Lael Morgan for discovering the identity of John A. Parker and sharing the fruits of her research.

52 Brown, Indian Wars and Pioneers of Texas, 19. Unhappily, McCrory died only a few months after his wedding. In 1840 his widow, the former Mary Smith, wed Dr. Anson Jones and served as first lady during her husband's tenure

NOTES 239

as the last president of the Texas Republic. Sam Houston to Robert A. Irion, March 19, 1837, in Williams, ed., *Writings of Sam Houston*, 2:74; Looscan, "Harris County, 1822–1845," 402.

53 Holley, *The Texas Diary*, 36.

54 Rebecca Smith Lee, *Mary Austin Holley: A Biography* (Austin: University of Texas Press, 1962), 291; Hatcher, ed., *Letters of an Early American Traveller*, 70.

In 1837, eggnog was not today's packaged concoction. Mrs. Allen's recipe would have resembled the following:

> Beat yolks of twelve eggs well. Add two and a fourth cups of sugar and continue to beat well. Add one quart of good Brandy, one pint of Jamaica Rum alternately and slowly. To this add three quarts of heavy cream and fold in half of the beaten egg whites. Beat remaining six eggs whites very stiff and add one cup powdered sugar. Then stir lightly into this one quart of cream and fold this mixture into the other ingredients. Let stand from six to twelve hours in a cold place before serving.

See Mrs. Helen Bullock, *The Williamsburg Art of Cookery or, Accomplish'd Gentlewoman's Companion: Being a Collection of upwards of Five Hundred of the most Ancient & Approv'd Recipes in Virginia Cookery* (Williamsburg: Published by Colonial Williamsburg, and printed by The Dietz Press in Richmond, Va., 1938), 241–42.

55 Hatcher, ed., *Letters of an Early American Traveller*, 70.

56 Muir, ed., *Texas in 1837*, 42; Herndon Diary, March 15, 1838; [Millie Gray], *Diary of Millie Gray*, 152.

57 Stiff, *Texan Emigrant*, 80.

58 "Old Diseases Defined" online at www.carolyar.com/Illinois/diseases.htm [accessed September 30, 2007]; *Telegraph and Texas Register* (Houston), August 30, 1836; "Malaria," online at Emedicine Consumer Health, www.emedicinehealth.com /articles/13140–2.asp [accessed September 29, 2007]; Allen, *The City of Houston From Wilderness to Wonder*, 1–2; Maillard, *History of the Republic of Texas*, 330.

59 Leonard Wolf, ed., *The Essential Frankenstein* (New York: ibooks, 2004), 20, 145; Susan Coulter, "Frankenstein—a cautionary tale of bad parenting," online at www.kimwoodbridge.com/maryshel/coulter.shtml [accessed January 30, 2007].

240   NOTES

CHAPTER FOUR

[1] Matilda Charlotte (Jesse) Fraser Houstoun, *Texas and the Gulf of Mexico; or, Yachting in the New World*, edited by Marilyn McAdams Sibley (London: John Murray, Albemarle Street, 1844; rpt. ed., Austin: W. Thomas Taylor, 1991), 178.

[2] William M. Gouge, *The Fiscal History of Texas: Embracing an Account of its Revenues, Debts, and Currency from the Commencement of the Revolution in 1834 to 1851–52, with Remarks on American Debts* (Philadelphia: Lippincott, Grambo, and Co., 1852; rpt. ed., New York: Burt Franklin, 1969), 27; Joseph Milton Nance, *After San Jacinto: The Texas Mexican Frontier, 1836–1841* (Austin: University of Texas Press, 1963), 16–19.

[3] Thomas W. Cutrer quotes Eugene C. Barker's "true friend" opinion in "HUSTON, FELIX," *Handbook of Texas Online*, www.tsha.edu/handbook/online/articles/HH /fhu46html [accessed January 30, 2006]; William Kennedy, *Texas: The Rise, Progress, and Prospects of the Republic of Texas* (London: R. Hastings, 1841; rpt. ed., Fort Worth: The Molyneaux Craftsmen, Inc., 1925), 609–10; James L. Haley, *Sam Houston* (Norman: University of Oklahoma Press, 2002), 162–63.

[4] Hubert Howe Bancroft, *History of the North Mexican States and Texas*, 2 vols. (San Francisco: The History Company, Publishers, 1889), 2:289–90; "ARMY OF THE REPUBLIC OF TEXAS," *Handbook of Texas Online*, www.tsha.utexas.edu/handbook /online/articles/AA/qja3.html [accessed January 30, 2006]; Philip Graham, *Life and Poems of Mirabeau B. Lamar* (Chapel Hill: University of North Carolina Press, 1938), 33.

[5] "HUSTON, FELIX," *Handbook of Texas Online*; Stanley Siegel, *A Political History of the Texas Republic, 1836–1845* (Austin: University of Texas Press, 1956), 41–42; "ARMY OF THE REPUBLIC OF TEXAS, *Handbook of Texas Online*; Henderson Yoakum, *History of Texas from its First Settlement in 1685 to its Annexation to the United States in 1846*, 2 vols. (New York: Redfield, 34 Beekman Street, 1855), 2:183. Sadly, Yoakum did not bother to identify the "eye-witness" responsible for the quotation. Sam Houston to Thomas Jefferson Green, December 27, 1836, in Amelia Williams and Eugene C. Barker, eds., *The Writings of Sam Houston*, 8 vols. (Austin: University of Texas Press, 1938–1943), 5:7–9; William Preston Johnston, *The Life of Gen. Albert Sidney Johnston, Embracing His Services in the Armies of the United States, The Republic of Texas, and the Confederate States* (New York: D. Appleton & Company, 549 and 551 Broadway, 1878; rpt. ed., New York: Da Capo Press, 1997), 75.

[6] William Fairfax Gray, *The Diary of William Fairfax Gray: From Virginia to Texas, 1835–1837*, ed., intro., and notes by Paul Lack (Dallas: De Golyer Library & William P.

Clements Center for Southwest Studies, Southern Methodist University, 1997), 210; Johnston, *Life of Albert Sidney Johnston*, 75.

[7] Felix Huston to Sam Houston, November 5, 1836, Sam Houston Papers, Catholic Archives of Texas, Austin.

[8] Sam Houston to Thomas J. Rusk, August 8, 1836, in Williams and Barker, eds., *The Writings of Sam Houston*, 1:443–45.

[9] Huston to Houston, December 16, 1836, Sam Houston Papers, Catholic Archives of Texas.

[10] Edward Stiff, *The Texan Emigrant: Being a Narration of the Adventures of the Author in Texas, and a Description of the Soil, Climate, Productions, Minerals, Towns, Bays, Harbors, Rivers, Institutions, and Manners and Customs of the Inhabitants of That Country; Together with the Principal Incidents of Fifteen Years Revolution in Mexico: and Embracing a Condensed Statement of Interesting Events in Texas, From the First European Settlement in 1692, Down to the Year 1840* (Cincinnati: Published by George Conclin, 1840; rpt. ed., Waco: Texian Press, 1968), 50; Francis Trollope, *Domestic Manners of the Americans*, edited by Donald Smalley (New York: Alfred A. Knopf, 1949), 17.

[11] Huston to Houston, November 14, 1836, Sam Houston Papers, Catholic Archives of Texas; Yoakum, *History of Texas*, 2:194; Andrew Forest Muir, ed., *Texas in 1837: An Anonymous, Contemporary Narrative* (Austin: University of Texas Press, 1958), 147; Johnston, *Life of Albert Sidney Johnston*, 70.

[12] Siegel, *Political History of the Texas Republic*, 66; "JOHNSTON, ALBERT SIDNEY," Handbook of Texas Online, www.tsha.utexas.edu/handbook/online/articles/jj/fjo32.html [accessed January 30, 2006].

[13] Johnston, *Life of Albert Sidney Johnston*, 75–78; "DUELING IN THE REPUBLIC OF TEXAS," Handbook of Texas Online, www.tsha.utexas.edu/handbook/online/articles/DD/jgd1.html [accessed January 30, 2006].

[14] Huston to Houston, December 3, 1836, Sam Houston Papers, Catholic Archives of Texas; Seymour V. Connor, *Adventure in Glory* (Austin: Steck-Vaughn Company, 1965), 34.

[15] Henry Teal to Sam Houston, March 5, 1837, A. J. Houston Collection, Texas State Library and Archives, Austin; Daniel Elam to Sam Houston, January 3, 1837, A. J. Houston Collection; Sam Houston to Thomas Toby & Brother, March 10, 1837, in Williams and Barker, eds., *Writings of Sam Houston*, 2: 65; Sam Houston to Captain B. J. White, February 12, 1837, in Ibid., 2:51–52.

242 NOTES

[16] Johnston, *Life of Albert Sidney Johnston*, 70; Henry Teal to Sam Houston, March 5, 1837, A. J. Houston Collection, Texas State Library and Archives.

[17] [Sam Houston], Address to the Army of Texas, May 20, 1837, in Williams and Barker, eds., *Writings of Sam Houston*, 2:97–99.

[18] Johnston, *Life of Albert Sidney Johnston*, 81; Haley, *Sam Houston*, 194; Charles P. Roland, *Albert Sidney Johnston: Soldier of Three Republics* (Austin: University of Texas Press, 1964), 64.

[19] Felix Huston to Sam Houston, March 16, 1837; Felix Huston and Albert Sidney Johnston to Sam Houston [received May 24, 1837], Sam Houston Papers, Catholic Archives of Texas. Recognition is due to James Haley as the first historian to untangle the events surrounding Houston's furloughing of the Texas army. See Haley, *Sam Houston*, 193–95.

[20] Sam Houston to William S. Fisher, May 19, 1837, A. J. Houston Collection, Texas State Library and Archives.

[21] William S. Fisher to Sam Houston, May 24, 1837, A. J. Houston Collection, Texas State Library and Archives.

[22] Ibid.; Nance, *After San Jacinto*, 37; Francis R. Lubbock, *Six Decades in Texas; Or, Memoirs of Francis Richard Lubbock, Governor of Texas in War Time, 1861–63. A Personal Experience in Business, War, and Politics* (Austin: Ben C. Jones and Co., 1900), 74.

[23] Felix Huston to Sam Houston, June 3, 1837, Sam Houston Papers, Catholic Archives of Texas.

[24] Stiff, *Texan Emigrant*, 57.

[25] Muir, ed., *Texas in 1837*, 35.

[26] Gustav Dresel, *Gustav Dresel's Houston Journal: Adventures in North America and Texas, 1837–1841*, trans. and ed. by Max Freund (Austin: University of Texas Press, 1954), 32; W. Eugene Hollon, *Frontier Violence: Another Look* (New York: Oxford University Press, 1974), 36–37.

[27] A hogshead is a large cask holding between 63 and 140 gallons of liquid. Since the cask appeared in Houston, one need not speculate regarding its previous contents. John Hunter Herndon Papers, 1814–1872, Center for American History, University of Texas at Austin, Diary, 1837–1838, March 17, 1838. Hereinafter, Herndon Diary; Ray Allen Billington, *America's Frontier Heritage* (New York: Holt, Rinehart and Winston, 1966), 122.

[28] Andrew Davis Narrative, undated, Archives and Manuscripts, Center for American History; W. J. Cash, *The Mind of the South* (New York: Alfred A. Knopf, 1941), 42–44.

NOTES 243

29 Trollope, *Domestic Manners of the Americans*, 329–30.

30 Nicholas Doran P. Maillard, *A History of the Republic of Texas, From the Discovery of the Country to the Present Time; and the Cause of Her Separation from the Republic of Mexico* (London: Smith, Elder, and Co., Cornhill, 1842), 207–208. My readiness to employ this account will surprise many students of Texas history. Maillard was unquestionably biased; he despised everyone in and everything about the Republic of Texas. He wrote the book to counter William Kennedy's *Texas: The Rise, Progress, and Prospects of the Republic of Texas* (1841), which was supportive in tone. The late Texas bibliophile John H. Jenkins said of Maillard: "This is the most vitriolic denunciation of the Republic of Texas, written with absolutely no regard for the truth." John H. Jenkins, *Basic Texas Books: An Annotated Bibliography of Selected Works for a Research Library* (Austin: Jenkins Publishing Company, 1983), 362–64. Small wonder so few historians have bothered to consult it. Yet, Jenkins overstated the case. While Maillard had entire crates of axes to grind, the book is not wholly without merit. It is, for example, a rich source of social history and colorful period expressions. Old Texians themselves corroborated many of Maillard's observations. When that is the case (as it is here), I cite him. When he takes off on flights of baseless diatribe, I do not. When citing Maillard, responsible historians should approach the book as they would any primary document and verify, verify, verify. Nevertheless, having done that, it would seem unnecessarily finicky to discount *everything* the man had to say.

31 Stiff, *Texan Emigrant*, 71.

32 Joe B. Frantz, ed., "Moses Lapham: His Life and Some Selected Correspondence, II," *Southwestern Historical Quarterly* 54 (April 1951): 469.

33 Kelsey H. Douglass to Minerva Douglass, Houston, December 10, 1837, Kelsey H. Douglass Papers, Center for American History; Nance, *After San Jacinto*, 201; Gouge, *Fiscal History of Texas*, 28.

34 Dresel, *Houston Journal*, 32, 131.

35 Howard Beeth and Cary D. Wintz, eds., *Black Dixie: Afro-Texan History and Culture in Houston* (College Station: Texas A&M University Press, 1992), 15. Houston's city fathers did not welcome free blacks. The grand jury charged free blacks for being criminals, indigent, abolitionists, or as poor role models for their fellow blacks who remained in bondage. Neither slaves nor free blacks could hold dances without the mayor's leave. See Alwyn Barr, *Black Texans: A History of African Americans in Texas,*

1528–1995 (Austin: Jenkins Book Publishing Company, Inc., 1973; 2nd ed., Norman: University of Oklahoma Press, 1996), 8–9.

36 Muir, ed., *Texas in 1837*, 35; Lubbock, *Six Decades in Texas*, 54–55; Kelsey H. Douglass to Minerva Douglass, Houston, December 10, 1837, Kelsey H. Douglass Papers, Center for American History.

37 Lubbock, *Six Decades in Texas*, 57.

38 Stiff, *Texan Emigrant*, 70.

39 Ibid.

40 Ibid., 69; Maillard, *A History of the Republic of Texas*, 104; Houstoun, *Texas and the Gulf of Mexico*, 146–47; Francis Sheridan, *Galveston Island, Or, A Few Months Off the Coast of Texas: The Journal of Francis C. Sheridan, 1839–1840*, edited by Willis W. Pratt (Austin: University of Texas Press, 1954), 100; for a history of the Bowie knife and its place in American history, see Raymond W. Thorp, *Bowie Knife* (Williamstown, NJ: Philips Publications, 1991).

41 Sheridan, *Galveston Island*, 100.

42 Jonnie Lockhart Wallis and Laurance L. Hill, eds., *Sixty Years on the Brazos: The Life and Letters of Dr. John Washington Lockhart, 1824–1900* (Los Angeles: Privately Printed, 1930), 80; Sheridan, *Galveston Island*, 36.

43 Muir, ed., *Texas in 1837*, 35; William Ransom Hogan, *The Texas Republic: A Social and Economic History* (Norman: University of Oklahoma Press, 1946), 129; Herndon Diary, January 24 and 26, 1838.

44 *Telegraph and Texas Register* (Houston) October 27, 1837; *American Turf Register and Sporting Magazine*, 9 (February 1838), 51–52.

45 Sheridan, *Galveston Island*, 112.

46 Stiff, *Texan Emigrant*, 76.

47 Although Lubbock did not specifically date the incident, Houston historian A. Pat Daniels places the episode in November 1837. A. Pat Daniels, *Texas Avenue at Main Street: The Chronological Story of a City Block in Houston, The Most Significant Block in the History of Texas. An informal but factual history of the block now occupied by the Rice Hotel, site of the Capitol Building of the Republic of Texas when Sam Houston was President* (Houston: Allen Press, 2803 Fannin, a Division of Allen Printing and Letter Service, Publisher, 1964), 13–14.

48 Lubbock, *Six Decades in Texas*, 55–56.

49 Stiff, *Texan Emigrant*, 70.

50 Sheridan, *Galveston Island*, 100; Lubbock, *Six Decades in Texas*, 70.

NOTES 245

CHAPTER FIVE

1 Francis Lubbock, *Six Decades in Texas: The Memoirs of Francis R. Lubbock; or, Memoirs of Francis Richard Lubbock, Governor of Texas in War Time, 1861–63. A Personal Experience in Business, War, and Politics* (Austin: B. C. Jones & Co., Printers, 1900), 57.

2 Marilyn McAdams Sibley, *Lone Stars and State Gazettes: Texas Newspapers before the Civil War* (College Station, Texas A&M University Press, 1983), 86–87; A. C. Gray, "A History of the Texas Press," in Dudley Wooten, ed., *A Comprehensive History of Texas, 1685–1897*, 2 vols. (Dallas: William G. Scarff, 1898), 2:374.

3 William Preston Johnston, *The Life of Gen. Albert Sidney Johnston, Embracing His Services in the Armies of the United States, The Republic of Texas, and the Confederate States* (New York: D. Appleton & Company, 549 and 551 Broadway, 1878; rpt. ed., New York: Da Capo Press, 1997), 70–71.

4 *Telegraph and Texas Register* (Houston), May 9, 1837.

5 *Telegraph and Texas Register* (Houston), May 30, 1837; Joe B. Frantz, *Gail Borden: Dairyman to a Nation* (Norman: University of Oklahoma Press, 1951), 126.

6 "WE LABOR FOR OUR COUNTRY" was the masthead motto for the *Telegraph and Texas Register*. By echoing the familiar creed, Moore was assuring readers that he would LABOR every bit as hard as the Bordens. *Telegraph and Texas Register* (Houston), June 13 and June 24, 1837.

7 "CRUGER, JACOB W.," *Handbook of Texas Online*, www.tsha.utexas.edu/handbook /online/articles/CC/fcr37.html [accessed June 25, 2006].

8 Harriett Smither, ed., *Journals of the Fourth Congress of the Republic of Texas, 1839–1840*, 3 vols. (Austin: Von Boeckmann-Jones Co., 1929), 3:94. To twenty-first century ears, this statement sounds more than a little homoerotic. It is probably idle to speculate, since, so far removed from the man and events, historians rarely know what was in their subject's head and heart. Here, however, are the facts. There are abundant examples of Moore's prose style. In the nineteenth century, people wrote in a more florid fashion—and, even by the standards of his day, Moore's style was extravagant. When he described his affection toward Cruger, he probably employed the same rhetorical excess with which he approached most topics. Also consider this: on an 1839 visit to Bath, New York, Moore rekindled an earlier relationship with Elizabeth Mofat Wood. They wed in 1840 and he subsequently fathered nine children by her. On the other hand, Jacob W. Cruger never married, which, in and of itself, signifies nothing.

9 *Telegraph and Texas Register* (Houston), May 15, 1839.

246   NOTES

10 The "same pair of stitchdowns" refers to Moore's footwear. This mode of
construction involved the cobbler turning the upper leather outward around
its bottom edge to form a flange. He then stitched the flange to the sole.
Although this technique dates as far back at the medieval period, the term
"stitchdown" (frequently spelled "stitch down") had been in use since the 1700s.
Less finished than other shoes, stitchdowns were also less expensive. This was
probably Stiff's reason for identifying them by name. For all of his airs and graces,
Moore wore cheap shoes. Edward Stiff, *The Texas Emigrant: Being a Narration of the
Adventures of the Author in Texas and a Description of the Soil, Climate, Productions, Minerals,
Towns, Bays, Harbors, Rivers, Institutions, and Manners and Customs of the Inhabitants of
that Country; Together with the Principal Incidents of Fifteen Years Revolution in Mexico: and
Embracing a Condensed Statement of Interesting Events in Texas, From the First European
Settlement in 1692 to the Year 1840* (Cincinnati: Published by George Conclin, 1840;
rpt. ed., Waco: Texian Press, 1968), 95.

11 In Greek mythology, Proteus was a prophetic sea god who had the ability to shift
shape to evade capture. From this feature derives the adjective *protean*, meaning:
variable, often changing, versatile. William D. Redd to Mirabeau B. Lamar,
Columbus, Georgia, August 10, 1839, in Charles A. Gulick, et al., eds., *The Papers of
Mirabeau Buonaparte Lamar*, 6 vols. (Austin: A. C. Baldwin & Sons, 1921–1927), 5:30;
Amelia W. Williams and Eugene C. Barker, eds., *The Writings of Sam Houston*, 8 vols.
(Austin: University of Texas Press, 1938–1943), 6:11.

12 *Telegraph and Texas Register* (Houston), September 23, 1837.

13 Ibid., September 30, 1837.

14 Kelsey H. Douglass to Minerva Douglass, Houston, October 15 and [October?] 27,
1837, Kelsey H. Douglass Papers, Center for American History, University of Texas
at Austin; *Telegraph and Texas Register* (Houston), October 14, 1837.

15 Sibley, *Lone Stars and State Gazettes*, 90.

16 Marie Lee Phelps, *A History of Early Houston* (Houston: The Harris County
Heritage Society, 1959), [2–3].

17 Boswell and Herndon shared many traits. Both were lawyers; both were young
men about town; both attended church services to ogle the ladies; both were bon
viveurs who enjoyed strong drink, ribald stories, and outlandish companions.
Neither could resist a hanging and their journals include vivid descriptions of
contemporary executions. The best edition remains James Boswell, *Boswell's London*

NOTES 247

Journal, 1762–1763, edited by Frederick A. Pottle (New York: McGraw-Hill Book Company, Inc., 1950).

[18] Andrew Forest Muir, ed., "Diary of a Young Man in Houston," *Southwestern Historical Quarterly*, 53 (January 1950): 277–78. It is fitting that I acknowledge this remarkable scholar. This article was my introduction to the Jones–Quick hanging. As my research came together, I recalled that Muir had also edited *Texas in 1837: An Anonymous, Contemporary Narrative*, the "earliest written account of Texas as a republic." What bibliophile John H. Jenkins wrote about that volume and its editor in 1983 remains true today: "The Muir edition is the first in book form, and it is a masterpiece of editing—one of the best-edited and best-annotated of all Texas books. Andrew Forest Muir was one of those meticulous researchers with a genius for following up clues but who unfortunately seldom publish the results of their findings. In this case, his introduction and annotations are as valuable as the text itself." John H. Jenkins, *Basic Texas Books: An Annotated Bibliography of Selected Works for a Research Library* (Austin: Jenkins Publishing Company, 1983), 394. Simply stated, I could not have written this book without Muir's groundbreaking research. My debt to him is immense.

[19] John Hunter Herndon Papers, 1814–1872, Center for American History, University of Texas at Austin, Diary, 1837–1838, passim. Hereinafter Herndon Diary.

[20] Ibid.

[21] Herndon Diary, February 11 and 21, 1838; R. M. Farrar, *The Story of Buffalo Bayou and the Houston Ship Channel* (Houston: Chamber of Commerce, [1926]), [6–7].

[22] Herndon Diary, February 17, 1838. Dr. Robert H. Watson was a member of the Medical and Surgical Society of Houston, which local physicians formed in 1838. His name still appeared on its membership roll in 1840. See Pat Ireland Nixon, *The Medical Story of Early Texas, 1528–1853* ([Lancaster, PA]: Mollie Bennett Lupe Memorial Fund, 1946), 462–63.

[23] Dorman Hayward Winfrey, comp., *A History of The Philosophical Society of Texas, 1837–1897* (Austin: The Philosophical Society of Texas, 1987), 37; Ashbel Smith to Muller, Houston, December 6, 1837, Letter Book, Ashbel Smith Papers, Center for American History; "PHILOSOPHICAL SOCIETY OF TEXAS," *Handbook of Texas Online*, www.tsha.utexas.edu/handbook/online/articles/PP/vtp4.html [accessed July 11, 2006]; Harry Huntt Ransom, *The Other Texas Frontier* (Austin: University of Texas Press, 1984), 40; Dora Fowler Arthur, ed., "Jottings from the Old Journal of Littleton Fowler," *Quarterly of the Texas State Historical Association*, 2 (July 1898): 80.

248 NOTES

24 Ashbel Smith to Henry Barnard, Houston, December 22, 1837, Letter Book, Ashbel Smith Papers, Center for American History; Llerena B. Friend, Sam Houston: The Great Designer (Austin: University of Texas Press, 1954), 88; Ransom, The Other Texas Frontier, 40; Winfrey, comp., History of the Philosophical Society of Texas, 37.

25 Lubbock, Six Decades in Texas, 70. The Philosophical Society "dissolved," according to Francis Lubbock, "on the next removal of the capital." That is to say, the removal to Austin.

26 William Christy quoted in Marshall De Bruhl, Sword of San Jacinto: A Life of Sam Houston (New York: Random House, 1993), 247.

27 Arthur, ed., "Jottings from the Old Journal of Littleton Fowler," Quarterly of the Texas State Historical Association, 2 (July 1898): 82.

28 Frank B. Sexton quoted in ibid., 76; Winfrey, comp., History of the Philosophical Society of Texas, 17; "FOWLER, LITTLETON," Handbook of Texas Online, www.tsha.utexas.edu /handbook/online/articles/FF/ffo25.html [accessed July 24, 2006].

29 When Reverend Fowler recounted that the "great men" stripped themselves to their "linen," he meant their linen shirts. In the 1830s, "pantaloons" were tight trousers extending from waist to ankle with straps passing under the instep. This was a shocking affront to contemporary standards of decency. In Fowler's day, people considered a man's shirt part of his underclothing. Under normal circumstances a gentleman would wear a waistcoat (vest), coat, and cravat over his shirt. The only portion of the shirt visible to public view would be the collar points peeking above the cravat. In a time when propriety reigned supreme, a man appearing in society dressed only in shirtsleeves and trousers would be akin to someone nowadays arriving at the prom in his briefs and wife-beater undershirt. For more on nineteenth-century fashion mores, see C. Willet and Phillis Cunnington, The History of Underclothes (Mineola, NY: Dover Publications, Inc., 1992), 120–34. See also Elisabeth McClellan, History of American Costume, 1607–1870: With an Introductory Chapter on Dress in the Spanish and French Settlements in Florida and Louisiana (New York: Tudor Publishing Company, 1942), 583–96.

30 Arthur, ed., "Jottings," 82.

31 Writers Program of the Work Projects Administration, Houston: A History and Guide (Houston: The Anson Jones Press, 1942), 42–43; Charles S. Taylor to James H. Starr, August 38, 1839, Starr Papers, Center for American History; see also Stephen L. Hardin, comp. and ed., Lone Star: The Republic of Texas, 1836–1846 (Carlisle, MA: Discovery Enterprises, Ltd., 1998), 29.

32 Muir, ed., *Texas in 1837*, 38.

33 Ibid. J. De Cordova, *Texas: Her Resources and her Public Men: A Companion for J. De Cordova's New and Correct Map of the State of Texas* (Philadelphia: Printed by E. Crozet, Cor. Thirteenth & Market, 1858; rpt. ed., Waco: Texian Press, 1969), 161; Adele B. Looscan, "Harris County, 1822–1845," *Southwestern Historical Quarterly* 19 (July 1915): 41.

34 Harnett T. Kane, *Gentlemen, Swords and Pistols* (New York: Bonanza Books, 1951), xi.

35 Houston's dueling ground lay within yards of the capitol, just outside town near the junction of Main and Texas streets. Today it would be located near the vicinity of 610 Main Street. Jim Glass, "The City of Houston, December, 1837." Copy in author's possession. The author is indebted to Mr. Glass for providing this invaluable research tool. A copy of this map is on file in the Texas Room, Houston Public Library.

36 Muir, ed., *Texas in 1837*, 38–39.

37 *Telegraph and Texas Register* (Houston) May 16, 1837.

38 Ibid., June 3 and 8, 1837.

39 William Fairfax Gray, *The Diary of William Fairfax Gray: From Virginia to Texas, 1835–1837*, edited with an introduction and notes by Paul Lack (Dallas: De Golyer Library & William P. Clements Center for Southwest Studies, Southern Methodist University, 1997) 48; Florence King, *With Charity Toward None: A Fond Look at Misanthropy* (New York: St. Martin's Press, 1992), 146.

40 Muir, ed., *Texas in 1837*, 39; see also Nixon, *Medical Story of Early Texas*, 436.

41 Muir, ed., *Texas in 1837*, 40.

42 Ibid.; William Ransom Hogan, "Rampant individualism in the Republic of Texas," *Southwestern Historical Quarterly* 44 (April 1941): 467.

43 Goodrich to Smith, Fort Bend, June 30, and San Antonio, August 24, 1837, Ashbel Smith Papers, Center for American History.

44 Goodrich to Smith, Fort Bend, June 30, 1837, Ashbel Smith Papers, Center for American History; Dickson D. Bruce, Jr., *Violence and Culture in the Antebellum South* (Austin: University of Texas Press, 1979), 40–41.

45 *Telegraph and Texas Register* (Houston), July 1, 1837.

46 Law quoted in Suzanne M. Shultz, *Body Snatching: The Robbing of Graves for the Education of Physicians in Early Nineteenth Century America* (Jefferson, NC: McFarland & Company, Inc., Publishers, 1992), 8.

47 *Telegraph and Texas Register* (Houston), July 1, 1837.

250   NOTES

48 Ibid., September 16, 1837; William Ransom Hogan, *The Texas Republic: A Social and Economic History* (Norman: University of Oklahoma Press. 1946), 279.

49 *Telegraph and Texas Register* (Houston), October 14, 1837.

50 Bertram Wyatt-Brown, *Southern Honor: Ethics and Behavior in the Old South* (Oxford: Oxford University Press, 1982), 351, 355; Hogan, "Rampant Individualism in the Republic of Texas," 478; James L. Haley, *Sam Houston* (Norman: University of Oklahoma Press, 2002), 226; Jack K. Williams, *Dueling in the Old South: Vignettes of Social History* (College Station: Texas A&M University Press, 1980), 26–39. Also useful is Kenneth S. Greenberg, *Honor & Slavery: Lies, Duels, Noses, Masks, Dressing as a Woman, Gifts, Strangers, Humanitarianism, Death, Slave Rebellions, The Proslavery Argument, Baseball, Hunting and Gambling in the Old South* (Princeton: Princeton University Press, 1966), xi–xii, 7–9, 35–36, 54–60, 81–82.

CHAPTER SIX

1 *Telegraph and Texas Register* (Houston), November 18, 1837. Editor Moore, perhaps purposely, did not identify the horse's owner.

2 Ibid. In this issue, Moore reported victim's first name as "William," but corrected the error in future issues.

3 Ibid. Wood died on November 13, 1837.

4 Marilyn McAdams Sibley, *Lone Stars and State Gazettes: Texas Newspapers before the Civil War* (College Station: Texas A&M Press, 1983), 116–17.

5 Daughters of the Republic of Texas, *Muster Rolls of the Texas Revolution* (Lubbock: Printed by Craftsman Printers, 1986), 43–45; for more on Cooke's company, see Alwyn Barr, *Texans in Revolt: The Battle for San Antonio, 1835* (Austin: University of Texas Press, 1990), 44–45, 53–54, 56, 62, 65, 69, 71; see also Edward L. Miller, *New Orleans and the Texas Revolution* (College Station: Texas A&M University Press, 2004), 113, 122, 152, 166; Louis Wiltz Kemp, *The Signers of the Texas Declaration of Independence* (Salado, Tenn. The Anson Jones Press, 1944), 27; Andrew Forest Muir, ed. "Diary of a Young Man in Houston," *Southwestern Historical Quarterly* 53 (January 1950): 297; Allen Johnson and Dumas Malone, eds., *Dictionary of American Biography*, 20 vols. (New York: Charles Scribner's Sons, 1937), 20:456–57; *Biographical Directory of the American Congress, 1794–1927* (Washington, DC: United States Government Printing Office, 1928), 1724.

6 For the effects of the depression in the United States, see Reginald Charles McGrane, *Panic of 1837: Some Financial Problems of the Jacksonian Era* (Chicago:

NOTES   251

University of Chicago Press, 1965) and James Roger Sharp, *The Jacksonians versus the Banks: Politics in the States after the Panic of 1837* (New York: Columbia University Press, 1970). For its impact on Texas, see William Ransom Hogan, *The Texas Republic: A Social and Economic History* (Norman: University of Oklahoma Press, 1946), 82, 87–89; Joseph Milton Nance, *After San Jacinto: The Texas-Mexican Frontier, 1836–1841* (Austin: University of Texas Press, 1963), 208; and, Mark E. Nackman, *A Nation Within a Nation: The Rise of Texas Nationalism* (Port Washington, NY: Kennikat Press, 1975), 38; for John Quincy Adams's opposition to Texas annexation, see Frederick Merk, *Slavery and the Annexation of Texas* (New York: Alfred A. Knopf, 1972), 136, 159, 180–81, 209, 243–44.

[7] *Daily Picayune* (New Orleans), June 18, 1837.

[8] Ashbel Smith to Muller, Houston, December 6, 1837, Letter Book, Ashbel Smith Papers, Center for American History, University of Texas at Austin. Houston, at times an affable drinking companion, could also be a sloppy drunk. Dr. John Washington Lockhart chronicled one especially destructive episode: "While under the influence of wine he was very self-willed; for instance, on a certain day as he was lying on a fine bedstead, he conceived an idea that one of the posts obstructed his breathing, so he made his servant bring in an ax and cut the post off even with the bed. This was the first time that I ever saw him under the influence of any kind of liquor, and I dare say that if Mrs. Houston had been at home this would not have occurred." To make matters worse, it was Dr. Lockhart's guest bed that Houston demolished. See James L. Haley, *Sam Houston* (Norman: University of Oklahoma Press, 2002), 265.

[9] Ashbel Smith to [Eugene] Rousseau, Houston, December 18, 1837, Letter Book, Ashbel Smith Papers, Center for American History.

[10] Edward Stiff, *Texan Emigrant: Being a Narration of the Adventures of the Author in Texas, and a Description of the Soil, Climate, Productions, Minerals, Towns, Bays, Harbors, Rivers, Institutions, and Manners and Customs of the Inhabitants of that Country; Together with the Principal Incidents of Fifteen Years Revolution in Mexico: And Embracing a Condensed Statement of Interesting Events in Texas, From the First European Settlement in 1692, Down to the Year 1840* (Cincinnati: Published by George Conclin, 1840; rpt. ed., Waco: Texian Press, 1968), 86.

[11] Gustav Dresel, *Gustav Dresel's Houston Journal: Adventures in North America and Texas, 1837–1841*, trans. and ed. by Max Freund (Austin: University of Texas Press, 1954), 36–37.

252   NOTES

12 John W. Moore, Audited Republic Claims, Archives and Information Services Division, Texas State Library and Archives, Austin.

13 *Telegraph and Texas Register* (Houston), August 5, 1837, and February 17, 1838.

14 Andrew Forest Muir, ed., *Texas in 1837: An Anonymous, Contemporary Narrative* (Austin: University of Texas Press, 1958), 35; William M. Gouge, *The Fiscal History of Texas: Embracing an Account of its Revenues, Debts, and Currency From the Commencement of the Revolution in 1834 to 1851–52, With Remarks on American Debts* (Philadelphia: Lippincott, Grambo, and Co., 1852; rpt. ed., New York: Burt Franklin, 1969), 27–28; Dresel, *Houston Journal*, 32.

15 Dr. S. O. Young, *A Thumb-nail History of the City of Houston Texas: From its Founding in 1836 to the Year 1912* (Houston: Press of Rein & Sons Company, 1912), 11.

16 "BRIGHAM, MOSES ," San Jacinto Museum of History Biographies, online at www.sanjacinto-museum.org/Herzstein_Library/Veteran_Biographies/biographies /defalt.asp?action=bio&id+2937 [accessed April 21, 2007]; *Telegraph and Texas Register* (Houston), January 20, 1838.

17 *Telegraph and Texas Register* (Houston), January 20, 1838.

18 Ibid.

19 Ibid.

20 Ibid., May 15, 1839.

21 Ibid., March 24, 1836.

22 Herndon Diary, March 22, 1838; Kemp Veteran Biographies, San Jacinto Museum of History website, www.sanjacinto-museum.org/Herzstein_library/ [accessed April 21, 2007]; E. R. Lindley, comp., *Biographical Directory of the Texan Conventions and Congresses, 1832–1845* (Huntsville: Printed by order of the House of Representatives, 1941), 160.

23 Herndon Diary, March 22, 1838; Augustus M. Tomkins, Audited Republic Claims, claim no. 647, Archives and Information Services Division, Texas State Library and Archives, Austin; E. H. Winfield, Audited Republic Claims, claim no. 1763, Archives and Information Services Division, Texas State Library and Archives, Austin.

24 *Telegraph and Texas Register* (Houston), March 24, 1838; Francis Richard Lubbock, *Six Decades in Texas, or, Memoirs of Francis Richard Lubbock, Governor of Texas in Wartime, 1861–63. A Personal Experience in Business, War, and Politics* (Austin: Ben C. Jones & Co., Printers, 1900), 56.

25 *Telegraph and Texas Register* (Houston), March 24 and 13, 1838; Herndon Diary, March 23, 1838.

NOTES   253

[26] In 1838, Texana, in south central Jackson County, was an important settlement and county seat. In 1883, however, the New York, Texas and Mexican Railway bypassed the town, triggering its decline. Voters moved the county seat to Edna; by 1884, Texana was a virtual ghost town. Nowadays, the town site lies under the waters of Lake Texana. Herndon Diary, March 28, 1838; Augustus M. Tomkins, Audited Republic Claims, claim no. 647, Archives and Information Services Division, Texas State Library and Archives; E. H. Winfield, Audited Republic Claims, claim no. 1763, Archives and Information Services Division, Texas State Library and Archives, Austin.

[27] Herndon Diary, March 24, 1838. Francis Lubbock related an anecdote that has occasionally appeared in secondary accounts: "It had been reported to the court that the jail was very insecure, the weather was cold, and the prisoners quite uncomfortable, particularly as they had to be kept ironed for security. So the judge pronounced sentence that the two men, 'the prisoners, in consequence of the insecurity of the jail, the extreme cold weather, and their uncomfortable situation,' be hung on the Friday following their conviction, which was done." Lubbock's memory failed him, for this lively tale is wrong on many key points. As noted earlier, in March 1838, Houston had no jail. But no need to quibble. Lubbock probably meant the structure that *served* as a jail. He was certainly on the nose when he recalled it was "very insecure."

Other parts of his story, however, are more worrisome. Although the winter of 1838 was exceptionally bitter, the entire week surrounding the trial and execution of Jones and Quick was quite agreeable. Herndon declared Thursday, the day of Jones's conviction, a "Fine day." The following Saturday, when Judge Robinson passed sentence, was "Cloudy but pleasant." Sunday was "fair" and "fine." Herndon actually found Tuesday "warm." Therefore, what Lubbock recalled as "the extreme cold weather" was anything but and did not sway Robinson's sentence. Most damning, a cursory review of the *Telegraph and Texas Register* and Herndon's diary reveals that Judge Robinson passed sentence on March 24, and on March 28, the condemned kept their scheduled appointment with the hangman. Lubbock's assertion that Robinson ordered the pair "be hung on the Friday following their conviction" is at odds with all other evidence. Lubbock, *Six Decades in Texas*, 56–57.

The late John H. Jenkins contributed to this myth when he quoted a passage from an uncited Mississippi newspaper that claimed to report Judge Robinson's remarks:

254   NOTES

> The fact is, Jones, that the court did not intend to order you to be executed
> before next spring, but the weather is very cold—our jail, unfortunately,
> is in very bad condition—much of the glass in the windows is broken—the
> chimneys are in such a dilapidated state that no fire can be made to render
> your apartments comfortable; besides, owing to the great number of prisoners,
> not more than one blanket can be allowed to each; to sleep soundly and
> comfortably, therefore, will be out of the question. In consideration of these
> circumstances, and wishing to lessen your sufferings as much as possible, the
> Court, in the exercise of its humanity and compassion, do hereby order you to
> be executed tomorrow morning, as soon after breakfast as may be convenient
> to the Sheriff and agreeable to you.

The tone of the above passage is tongue-in-cheek; it is also incorrect on many key features. As noted, the weather was not "very cold" and the sheriff did not hang Jones and Quick the following day "after breakfast." Since what it reports is obviously twaddle, the author has made no effort to identify the unnamed Mississippi newspaper. John H. Jenkins, *Audubon and Other Capers: Confessions of a Texas Bookmaker* (Austin: The Pemberton Press, 1976), 53.

Early Houston historian, Dr. S. O. Young weighed in on the debate: "It is an historical fact that at the first session of court held in Harrisburg County, as Harris [County] was then called, two men were found guilty of murder and sentenced to death. It is stated that those two men were hanged immediately because the jail was uncomfortably cold and the kind-hearted judge did not want the prisoners to suffer unduly." He concluded, "The court sentence is true, no doubt, but the story about the jail being too uncomfortable must be taken with a large pinch of salt, since there was no jail to be uncomfortable." See Dr. S. O. Young, *True Stories of Old Houston and Houstonians: Historical and Personal Sketches* (Galveston: Oscar Springer, Publisher, 1913), 7.

Professor Andrew Forest Muir also confirmed that Houston had no jailhouse during the period in question. "Having no prison to which the convicted could be sent, the court assessed two sentences of hanging, both for murder; thirteen fines, totaling $1,040, in nine cases of gambling and four of assault; and 139 lashes, in six cases of crimes against property." Andrew Forest Muir, "Augustus M. Tomkins, Frontier Prosecutor," *Southwestern Historical Quarterly*, 54 (January 1951): 316–23.

[28] Herndon Diary, March 22 and 25, 1838.

NOTES 255

29 Ibid., March 26, 1838.

30 Ibid., March 27, 1838.

31 Ibid.

32 Ibid.

33 Ibid.

34 V. A. C. Gatrell, *The Hanging Tree: Execution and the English People, 1770–1868* (Oxford: Oxford University Press, 1994), 104, 246–47; *Telegraph and Texas Register* (Houston), March 31, 1838.

35 John W. Moore, Audited Republic Claims, claim no. 1817, Archives and Information Services Division, Texas State Library and Archives.

36 When Moore called the gallows "the fatal trees," he was speaking metaphorically. Both he and Herndon made numerous references to the "gallows." Moore was attempting to be poetic; many ballads spoke of the "gallows tree." The term "gallows pole" was also in usage. Readers of a certain age may recall that the British super group, Led Zeppelin, featured the ballad "Gallows Pole" on their third album. Herndon Diary, March 28, 1838; *Telegraph and Texas Register* (Houston), March 31, 1838.

On December 30, 2006, as the author was writing this chapter, news arrived that the Iraqi dictator Saddam Hussein had died on the end of a rope. The execution of Saddam was a grim reminder that hanging is not a morbid vestige of the past. At the dawn of the twenty-first century, millions of people still hover under the shadow of the gallows.

In the wake of the executions of Saddam Hussein and two of his accomplices, the U.S. press rediscovered hanging. Maria Cheng of the Associated Press reported, "There is nothing kind or gentle about a hanging. It is a process scientifically designed to break the neck and choke a person to death as efficiently as possible." That she had to explain what would appear obvious, suggests how far removed Americans are from their own history. *Victoria Advocate* (Victoria, Texas), January 16, 2007. The gristly details surrounding the deaths of Barzan Ibrahim, Saddam's chief of intelligence, and Awad Hamed al-Bandar, the head of the dictator's Revolutionary Court, shocked the world. "After the trap doors beneath them opened, Bander dangled from the rope, but the shock of the rope going taut severed Ibrahim's head from his body." *Houston Chronicle,* January 16, 2007.

37 Herndon Diary, March 28, 1838. This was Dr. J. Hervey Price, who was later a member of the Medical and Surgical Society of Houston. Dr. Robert H.

256   NOTES

Watson was, of course, Herndon's traveling companion who had earlier drunk whisky from a skull. In December 1837, President Houston nominated him as a surgeon in the army. The Senate—for reasons documents fail to record—requested the president to withdraw Watson from consideration and he apparently did so. Watson was a member of the Medical and Surgical Society of Houston. In 1842, he was one of the surgeons attached to the Mier Expedition and participated in the infamous Black Bean Episode. Watson drew a white bean and endured incarceration in Perote prison until paroled in 1844. By 1840, Dr. Charles B. Snow served as surgeon aboard the *San Bernard*, a ship in the Texas Navy. The author was unable to discover the identity of Cavanaugh, but he appears not to have been a physician. Like Herndon, he was likely a gentleman phrenologist. For more concerning the three Houston physicians, see Pat Ireland Nixon, *The Medical Story of Early Texas, 1528–1853* ([Lancaster, PA].: Published by the Mollie Bennett Lupe Memorial Fund, 1946), 445, 463; see also Joseph D. McCutchan, *Mier Expedition Diary: A Texan Prisoners Account*, edited by Joseph Milton Nance (Austin: University of Texas Press, 1978), 60–61.

38 Gatrell, *The Hanging Tree*, 263, 518. English courts sanctioned hanging in chains—or gibbeting—from the Murder Act of 1752 until 1834. According to custom, executioners placed the remains of hanged felons in metal cages, which conserved them against the elements or efforts to recover them. Normally, authorities gibbeted the body near the crime scene as a warning to others. Since officials intended the gibbeted corpse to be a deterrent, they worried that decomposition might occur too quickly. They, therefore, ordered executioners to dip the remains in tar to preserve them for maximum exposure. Bodies remained on view for months until the bones collapsed. Gibbeting, as such, never caught on in the United States. Americans, however, occasionally displayed criminal remains—or at least parts of them—as admonitions. In 1799, Moses Stegall decapitated the notorious frontier serial killer, Micajah "Big" Harpe, with the same butcher knife the murderer had used to dispatch many of his victims. Would that all justice be so poetic. Afterward, Stegall nailed Harpe's head to a tree in Highland Lick, Kentucky. "The spot is still called 'Harpes Head,' and for many years the skull hung there, rotted and rain–whitened, grinning down at the traveler." For more on the crimes of the Harpe brothers, see Robert M. Coates, *The Outlaw Years: the History of the Land Pirates of the Natchez Trace* (New York: The Macaulay Company, 1930).

NOTES   257

39 Legislation quoted in Leon Radzinowich, *A History of English Common Law* 5 vols. (London: Stevens and Sons Limited, 1943), 1:206.

40 Binding books in human skin was so common, that bibliophiles even have a term to describe it: anthropodermic bibliopegy. According to English historian V. A. C. Gatrell, visitors to the Bury St. Edmunds museum may still view this flesh-bound volume "neatly exhibited in a glass case." *Bell's Life in London*, May 24, 1829, quoted in Gatrell, *The Hanging Tree*, 257.

41 Suzanne M. Shultz, *Body Snatching: The Robbing of Graves for the Education of Physicians in Early Nineteenth Century America* (McFarland & Company, Inc., Publishers, 1992), 13.

42 Ibid., ix, 14–21, 31–32, 41.

43 Ambrose Bierce, *The Devil's Dictionary* (New York: Oxford University Press, 1999), 69. Grave robbing is not entirely a sin of the past. It has made a comeback, although today's "sack-'em-up-men" are more likely to harvest body parts rather than the entire cadaver. The 2004 passing of Alistair Cooke, the silver-haired host of "Masterpiece Theatre" from 1971 until his retirement in 1992, saddened many viewers who admired his wit and erudition. Yet, their grief turned to shock and outrage when his daughter, Susan Cooke Kittredge, revealed that, prior to his cremation, thieves stole his legs, the bones of which later sold for more than $7,000. Mrs. Kittredge lamented: "Just last week I discovered the unsettling details that it was my father's legs that were cut off and sold. To know his bones were sold was one thing, but to see him standing truncated before me is another thing . . . we remain haunted by the body's gruesome fate." New York authorities charged four men, including an embalmer and a dentist, with stealing skin, bones, heart valves, and assorted tissue from 1,077 corpses. According to published reports, there is a steady demand for "recycled" body parts. "A shoulder can fetch as much as $650. Knees go for between $450 and $650 each. A head with its brain intact can cost $900." "Corpse Thieves Thrive as 'Body Brokers'; $900 for Severed Head," Taphophilia website, www.taphophilia.com/modules.php?name =News&file=articles&sid=3147 [accessed April 4, 2007]; see also "Body-snatching gang cut legs off Alistair Cooke 'to sell bones,' *The Independent*, March 6, online at http://news.independent.co.uk/world/americas/article349595.ece [accessed April 2, 2007]. For a modern expose of the practice, see Annie Cheney, *Body Brokers: Inside the Underground Trade in Human Remains* (New York: Broadway Books, 2006).

258   NOTES

[44] John van Wyhe, "The History of Phrenology on the Web," online at *http://pages* *.britishlibrary.net/phrenology/overview.htm* [accessed December 28, 2007].

[45] Ibid.

[46] Phrenological orthodoxy maintained the size of the brain's "organ" determined a person's inclinations. Since the portion of Jones's brain that targeted anger and self-preservation (traits associated with "animal" behavior) was "well developed"—that is to say, large—he was innately inclined toward crime and violence. All the more so, since the portions of his brain that governed reason and morality were "very deficient." Phrenologists would have believed Jones a victim of his organs. Even if he had tried, he would have been unable to control his violent tendencies. In Herndon's opinion, science validated Judge Robinson's sentence: Jones was born to hang. Herndon Diary, March 29, 1838.

[47] Ibid., March 30, 1838.

[48] Ibid., March 31, 1838.

EPILOGUE

[1] *Telegraph and Texas Register* (Houston), March 31, 1838.

[2] Ibid.

[3] Ibid.

[4] *Morning Star* (Houston), May 11, 1839.

[5] Francis Richard Lubbock, *Six Decades in Texas, or Memoirs of Francis Richard Lubbock, Governor of Texas in War-time, 1861–63. A Personal Experience in Business, War, and Politics* (Austin: Ben C. Jones & Co. Printers, 1900), 57; "SAN JACINTO MONUMENT AND MUSEUM," *Handbook of Texas Online*, www.tsha.utexas.edu/handbook/online /articles/SS/lbs1.html [accessed February 20, 2007]; San Jacinto Museum of History website, www.sanjacinto-museum.org/Herzstein_Library/Veterans_Biographies /Browse_Biographies/biographies/default.asp?action=bio&id=3282 [accessed December 29, 2006]; Directors of the San Jacinto Monument have included Jones's name to the official list of veterans that they sell in the gift shop. See *The Honor Roll of the Battle of San Jacinto: The Complete List of Participants and Personnel on Detached Services* (La Porte: San Jacinto Museum of History Association, 1993), [6].

[6] John Hunter Herndon Papers, 1814–1872, Center for American History, University of Texas at Austin, Diary, 1837–1838, April 7, 1838. Hereinafter Herndon Diary.

[7] Andrew Forest Muir, ed., "Diary of a Young Man in Houston, 1838," *Southwestern Historical Quarterly*, 53 (January 1950), 279.

NOTES   259

8   "HERNDON, JOHN HUNTER," The Handbook of Texas Online, www.tsha.utexas
    .edu/handbook/online/articles/HH/fth30.html [accessed January 22, 2007].

9   "STIFF, EDWARD," The Handbook of Texas Online, www.tsha.utexas.edu/handbook/online
    /articles/SS/fst56.html [accessed January 23, 2007].

10 Telegraph and Texas Register (Houston), March 2, 1842.

11 John H. Jenkins, Basic Texas Books: An Annotated Bibliography of Selected Works for a
    Research Library (Austin: Jenkins Publishing Company, 1983), 525.

12 "DRESEL, GUSTAV," Handbook of Texas Online, www.tsha.utexas.edu/handbook
    /online/articles/DD/fdr2.html [accessed January 23, 2007].

13 James Wilson Nichols, Now You Hear My Horn: The Journal of James Wilson
    Nichols, 1820–1887, edited by Catherine W. McDowell (Austin: University of Texas
    Press, 1967), 60.

14 Dudley G. Wooten, A Comprehensive History of Texas, 1685 to 1897, 2 vols. (Dallas:
    William G. Scarff, 1898), 1:361–65.

15 Ibid. Robert Hall, Life of Robert Hall: Indian Fighter and Veteran of Three Great Wars, (Austin:
    Ben C. Jones & Company, 1898; rpt. ed., Austin: State House Press, 1992), 56.

16 "HUSTON, FELIX," The Handbook of Texas Online, www.tsha.utexas.edu
    /handbook/online/articles/HH/fhu46.html [accessed February 8, 2007].

17 Flora Agatha Davie, "The Early History of Houston, Texas," thesis, University
    of Texas at Austin, 1940, 44.

18 Telegraph and Texas Register (Houston), September 27, 1843; C. Richard King,
    Susanna Dickinson: Messenger of the Alamo (Austin: Shoal Creek Publishers,
    Inc., 1976), 63.

19 No. 3618, Peter Bellows vs. Susanna Bellows, 11th Judicial Court, Granted
    6/5/[18]57, recorded Vol. H, page 479, Minutes of Courts, Harris County.

20 King, Susanna Dickinson, 74–75, 87–90.

21 DICKINSON, ANGELINA ELIZABETH," The Handbook of Texas Online, www
    .tsha.utexas.edu/handbook/online/articles/DD/fdi36.html [accessed January 23,
    2007].

22 King, Susanna Dickinson, 117–19.

23 Rebecca Smith Lee, Mary Austin Holley: A Biography (Austin: University of Texas
    Press, 1962), 298–99, 312, 315–16, 323.

24 Ibid., 349, 362.

25 Adolphus Sterne, Hurrah for Texas!: The Diary of Adolphus Sterne, 1838–1851, edited
    by Archie P. McDonald (Austin: Eakin Press, 1986), 3; "DOUGLASS, KELSEY

260   NOTES

HARRIS," *Handbook of Texas Online*, www.tsha.utexas.edu/handbook/online/articles/DD/fdo25.html [accessed January 24, 2007]; William Ransom Hogan, *The Texas Republic: A Social and Economic History* (Norman: University of Oklahoma Press, 1946), 187.

26 Frank W. Johnson, *A History of Texas and Texans*, 5 vols. (Chicago: American Historical Society, 1916), 1:543.

27 Ibid., 2:1082–83.

28 Lubbock, *Six Decades in Texas*, 70.

29 "EPIDEMIC DISEASES," *Handbook of Texas Online*, www.tsha.utexas.edu/handbook/online/articles/EE/sme1.html [accessed January 27, 2007].

30 Elizabeth Silverthorne, *Ashbel Smith of Texas: Pioneer, Patriot, Statesman, 1805–1886* (College Station: Texas A&M University Press, 1982), 54–55.

31 John H. Jenkins, *Basic Texas Books: An Annotated Bibliography of Selected Works for a Research Library* (Austin: Jenkins Publishing Company, 1983), 493.

32 Silverthorne, *Ashbel Smith of Texas*, 147–59.

33 Ashbel Smith Journal, February 2, 1831, Ashbel Smith Papers, Center for American History, University of Texas at Austin; James L. Haley, *Sam Houston* (Norman: University of Oklahoma Press, 2002), 472, 50n.

34 Silverthorne, *Ashbel Smith of Texas*, 225.

35 Texas State Cemetery website, www.cemetery.state.tx.us/html/history.htm [accessed February 7, 2007].

36 Kemp Veteran Biographies, San Jacinto Museum of History website, www.sanjacinto-museum.org/Herzstein_library/ [accessed April 21, 2007].

37 Marilyn McAdams Sibley, *Lone Stars and State Gazettes: Texas Newspapers before the Civil War* (College Station: Texas A&M University Press, 1983), 84–110, 121, 161, 178, 188, 298–99; S. W. Geiser, "Note on Dr. Francis Moore (1808–1864)," *Southwestern Historical Quarterly* 47 (April 1944), 419–25; Dudley G. Wooten, ed., *A Comprehensive History of Texas, 1685 to 1897*, 2 vols. (Dallas: William G. Scarff, 1898; rpt. ed., Austin: Texas State Historical Association, 1986), 2:373–75; "FRANCIS MOORE, JR.," *Handbook of Texas Online*, www.tsha.utexas.edu/handbook/online/articles/MM/fmo26.html [accessed February 9, 2007].

38 *Telegraph and Texas Register* (Houston), April 17, 1839.

39 [Millie Gray], *The Diary of Millie Gray, 1832–1840 (nee Mildred Richards Stone, Wife of Wm. Fairfax Gray) Recording her Family Life before, during, and after Col. Wm. F. Gray's Journey to Texas in 1835, and the Small Journal giving Particulars of all that occurred during the Family's Voyage to Texas in 1838* (Houston: The Fletcher Young Publishing Company, 1967),

134; David G. McComb, *Houston: The Bayou City* (Austin: University of Texas Press, 1969), 88; Stanley Siegel, *A Political History of the Texas Republic, 1836–1845* (Austin: University of Texas Press, 1956), 112; D.W. Meinig, *Imperial Texas: An Interpretive Essay in Cultural Geography* (Austin: University of Texas Press,1969), 121.

[40] A colloquialism even in the 1830s, the word "callithumpian" has passed out of modern usage. At the time it meant "disturbers of order at Parliamentary elections" or "designating, pertaining to, or resembling a band of discordant instruments." Clearly, the Houston Callithumpian Society had both definitions covered. *Telegraph and Texas Register* (Houston), March 31, 1838; James Harper Starr, memo book, 1839–1840 to February 23, 1841, James Harper Starr Papers, 5–6 (typescript), Center for American History, University of Texas at Austin; *Morning Star* (Houston), September 18, 1839; Smith quoted in Silverthorne, *Ashbel Smith of Texas*, 54.

[41] HOUSTON, TEXAS," *Handbook of Texas Online*, www.tsha.utexas.edu/handbook/online/articles/HH/hdh.3.html [accessed January 24, 2007].

[42] "HOUSTON SHIP CHANNEL," *Handbook of Texas Online*, www.tsha.utexas.edu/handbook/online/articles/HH/rhh11.html [accessed January 29, 2007].

[43] "HOUSTON, TEXAS," *Wikipedia Online*, http://en.wikipedia.org/wiki/Houston_Texas [accessed January 29, 2007].

[44] T. S. Eliot, *Murder in the Cathedral* (New York: Harcourt, Brace and Company, 1935), 44.

Chronology

1835

OCTOBER

2   Texian settlers grapple with centralist troops outside Gonzales, in the opening skirmish of the War for Texas Independence.

28   Texian volunteers under James Bowie and James W. Fannin, Jr., are victorious in a battle near Mission Concepción, outside San Antonio de Béxar.

DECEMBER

1–9   Texian volunteers under Ben Milam and Francis W. Johnson storm Béxar and engage in intense house-to-house fighting.

10   Brigadier General Martín Perfecto de Cos, commander of the centralist garrison, surrenders Béxar and agrees to withdraw his troops south of the Rio Grande. With this victory, many Texians naively believe the war is finished and return to their homes.

21   David James Jones joins the Texas Auxiliary Volunteer Corps.

1836

JANUARY

3   Governor Henry Smith informs the Council that he has ordered Texian volunteers on an expedition against the town of Matamoros.

11   In a proclamation addressed to the "People of Texas," the General Council announces that it has impeached Governor Smith and declares James W.

264 CHRONOLOGY

Robinson acting governor. Smith, however, refuses to recognize the Council's authority to dismiss him and continues to issue orders as governor. Texians are unclear who, if any one, claims legal authority.

FEBRUARY

1–5 Fannin and his American volunteers march to Refugio to join the Matamoros Expedition.

2 James W. Fannin, Jr., lands at Copano Bay with some two hundred American volunteers.

9 David James Jones, a member of a ten-man squad of American volunteers, arrives in San Felipe de Austin. Don Carlos Barrett, chairman of the Advisory Committee of the General Council, dispatches the unit to Copano Bay where it is to join the Matamoros Expedition.

16 Generalissimo Antonio López de Santa Anna crosses the Rio Grande and drives his centralist force toward Béxar.

17 General José Cosme de Urrea fords the Rio Grande at Matamoros with five hundred men and advances northward up the Atascosito Road.

23 Santa Anna arrives in Béxar and begins the thirteen-day siege of the Alamo.

24 Jones and the other members of the squad that departed San Felipe on February 9, arrive in Goliad by this date. Jones joins the San Antonio Greys, which, after February 15, Captain Samuel O. Pettus commands.

27 Urrea surprises Francis W. Johnson and his command at San Patricio. Johnson escapes but Urrea's force kills or captures most of the Texian garrison.

MARCH

2 Texian delegates at the Town of Washington declare Texas independence. General Urrea ambushes Dr. James Grant's command at El Puerto de Los Cuates de Agua Dulce.

4 Delegates confirm Sam Houston as commander of all Texian military forces.

6 Santa Anna launches a final assault on the Alamo. His soldiers kill every Texian combatant.

11 Colonel James W. Fannin, Jr., commander of the Goliad garrison, orders Captain Amon King to Refugio to evacuate Texian settlers.

12 King's men skirmish with Urrea's ranchero scouts.

CHRONOLOGY 265

13   King, still in Refugio, sends a courier to Fannin to request reinforcements. Fannin dispatches the Georgia Battalion to assist King.

14   Urrea arrives in Refugio at the head of 1,500 soldados. The Georgia Battalion manages a getaway, but King's men fall captive.

16   Urrea orders the execution of King and his men. Delegates of the Independence Convention adopt the constitution of the Republic of Texas. Officers of the ad interim government take their oaths of office. In the early morning hours of March 17, the Convention concludes its business and hurriedly adjourns.

17   In Goliad, Fannin learns of the Refugio debacle.

19   Fannin abandons Fort Defiance and retreats toward Victoria. Urrea's forces overtake Fannin's command on the open prairie and the battle of Coleto Creek ensues. David James Jones experiences his first combat.

20   Fannin surrenders to General Urrea, who marches the Texian prisoners of war back to Fort Defiance.

27   In what becomes infamous as the Goliad Massacre, Mexican soldiers gun down some 342 Texian prisoners of war. Jones escapes the slaughter.

APRIL

1   David James Jones joins Houston's army at Groce's Landing.

20   Texian and Mexican forces arrive at Lynch's Ferry. An exchange of artillery fire and a clash of cavalry prove indecisive.

21   Texians assault the Mexican camp and win the battle of San Jacinto. Although attached to Captain Joseph B. Chance's company, which Houston directs to serve as baggage guard at Camp Harrisburg, Jones ignores that order and participates in the battle.

22   Texians capture Santa Anna, who orders the withdrawal of all Mexican forces from Texas.

26   The undefeated remnant of the Mexican army begins its retreat toward the Rio Grande.

MAY

14   Santa Anna and ad interim President David G. Burnet sign the Treaties of Velasco, which establishes the Rio Grande as the southern boundary of Texas. The Mexican government subsequently refuses to ratify the treaties.

266   CHRONOLOGY

18   Comanche, Kiowa, and Kichai warriors attack Fort Parker and kill or kidnap several of its inhabitants. The attack heralds the beginning of almost forty years of Comanche–Texian conflict.

JUNE

1   Texian officials place Santa Anna aboard the schooner *Invincible*, moored at the mouth of the Brazos River, for return to Mexico.

2   At Goliad, General Thomas J. Rusk conducts a military funeral for the victims of the March 27 massacre.

3   An angry mob, including newly arrived volunteers from New Orleans, defy Burnet and forcibly remove Santa Anna from the *Invincible*. The incident further illustrates the weakness of the ad interim government.

4   Army units demand redress in a threatening letter to ad interim President Burnet.

JULY

1   David James Jones enrolls in Captain Elliott's Company. He eventually serves three months.

2   Felix Houston and Rezin P. Bowie arrive in Texas at the head of five to seven hundred U.S. volunteers.

18   Major General Mirabeau B. Lamar resigns as commander-in-chief of the Texian Army when the volunteers refuse to accept him in the position.

23   Ad interim President David G. Burnet issues an election proclamation for September. Texians will elect national and county officials, ratify the constitution, and consider the issue of annexation in a straw vote. Candidates for office begin active campaigning.

AUGUST

30   Augustus and John Allen run an ad in the *Telegraph and Texas Register* advertising the "Town of Houston" as the "great interior commercial emporium of Texas." On this date, no town yet exists.

SEPTEMBER

1   Texians go to the polls and elect Sam Houston president with 5,119 votes. Henry Smith receives 743 and Stephen F. Austin only garners 587. Mirabeau B. Lamar wins election as vice president. In the straw vote, Texians favor annexation to the

United States by a vote of more than 6,000. Only 93 voters oppose. According to constitutional dictate, the newly elected candidates are to assume office on the second Monday in December.

OCTOBER

1   The First Congress of the Republic of Texas convenes at Columbia. David James Jones receives his honorable discharge from the army of the Republic of Texas.

21 Ad interim Vice President Lorenzo de Zavala resigns.

22 Under enormous pressure—and ignoring the constitutional niceties—Burnet resigns as ad interim president, allowing Houston to take the oath as the first constitutionally elected president of the Republic of Texas. Lamar also takes the oath as vice president. Houston names his cabinet: Stephen F. Austin as secretary of state, Henry Smith as secretary of the treasury, Thomas J. Rusk as secretary of war, S. Rhoads Fisher as secretary of the navy, James Pinckney Henderson as attorney general, and Robert Barr as postmaster general.

NOVEMBER

23 President Houston orders the release of Santa Anna. The former dictator travels to Washington, DC, where he pledges to work on behalf of Texas with President Andrew Jackson. After meetings with Old Hickory, which accomplish little, Santa Anna, who has now fallen out of favor in Mexico City, returns to his homeland aboard a U.S. Navy vessel.

30 Meeting in Columbia, the Texas Congress chooses the town of Houston as the temporary seat of government until at least 1840.

DECEMBER

20 President Houston appoints Felix Huston junior brigadier general and temporary commander of the Texas Army.

27 Stephen F. Austin dies of pneumonia at Columbia; James Pinckney Henderson succeeds him as secretary of state.

1837

JANUARY

1   Francis R. Lubbock arrives at the Houston town site in a yawl. The steamboat *Laura*, the first to dock at the new town, follows later in the day.

CHRONOLOGY

18 Captain Robert Boyce arrives in Houston. He finds only a scattered array of "clapboard camps and tents."

FEBRUARY

7 General Felix Huston seriously wounds General Albert Sidney Johnston in a duel.

16 Citizens of Houston suffer bitterly cold temperatures; on this date, the mercury plummets to "within ten degrees of zero."

MARCH

3 The United States recognizes Texas independence when President Andrew Jackson signs the congressional resolution and appoints Alcée La Branche as chargé d'affaires to the Republic of Texas.

APRIL

1 Contractor Thomas William Ward and his crew begin construction of national capitol at Main Street and Texas Avenue.

21 Houston society celebrates the first anniversary of the battle of San Jacinto with an elaborate ball. Citizens also mark the date by erecting a tall flagpole in the middle of town.

28 Writing his friend Robert A. Irion, President Houston claims that his namesake town has grown to 100 houses and 1500 residents.

MAY

2 The first issue of the *Telegraph and Texas Register* published in Houston hits the streets.

4 Ornithologist James J. Audubon visits President Houston in his presidential mansion, a "small log house consisting of two rooms."

5 The Texas Congress convenes at Houston following a five-day delay to allow the completion of a temporary cover for the roofless Capitol building.

18 President Houston, acting through Secretary of War William S. Fisher, furloughs the Texian Army to shut down General Felix Huston's scheme to invade Mexico.

CHRONOLOGY 269

JUNE

18 The New Orleans *Daily Picayune* reports that the town of Houston "is falling faster than it has risen."

12 Houstonians suffer the effects of a blistering summer. On this date, President Houston writes, "God keep me clear of the heat of the natural as well as the political season."

25 Dr. Chauncey Goodrich kills Levi L. Laurens in a duel that appalls most Houstonians.

JULY

8   Dr. Ashbel Smith reports that Houston now "contains a handsome Capitol, about 200 houses and more than 2000 inhabitants."

AUGUST

4   Texas minister to the United States Memucan Hunt petitions for Texas annexation. Three weeks later, U.S. Secretary of State John Forsyth replies with a resounding rejection.

SEPTEMBER

15 The *Telegraph and Texas Register* reports the murder of Dr. Chauncey Goodrich. Few in Houston mourn his passing.

30 President Houston approves a joint resolution of the Texas Congress suspending the opening of the General Land Office.

OCTOBER

27 Houston descends into squalor. On this date, Representative Kelsey H. Douglass condemns Houston as the "most misera[b]le place in the world."

NOVEMBER

11 David James Jones stabs Mandred Wood.

19 Reverend Littleton Fowler arrives in Houston and, to his dismay, finds "much vice, gaming, drunkenness, and profanity the commonest."

27 Susanna Dickinson marries John Williams.

CHRONOLOGY

DECEMBER

5 Twenty-six of Houston's finest gentlemen meet in the capitol building to organize the Philosophical Society of Texas.

20 Twenty-eight representatives of three Masonic lodges in Texas assemble in Houston to organize the Grand Lodge of the Republic of Texas. President Houston chairs the meeting; members elect Dr. Anson Jones Grand Master. Although less than a year old, the town already boasts three Masonic lodges.

25 Mary Austin Holley is a guest in the elegantly furnished home of Augustus and Charlotte Allen. Reports of an impending Mexican invasion roil the capital. The rumors prove false.

1838

JANUARY

20 In the pages of the *Telegraph and Texas Register*, Moore proposes the death penalty for Jones and Quick. The pair has yet to stand trial.

FEBRUARY

4 Houston's weather is bitterly cold. John Hunter Herndon records: "Several persons freeze to death."

17 Robert H. Watson drinks whiskey out of a skull "that had yet brains in it."

MARCH

19 Houston court indicts David James Jones for murder.

22 David James Jones stands trial. The jury takes an hour to return a guilty verdict.

23 John C. C. Quick stands trial for murder; the jury takes twenty minutes to find him guilty.

24 Judge James W. Robinson sentences Jones and Quick to hang on the following Wednesday.

25 While awaiting his execution Jones attempts to shoot himself; he botches the attempt.

27 Houston society celebrates the second anniversary of the Goliad Massacre with a commemorative ball.

28 That afternoon, Jones and Quick meet their scheduled appointment with the hangman and swing off the cart at two o'clock. That night, five of Houston's most

CHRONOLOGY 271

distinguished gentlemen return to the gallows to exhume the corpses of Jones and Quick. They decapitate the bodies and return to town with their bagged specimens.

31 After painstaking examination, John Hunter Herndon disposes of the severed heads of Jones and Quick.

APRIL

1 In Houston, Herndon records: "Strong evidences of reformation in this city."

16 The Grand Lodge of the Republic of Texas of the Masonic Order holds its first meeting in Houston. Grand Master Anson Jones presides.

MAY

1 Cherokee Chief Bowl (also spelled "Bowles") visits the town of Houston.

2 The *Texas and Telegraph Register* reports that the Texas Senate has authorized a loan of five million dollars.

JUNE

11 The first professional stock company in Houston opens its season with a production of the Sheridan Knowles comedy, *The Hunchback*. The company holds its performance in a building provided by local merchant, John Carlos. The players open by singing the new National Texian Anthem, which was explicitly written for the occasion.

JULY

21 The *Telegraph and Texas Register* reports, "The Comanches near Bexar have become quite hostile. They have lately committed many depredations in the neighborhood of that city and Gonzales."

AUGUST

11 The *Telegraph and Texas Register* announces that the town's theater will close for the season, to reopen in October or November.

272   CHRONOLOGY

SEPTEMBER

2   Texians go to the polls and elect General Mirabeau B. Lamar president. Lamar wins in a landslide, receiving 6,995 votes. Sam Houston's token candidate, Robert Wilson, receives 252 votes.

18   In Baltimore, Maryland, *American Museum* magazine publishes Edgar Allan Poe's short story "Ligeia." Set in an old castle redolent with moldy tapestries and "verdant decay," it embraces the conventions of traditional gothic horror.

NOVEMBER

17   Mayor Moore reportas that a "vessel richly freighted with British manufactured articles is now on her way from Liverpool to Galveston. We trust this is the harbinger of brighter days for Texian commerce."

DECEMBER

8   The *Telegraph and Texas Register* reports the circulation of "spurious bank bills" and counterfeited land scrip."

10   Mirabeau B. Lamar takes the oath as second president of the Republic.

1839

JANUARY

5   The Fourth Congress of the Republic passes an act establishing a public education system.

FEBRUARY

13   Bernard E. Bee announces his resignation as the Republic's secretary of state to accept an appointment as its Minister to the United States.

MARCH

29   A Texian unit under Edward Burleson intercepts a detachment of Mexican spies led by Vicente Córdova, who is attempting to incite Texas Indians to attack the Republic. Cordova escapes, but twenty of his men fall in the fight.

APRIL

13   Commissioners select the village of Waterloo as the site for the new capital. The village changes its name to Austin, to honor the "Father of Texas."

MAY

8   Representative of the Lamar administration, Bernard E. Bee arrives in Vera Cruz to seek peace and recognition from the Mexican government. His efforts prove unsuccessful.

26 Rangers under Captain John Bird engage Comanches on the Little River.

JUNE

9   Francis Moore, Jr., announces his candidacy for a seat in the Senate representing the Second District.

JULY

8   Lieutenant Edwin Ward Moore, age twenty-eight, tenders his resignation from the U.S. Navy to become commodore of the Texas Navy.

9   Texians and Cherokees clash at the battle of the Neches. Sam Houston's friend, Chief Bowl falls in the fight.

AUGUST

14 The *Telegraph and Texas Register* reports that Texian soldiers refuse to fight as infantry. "This great desire to be mounted on horseback, is doing our service more injury than every thing else."

SEPTEMBER

25 France signs a commercial treaty that recognizes the independence of the Texas Republic; Alphonse de Saligny wins appointment as chargé d'affaires.

OCTOBER

17 Republic officials arrive in Austin, which officially becomes the capital. Houston's tenure as the "temporary capital" becomes a part of history.

Bibliography

PRIMARY MATERIALS

MANUSCRIPTS

A. J. Houston Collection, Texas State Library and Archives, Austin.

Audited Republic Claims, Archives and Information Services Division, Texas State Library and Archives, Austin.

Davis (Andrew) Narrative, undated, Archives and Manuscripts, Center for American History, University of Texas at Austin.

Dickson Family Papers, Manuscript Collection, Daughters of the Republic of Texas Library at the Alamo.

Douglass (Kelsey H.) Papers, undated, Archives and Manuscripts, Center for American History, University of Texas at Austin.

Herndon (John Hunter) Papers, 1814–1872, Archives and Manuscripts, Center for American History, The University of Texas at Austin.

Houston (Sam) Papers, Catholic Archives of Texas, Chancery of the Austin Diocese, Austin.

Smith (Ashbel) Papers, 1830–1850, Archives and Manuscripts, Center for American History, The University of Texas at Austin.

Starr (James Harper) Papers, Archives and Manuscripts, Center for American History, The University of Texas at Austin.

Valentine O. King Collection, Texas State Library, Austin.

276   BIBLIOGRAPHY

NEWSPAPERS

Houston Chronicle, 2007.

[Houston] Morning Star, 1839.

[Houston] Telegraph and Texas Register, 1837–1839.

[New Orleans] Daily Picayune, 1837–1838.

Victoria Advocate, 2007

BOOKS

Barker, Eugene C., ed. The Austin Papers. 2 vols. Washington, DC: Government Printing
Office, 1924, 1928; 3rd vol. Austin: University of Texas, 1927.

Barnard, Joseph H. Dr. J. H. Barnard's Journal, December 1836–June 1836. Ed. and annotated
by Hobart Huson. n.p.: Goliad Bicentennial Edition, 1949.

Boswell, James. Boswell's London Journal, 1762–1763. Edited by Frederick A. Pottle. New
York: McGraw-Hill Book Company, Inc., 1950.

Breeden, James O., ed. A Long Ride in Texas: The Explorations of John Leonard Riddell. College
Station: Texas A&M University Press, 1994.

Brown, John Henry. Indian Wars and Pioneers of Texas. Austin, L. E. Daniel, Publisher,
[1892–1893]; reprint ed., Austin: State House Press, 1988.

[Coleman, Robert M.] Houston Displayed; or, Who Won the Battle of San Jacinto? By a Farmer in
the Army. Velasco Herald, 1837. Reprint, Austin: Brick Row Book Shop, 1964.

Daughters of the Republic of Texas. Muster Rolls of the Texas Revolution. Lubbock: Printed
by Craftsman Printers, Inc., 1986.

Day, James M., comp. The Texas Almanac, 1857–1873: A Compendium of Texas History. Waco:
Texian Press, 1967.

De Cordova, Jacob. Texas: Her Resources and Her Public Men: A Companion for J. De Cordova's
New and Correct Map of the State of Texas. Philadelphia: Printed by E. Crozet, Cor.
Thirteenth & Market, 1858. Reprint, Waco: Texian Press, 1969.

Dresel, Gustav. Houston Journal: Adventures in North America and Texas, 1837–1841. Translated
by Max Freund. Austin: University of Texas Press, 1954.

Duval, John C. Early Times in Texas, or the Adventures of Jack Dobell. Austin: H. P. N.
Gammell & Co., Publishers, 1892.

Ehrenberg, Hermann. With Milam and Fannin: Adventures of a German Boy in Texas's
Revolution. Dallas: Tardy Publishing Company, Inc., 1935.

Erath, George B. The Memoirs of Major George B. Erath, 1813–1891: As Dictated to Lucy A. Erath.
Waco: The Heritage Society of Waco, 1923; reprinted 1956.

BIBLIOGRAPHY 277

Gouge, William M. *The Fiscal History of Texas: Embracing an Account of its Revenues, Debts, and Currency from the Commencement of the Revolution in 1834 to 1851–52, With Remarks on American Debts.* Philadelphia: Lippincott, Grambo, and Co., 1852, Reprint, New York: Burt Franklin, 1969.

[Gray, Millie]. *The Diary of Millie Gray, 1832–1840 (nee Mildred Richards Stone, Wife of Col. Wm. Fairfax Gray) Recording her Family Life Before, During and After Col. Wm. F. Gray's Journey to Texas in 1835, and the Small Journal Giving Particulars of all that Occurred during the Family's Voyage to Texas in 1838.* Houston: The Fletcher Young Publishing Company, 1967.

Gray, William Fairfax. *The Diary of William Fairfax Gray: From Virginia to Texas, 1835–1837.* Edited from the original manuscript, with an Introduction and notes, by Paul Lack. Dallas: De Golyer Library & William P. Clements Center for Southwest Studies, Southern Methodist University, 1997.

Green, Rena Maverick, ed. *Samuel Maverick, Texan: 1803–1870. A Collection of Letters, Journals and Memoirs.* San Antonio: Privately Printed, 1952.

Gulick, Charles Adams, Jr., ed. *The Papers of Mirabeau Buonaparte Lamar.* 6 vols. Austin: Texas State Library, 1922.

Hall, Robert. *Life of Robert Hall: Indian Fighter and Veteran of Three Wars.* Austin: Ben C. Jones & Company, 1898. Reprint, Austin: State House Press, 1992.

Hansen, Todd, ed. *The Alamo Reader: A Study in History.* Mechanicsburg, PA: Stackpole Books, 2003.

Hatcher, Mattie Austin. *Letters of an Early American Traveller: Mary Austin Holley, Her Life and Her Works, 1784–1846.* Dallas: Southwest Press, 1933.

Holley, Mary Austin. *The Texas Diary, 1835–1838.* Edited with an introduction by J. P. Bryan. Austin: The Humanities Research Center, University of Texas, 1965.

Honor Roll of the Battle of San Jacinto: The Complete List of Participants and Personnel on Detached Services. La Porte: San Jacinto Museum of History Association, 1993.

Houstoun, Matilda Charlotte (Jesse) Fraser. *Texas and the Gulf of Mexico; or, Yachting in the New World.* Edited by Marilyn McAdams Sibley. Philadelphia: G. B. Zieber &. Co., 1845. Reprint, Austin: W. Thomas Taylor, 1991.

Johnson, Frank W. *A History of Texas and Texans.* 5 vols. Chicago: American Historical Society, 1916.

Johnston, William Preston. *The Life of General Albert Sidney Johnston, Embracing His Services in the Armies of the United States, The Republic of Texas, and the Confederate States.* New Introduction by T. Michael Parrish. New York: Da Capo Press, 1997.

278   BIBLIOGRAPHY

Jones, Anson. *Memoranda and Official Correspondence Relating to the Republic of Texas, Its History and Annexation: Including a Brief Autobiography of the Author.* New York: D. Appleton & Company, Inc., 1859.

Kennedy, William. *Texas: The Rise, Progress, and Prospects of the Republic of Texas.* London: R. Hastings, 1841; reprint ed., Fort Worth: Molyneaux Craftsmen, 1925.

Lawrence, A. B. *Texas in 1840: or the Emigrant's Guide to the New Republic.* New York: W. W. Allen, 1840.

Lubbock, Francis R. *Six Decades in Texas; or, Memoirs of Francis Richard Lubbock, Governor of Texas in War Time, 1861–63. A Personal Experience in Business, War, and Politics.* Edited by C. W. Raines. Austin: Ben C. Jones & Co., 1900.

Maillard, Nicholas Doran P. *The History of the Republic of Texas, From the Discovery of the Country to the Present Time; and the Cause of Her Separation from the Republic of Mexico.* London: Smith, Elder, and Co., 1842.

Manford, Erasmus. *Twenty-five Years in the West.* Chicago: E. Manford Publisher, 1867.

McCutchan, Joseph D. *Mier Expedition Diary: A Texan Prisoner's Account.* Edited by Joseph Milton Nance. Austin: University of Texas Press, 1978.

Mier y Terán, Manuel de. *Texas by Terán: The Diary Kept by General Manuel de Mier y Terán on his 1828 Inspection of Texas.* Edited by Jack Jackson. Austin: University of Texas Press, 2000.

Morrell, Z. N. *Fruits and Flowers from the Wilderness.* Boston: Gould and Lincoln, 1872.

Muir, Andrew Forest, ed. *Texas in 1837: An Anonymous, Contemporary Narrative.* Austin: University of Texas Press, 1958.

Nichols, James Wilson. *Now You Hear My Horn: The Journal of James Wilson Nichols, 1820–1887.* Edited by Catherine W. McDowell. Austin: University of Texas Press, 1967.

Sheridan, Francis C. *Galveston Island, Or, a Few Months off the Coast of Texas: The Journal of Francis Sheridan, 1839–1840.* Edited by Willis W. Pratt. Austin: University of Texas Press, 1954.

Smither, Harriet, ed. *Journals of the Fourth Congress of the Republic of Texas, 1839–1840.* 3 vols. Austin: Von Boeckman-Jones Co., 1929.

Sterne, Adolphus. *Hurrah for Texas!: The Diary of Adolphus Sterne, 1838–1851.* Edited by Archie P. McDonald. Austin: Eakin Press, 1986.

Stiff, Edward. *The Texan Emigrant: Being a Narration of the Adventures of the Author in Texas, and a Description of the Soil, Climate, Productions, Minerals, Towns, Bays, Harbors, Rivers, Institutions, and Manners and Customs of the Inhabitants of that Country; Together With* the Principal Incidents of Fifteen Years Revolution in Mexico: and Embracing a Condensed Statement of Interesting Events in Texas, From the First European Settlement in 1692, Down to the Year 1840. Cincinnati: G. Conclin, 1840.

Swisher, Col. John M. *The Swisher Memoirs*. Edited by Rena Maverick Green. San Antonio: The Sigmund Press, Inc., 1932.

Travis, William B. *The Diary of William Barret Travis: August 30, 1833–June 26, 1834*. Edited by Robert E. Davis. Waco: Texian Press, 1966.

Trollope, Francis. *Domestic Manners of the Americans*. Edited by Donald Smalley. New York: Alfred A. Knopf, 1949.

Wallis, Jonnie Lockhart, and Laurance L. Hill, eds. *Sixty Years on the Brazos: The Life and Letters of Dr. John Washington Lockhart*. Los Angeles: Dunn Brothers, 1930.

Webster, Noah. *An American Dictionary of the English Language: Intended to Exhibit. I. The Origin, Affinities and Primary Signification of English Words, as Far as They Have Been Ascertained. II. The Genuine Orthography and Pronunciation of Words, According to General Usage, or to Just Principles of Analogy. III. Accurate and Discriminating Definitions, With Numerous Authorities and Illustrations. To Which are Prefixed, an Introductory Dissertation on the Origin, History and Connection of the Languages of Western Asia and of Europe, and a Concise Grammar of the English Language*. New York: Published by S. Converse, 1828. Reprint, San Francisco: Foundations for American Christian Education, 1967 and 1995.

Williams, Amelia W. and Eugene C. Barker, eds. *The Writings of Sam Houston, 1813*. 8 vols. Austin: University of Texas Press, 1938–1943.

Wooten, Dudley. *Comprehensive History of Texas, 1685–1897*. 2 vols. Dallas: William G. Scarff, 1898. Reprint, Austin: Texas State Historical Association, 1986.

Yoakum, Henderson. *History of Texas From its First Settlement in 1685 to its Annexation to the United States in 1846*. 2 vols. New York: Redfield, 1855.

PERIODICALS

American Turf Register and Sporting Magazine, Vol. 9, No. 12 (December 1838).

Arthur, Dora Fowler, ed. "Jottings from the Old Journal of Littleton Fowler." *Quarterly of the Texas State Historical Association*, 2 (July 1898), 73–84.

Cox, C. C. "Reminiscences of C. C. Cox." *Southwestern Historical Quarterly* 6 (October 1902): 113–38.

Frantz, Joe B., ed. "Moses Lapham: His Life and Some Selected Correspondence." *Southwestern Historical Quarterly* 54 (January 1951): 324–332; (April 1951): 462–75.

Muir, Andrew Forest, ed. "Diary of a Young Man in Houston, 1838." *Southwestern Historical Quarterly* 53 (January 1950): 276–307.

"Reminiscences of Mrs. Dilue Harris." *Quarterly of the Texas State Historical Association* 4 (October 1900): 85–125; (January 1903): 204–35; 7 (January 1904): 214–22.

SECONDARY MATERIALS

BOOKS

Allen, Dr. O. F. *The City of Houston From Wilderness to Wonder.* No Place: privately printed, no date), 1–2.

Bailey, Brian. *Hangmen of England: A History of Execution from Jack Ketch to Albert Pierrepoint.* New York: Barnes & Noble Books, 1989.

Bancroft, Hubert Howe. *History of the North Mexican States and Texas.* 2 vols. San Francisco: The History Company, Publishers, 1889.

Barker, Eugene Campbell. *The Life of Stephen F. Austin, Founder of Texas, 1793–1836: A Chapter in the Westward Movement of the Anglo-American People.* Dallas: Cokesbury Press, Importers, 1925. Reprint, Austin: Texas State Historical Association, 1949.

Barr, Alwyn. *Black Texans: A History of African Americans in Texas, 1528–1995.* Austin: Jenkins Book Publishing Company, Inc., 1973; 2nd edition, Norman: University of Oklahoma Press, 1996.

———. *Texans in Revolt: The Battle for San Antonio, 1835.* Austin: University of Texas Press, 1990.

Beeth, Howard and Cary D. Wintz, eds. *Black Dixie: Afro-Texan History and Culture in Houston.* College Station: Texas A&M University Press, 1992.

Bierce, Ambrose. *The Devil's Dictionary.* (New York: Oxford University Press, 1999.

Billington, Ray Allen. *America's Frontier Heritage.* New York: Holt, Rinehart and Winston. 1966.

Biographical Directory of the American Congress, 1794–1927. Washington, DC: United States Government Printing Office, 1928.

Buchanan, James E., comp. and ed. *Houston: A Chronological & Documentary History.* Dobbs Ferry, New York: Oceana Publications, Inc., 1975.

Bruce, Jr., Dickson D. *Violence and Culture in the Antebellum South.* Austin: University of Texas Press, 1979.

Cantrell, Gregg. *Stephen F. Austin: Empresario of Texas.* New Haven: Yale University Press, 1999.

Cash, W. J. *The Mind of the South.* New York: Alfred A. Knopf, 1941.

BIBLIOGRAPHY   281

Cawthorne, Nigel. *Public Executions*. London: Arcturus Publishing Limited, 2006. Reprint, Edison, New Jersey: Chartwell Books, Inc., a Division of Book Sales, Inc., 2006.

Chartrand, René. *Santa Anna's Mexican Army, 1821–48*. Oxford: Osprey Publishing Ltd., 2004.

Cheney, Annie. *Body Brokers: Inside the Underground Trade in Human Remains*. New York: Broadway Books, 2006.

Clark, Sara. *The Capitols of Texas: A Visual History*. Austin: The Encino Press, 1975.

Coates, Robert M. *The Outlaw Years: The History of the Land Pirates of the Natchez Trace*. New York: The Macaulay Company, 1930.

Connor, Seymour V. *Adventure in Glory*. Austin: Steck-Vaughn Company, 1965.

Crisp, James E. *Sleuthing the Alamo: Davy Crockett's Last Stand and Other Mysteries of the Texas Revolution*. New York: Oxford University Press, 2005.

Daniels, A. P. *Texas Avenue at Main Street: The Chronological Story of a City Block in Houston, The Most Significant Block in the History of Texas. An informal but factual history of the block now occupied by the Rice Hotel, site of the Capitol Building of the Republic of Texas when Sam Houston was President*. Houston: Allen Press, 2803 Fannin, A Division of Allen Printing and Letter Service, Publishers, 1964.

Davis, John L. *Houston: A Historical Portrait*. Austin: The Encino Press, 1983.

Davis, William C. *Lone Star Rising: The Revolutionary Birth of the Texas Republic*. New York: Free Press, 2004.

——— *A Way Through the Wilderness: The Natchez Trace and the Civilization of the Southern Frontier*. New York: Harper Collins Publishers, 1995.

De Bruhl, Marshall. *Sword of San Jacinto: A Life of Sam Houston*. New York: Random House, 1993.

Dixon, Sam Houston and Louis Wiltz Kemp. *The Heroes of San Jacinto*. Houston: The Anson Jones Press, 1932.

Dylan, Bob. *Chronicles*. New York: Simon & Schuster, 2004.

Eaton, Clement. *The Mind of the Old South*. Baton Rouge: Louisiana State University Press, 1967.

Eliot, T. S. *Murder in the Cathedral*. New York: Harcourt, Brace and Company, 1935.

Farrar, R. M. *The Story of Buffalo Bayou and the Houston Ship Channel*. Houston: Chamber of Commerce, [1926].

Frantz, Joe B. *Gail Borden: Dairyman to a Nation*. Norman: University of Oklahoma Press, 1951.

282   BIBLIOGRAPHY

———— and Mike Cox. *Lure of the Land: Texas County Maps and the History of Settlement.* College Station: Texas A&M University Press, 1988.

———— and David G. McComb. *Houston: A Student's Guide to Localized History.* New York: Teachers College Press, Columbia University, 1971.

Friend, Llerena B. *Sam Houston: The Great Designer.* Austin: University of Texas Press, 1954.

Funk, Charles Earle. *A Hog on Ice and Other Curious Expressions.* New York: Harper & Row, Publishers, 1948.

Gatrell, V. A. C. *The Hanging Tree: Execution and the English People, 1770–1868.* Oxford, U.K.: Oxford University Press, 1996.

Garrett, Julia Kathryn. *Green Flag Over Texas: A Story of the Last Years of Spain in Texas.* New York: The Cordova Press, 1939. Reprint, Austin: The Pemberton Press, [1969].

Graham, Philip. *Life and Poems of Mirabeau B. Lamar.* Chapel Hill: University of North Carolina Press, 1938.

Greenberg, Kenneth S. *Honor & Slavery: Lies, Duels, Noses, Masks, Dressing as Women, Gifts, Strangers, Humanitarianism, Death, Slave Rebellions, The Proslavery Argument, Baseball, Hunting and Gambling in the Old South.* Princeton: Princeton University Press, 1996.

Haley, James L. *Passionate Nation: The Epic History of Texas.* New York: Free Press, 2006.

———— *Sam Houston.* Norman: University of Oklahoma Press, 2002.

Hardin, Stephen L. *The Alamo 1836: Santa Anna's Texas Campaign.* Oxford: Osprey Publishing Ltd., 2001.

———— comp. and ed. *Lone Star: The Republic of Texas, 1836–1846.* Carlisle, Massachusetts: Discovery Enterprises, Ltd., 1998.

———— *Texian Iliad: A Military History of the Texas Revolution, 1835–1836.* Austin: University of Texas Press, 1994.

Harris County Historical Society. *Houston: A Nation's Capital, 1837–1839.* Houston: D. Armstrong Co., Inc., 1985.

Hickox, Ron G. *Collectors' Guide to Ames U.S. Contract Military Edged Weapons: 1832–1906.* Union City, TN: Pioneer Press, 1984, 1992.

Hogan, William Ransom. *The Texas Republic: A Social and Economic History.* Norman: University of Oklahoma Press, 1946.

Hollon, W. Eugene. *Frontier Violence: Another Look.* New York: Oxford University Press, 1974.

Huffines, Alan C. *Blood of Noble Men: The Alamo Siege & Battle, An Illustrated Chronology.* Austin: Eakin Press, 1999.

Jackson, Donald. *Voyages of the Steamboat Yellow Stone*. New York: Ticknor & Fields, 1985.

Jenkins, John H. *Basic Texas Books: An Annotated Bibliography of Selected Works for a Research Library*. Austin: Jenkins Publishing Company, 1983.

———— *Audubon and Other Capers: Confessions of a Texas Bookmaker*. Austin: The Pemberton Press, 1976.

Johnson, Allen and Dumas Malone, eds. *Dictionary of American Biography*. 20 vols. New York: Charles Scribner's Sons, 1937.

Johnson, Marguerite. *Houston: The Unknown City, 1836–1946*. College Station: Texas A&M University Press, 1991.

Jordan, Jonathan W. *Lone Star Navy: Texas, the Fight for the Gulf of Mexico, and the Shaping of the American West*. Washington, DC: Potomac Books, Inc., 2006.

Kane, Harnett T. *Gentlemen, Swords and Pistols*. New York: Bonanza Books, 1951.

Keegan, John. *The Face of Battle*. New York: The Viking Press, 1976.

Kellaway, Jean. *The History of Torture and Execution*. London: Mercury Books, 2005.

Kemp, Louis Wiltz. *The Signers of the Texas Declaration of Independence*. Salado, Texas: The Anson Jones Press, 1944.

King, C. Richard. *Susanna Dickinson: Messenger of the Alamo*. Austin: Shoal Creek Publishers, Inc., 1976.

King, Florence. *With Charity Toward None: A Fond Look at Misanthropy*. New York: St. Martin's Press, 1992.

Kopel, Hal. *Today in the Republic of Texas*. Waco: Texian Press, 1986.

Lack, Paul D. *The Texas Revolutionary Experience: A Political and Social History, 1835–1836*. College Station: Texas A&M University Press, 1992.

Lee, Rebecca Smith. *Mary Austin Holley: A Biography*. Austin: University of Texas Press, 1962.

Lindley, E. R., comp. *Biographical Directory of the Texan Conventions and Congresses*. Huntsville: Printed by order of the House of Representatives, 1941.

McClellan, Elisabeth. *History of American Costume, 1607–1870: With an Introductory Chapter on Dress in the Spanish and French Settlements in Florida and Louisiana*. New York: Tudor Publishing Company, 1942.

McComb, David G. *Houston: A History*. Austin: University of Texas Press, 1981.

———— *Houston: The Bayou City*. Austin: University of Texas Press, 1969.

McDonald, Archie P. *The Trail to San Jacinto*. Boston: American Press, 1982.

McGrane, Reginald Charles. *Panic of 1837: Some Financial Problems of the Jacksonian Era*. Chicago: University of Chicago Press, 1965.

284 BIBLIOGRAPHY

McLean, Malcolm D. *Fine Texas Horses: Their Pedigrees and Performance, 1836–1845.* Fort Worth: Texas Christian University Press, 1966.

Meinig, D. W. *Imperial Texas: An Interpretive Essay in Cultural Geography.* Austin: University of Texas Press, 1969.

Merk, Frederick. *Slavery and the Annexation of Texas.* New York: Alfred A. Knopf, 1972.

Miller, Edward L. *New Orleans and the Texas Revolution.* College Station: Texas A&M University Press, 2004.

Miller, Thomas Lloyd. *Bounty and Donation Land Grants of Texas, 1835–1888.* Austin: University of Texas Press, 1967.

Moore, Stephen L. *Eighteen Minutes: The Battle of San Jacinto and the Texas Independence Campaign.* Dallas: Republic of Texas Press, 2004.

Murry, Ellen N. *Notes On The Republic: An anthology of essays from the Star of the Republic Museum's quarterly journal, the Notes.* Washington, TX: Star of the Republic Museum, 1991.

Nackman, Mark E. *A Nation Within a Nation: The Rise of Texas Nationalism.* Port Washington, New York: Kennikat Press, 1975.

Nance, Joseph Milton. *After San Jacinto: The Texas-Mexican Frontier, 1836–1841.* Austin: University of Texas Press, 1963.

——— *Dare-Devils All: The Texan Mier Expedition, 1842–1844.* Austin: Eakin Press, 1998.

Neven, David. *The Texans.* New York: Time Life Books, 1975.

Nixon, Patrick Ireland. *The Medical Story of Early Texas, 1528–1853.* [Lancaster, Pa.]: Published by the Mollie Bennett Lupe Memorial Fund, 1946.

Nosworthy, Brent. *With Musket, Cannon and Sword: Battle Tactics of Napoleon and His Enemies.* New York: Sarpedon, 1996.

Oberste, William Herman. *Remember Goliad.* Austin: Von Boeckman-Jones Co., 1949.

O'Connor, Kathryn Stoner. *The Presidio La Bahía del Espiritu Santo de Zuniga, 1721–1846.* Austin: Von Boeckmann-Jones, 1966.

Phelps, Marie Lee. *A History of Early Houston.* Houston: The Harris County Heritage Society, 1959.

Pierce, Gerald S. *Texas Under Arms: The Camps, Posts, Forts, & Military Towns of the Republic of Texas, 1836–1846.* Austin: Encino Press, 1969.

Pohl, James W. *The Battle of San Jacinto.* Austin: Texas State Historical Association, 1989.

Pruett, Jakie L. and Everett B. Cole, Sr. *Goliad Massacre: A Tragedy of the Texas Revolution.* Austin: Eakin Press, 1985.

BIBLIOGRAPHY 285

Ransom, Harry Huntt. *The Other Texas Frontier.* Austin: University of Texas Press, 1984.

Reid, Stuart. *The Secret War for Texas.* College Station: Texas A&M University Press, 2007.

Remington, Frederic. *Men with the Bark on.* New York: Harper & Brothers Publishers, 1900.

Richardson, Ruth. *Death, Dissection and the Destitute.* 2nd ed. Chicago: University of Chicago Press, 1987, 2000.

Roberts, Randy and James S. Olson. *A Line in the Sand: The Alamo in Blood and Memory.* New York: The Free Press, 2001.

Roell, Craig H. *Remember Goliad!* Austin: Texas State Historical Association, 1994.

Roland, Charles P. *Albert Sidney Johnston: Soldier of Three Republics.* Austin: University of Texas Press, 1964.

Sanchez Lamego, Miguel A. *The Siege & Taking of the Alamo.* Santa Fe: Printed by The Blue Feather Press for The Press of the Territorian, 1968.

Santos, Richard G. *Santa Anna's Campaign Against Texas, 1835–1836: Featuring the Field Commands Issued to Major General Vicente Filisola.* Waco: Texian Press, 1968.

Schmitz, Joseph William. *Texas Culture, 1836–1846: In the Days of the Republic.* San Antonio: The Naylor Company, 1960.

Sharp, Roger. *The Jacksonians versus the Banks: Politics in the States after the Panic of 1837.* New York: Columbia University Press, 1970.

Shultz, Suzanne M. *Body Snatching: The Robbing of Graves for the Education of Physicians in Early Nineteenth Century America.* Jefferson, NC: McFarland & Company, Inc., Publishers, 1992.

Sibley, Marilyn McAdams. *Lone Stars and State Gazettes: Texas Newspapers before the Civil War.* College Station: Texas A&M University Press, 1983.

Siegel, Stanley. *A Political History of the Texas Republic, 1836–1845.* Austin: University of Texas Press, 1956.

Silverthorne, Elizabeth. *Ashbel Smith of Texas: Pioneer, Patriot, Statesman, 1805–1886.* College Station: Texas A&M University Press, 1982.

Thorp, Raymond W. *Bowie Knife.* Williamstown, New Jersey: Phillips Publications, 1991.

Tijerina, Andrés. *Tejanos & Texas Under the Mexican Flag, 1821–1836.* College Station: Texas A&M University Press, 1994.

Weber, David J. *The Mexican Frontier, 1821–1846: The American Southwest Under Mexico.* Albuquerque: University of New Mexico Press, 1982.

——— *Myth and the History of the Hispanic Southwest.* Albuquerque: University of New Mexico Press, 1988.

286 BIBLIOGRAPHY

Weems, John Edward. *Dream of Empire: A Human History of the Republic of Texas*, New York: Simon and Schuster, 1971.

────── *Men Without Countries: Three Adventurers of the Early Southwest*. Boston: Houghton Mifflin Company, 1969.

Wheeler, Kenneth W. *To Wear a City's Crown: The Beginnings of Urban Growth in Texas, 1836–1865*. Cambridge: Harvard University Press, 1968.

Willet, C. and Phillis Cunnington. *The History of Underclothes*. Mineola, NY: Dover Publications. Inc., 1992.

Williams, Jack K. *Dueling in the Old South: Vignettes of Social History*. College Station: Texas A&M University Press, 1980.

Winfrey, Dorman Hayward, comp. *A History of the Philosophical Society of Texas, 1837–1987*. Austin: The Philosophical Society of Texas, 1987.

Wolf, Leonard, ed. *The Essential Frankenstein*. New York: ibooks, 2004.

Wooten, Dudley G., ed. *A Comprehensive History of Texas, 1685 to 1897*. 2 vols. Dallas: William G. Scarff, 1898.

Writers' Program, Work Projects Administration. *Houston: A History and Guide*. Houston: Anson Jones Press, 1942.

Wyatt-Brown, Bertram. *Southern Honor: Ethics and Behavior in the Old South*. Oxford: Oxford University Press, 1982.

Young, Dr. S. O. *True Stories of Old Houston and Houstonians: Historical and Personal Sketches*. Galveston: Oscar Springer, Publisher, 1993.

────── *A Thumb-nail History of the City of Houston Texas: From its Founding in 1836 to the Year 1912*. Houston: Press of Rein & Sons Company, 1912.

PERIODICALS

Corner, William. "John Crittenden Duval: The Last Survivor of the Goliad Massacre." *Quarterly of the Texas State Historical Association*, vol. 1 (July 1897): 47–67.

Franz, Joe B., ed. "Moses Lapham: His Life and Some Selected Correspondence." *Southwestern Historical Quarterly*, vol. 54 (January 1951): 324–32; (April 1951): 462–75.

Garwood, Ellen. "Early Texas Inns: A Study in Social Relationships." *Southwestern Historical Quarterly*, vol. 60 (October 1956): 219–44.

Geiser, S. W. "Naturalists of the Frontier." *Southwest Review*, vol. 16 (Autumn 1930): 109–35.

────── "Notes on Dr. Francis Moore (1808–1864)." *Southwestern Historical Quarterly*, vol. 47 (April 1944): 419–25.

BIBLIOGRAPHY 287

Henson, Margaret Swett. "Politics and the Treatment of the Mexican Prisoners After the Battle of San Jacinto." *Southwestern Historical Quarterly*, vol. 94 (October 1990): 189–230.

Hogan, William Ransom. "Rampant Individualism in the Republic of Texas." *Southwestern Historical Quarterly*, vol. 44 (April 1941): 454–80.

Howren, Alleine. "Causes and Origin of the Decree of April 6, 1830." *Southwestern Historical Quarterly*, vol. 16 (April 1913): 378–422.

Looscan, Adele. "Harris County, 1822–1845." *Southwestern Historical Quarterly*, vols. 18 (April 1915): 399–409 and 19 (July 1915): 37–64.

Muir, Andrew Forest. "Augustus M. Tomkins, Frontier Prosecutor." *Southwestern Historical Quarterly*, vol. 54 (January 1951): 316–23.

———— "The Destiny of Buffalo Bayou." *Southwestern Historical Quarterly*, vol. 47 (October 1943): 91–106.

———— "The Intellectual Climate of Houston During the Period of the Republic." *Southwestern Historical Quarterly*, vol. 62 (January 1959): 312–21.

Robertson, Jane M. "Captain Amon B. King." *Southwestern Historical Quarterly*, vol. 29 (October 1925): 147–50.

Smith, Ruby Cumby. "James Walker Fannin, Jr., in the Texas Revolution." *Southwestern Historical Quarterly*, vol. 23 (October 1919): 80–90, (January 1920): 171–203, (April 1920): 271–84.

Smith, W. Roy. "The Quarrel between Governor Smith and the Council of the Provisional Government of the Republic." *Quarterly of the Texas State Historical Association*, vol. 5 (April 1902): 53–74.

Winkler, Ernest William. "The Seat of Government in Texas." *Quarterly of the Texas State Historical Association*, vol. 10 (October 1906): 164–71.

Winston, James E. "Notes on Commercial Relations Between New Orleans and Texas Ports, 1838–1839. *Southwestern Historical Quarterly*, vol. 34 (October 1930): 91–105.

THESES

Davie, Flora Agatha. "The Early History of Houston, Texas, 1836–1845." MA thesis, University of Texas at Austin, 1940.

WEBSITES

"Body-snatching gang cut legs off Alistair Cooke 'to sell bones.'" http://news.independent .co.uk/world/americas/article349595.ece

288 BIBLIOGRAPHY

Clark, Richard. "The history of judicial hanging in Britain." http://richard.clark32
.btinernet.co.uk/hanging1.html

"Corpse Thieves Thrive as 'Body Brokers'; $900 for Severed Head." www
.taphophilia.com/modules.php?name=News&file=article&sid=3147

Coulter, Susan. "Frankenstein—a cautionary tale of bad parenting," online at www
.kimwoodbridge.com/maryshel/coulter.shtml

Davenport, Harbert. "Notes from an Unfinished Study of Fannin and his Men, with
biographical sketches," online at www.tsha.utexas.edu/supsites/fannin/hd-home.html

Dunn, Jeff. "Emily West de Zavala and Emily D. West: Two Women or One?," The
Compass Rose, vol. 20 (Spring 2006) online at http://libraries.uta.edu/SpecColl/crose06
/CR-Spr2006.pdf

——— "One more Piece of the Puzzle: Emily West in Special Collections,"
The Compass Rose, vol. 19 (Spring 2005) online at http://libraries.uta.edu./SpecColl
/crose05/West.htm

The Handbook of Texas Online, www.tsha.utexas.edu/handbook/online

"Malaria," online at Emedicine Consumer Health, www.emedicinehealth.com
/articles/13140-2.asp

"Old Diseases Defined," online at www.carolyar.com/Illinois/diseases.htm

San Jacinto Museum of History website, www.sanjacinto-museum.org/Sons of Dewitt
Colony Texas website, www.tamu.edu/ccbn/dewitt/dewitt.htm

State House Press/McWhiney Foundation Press website, www.tfhcc.com/press

Texas State Cemetery website, www.cemetery.state.tx.us/

Wyhe, John van. "The History of Phrenology on the Web." http://pages.britishlibrary
.net/phrenology/overview.htm

Index

A

An Account of the Yellow Fever Which Appeared in the City of Galveston, Republic of Texas, In the Autumn of 1839 (1839), 206

ad interim government (Texas), 265, 266

Adams, James, 68

Adams, John Quincy, 165, 251 (n. 6)

Adelsverein, 199

Advisory Committee of the General Council, 13, 264

Age of Jackson, 112

Age of Reason (1795), 141

Agua Dulce, battle of, 20, 264

Alabama Red Rovers, 7, 14, 21, 23

Aláman, Lucas, 4

"Alamo City" (see San Antonio de Béxar, Texas)

Alamo, xvi, 9, 15, 18, 21-23, 44, 50, 88, 108, 170

Allen, ____ (murderer of Dr. Chauncey Goodrich), 155

Allen, Augustus C., 57-61, 66, 68-71, 73, 90, 92, 141, 150, 233 (n.7), 266, 270

Allen, Charlotte (Mrs. Augustus Allen), 90, 91 (portrait), 270

Allen, James L., 130

Allen, John Kirby, 57-61, 66, 68-71, 73, 92 (portrait), 93, 94, 150, 215, 233 (n. 3), 266

Allen, O. F., 73, 236 (n. 23)

Allen, Thomas G., 228 (n. 3)

American Museum (magazine), 272

American Turf Register and Sporting Magazine, 121, 244 (n. 44), 279

American volunteers (see United States' volunteers)

Anahuac, Texas, 25 (map), 52, 142 (map)

Anahuac Disturbance of 1835, 234 (n. 15)

Anthropodermic Bibliopegy (binding books in human skin), 257 (n. 40)

Appomattox, Virginia, 205

Army of the People, 5

290 INDEX

Arouet, Francois Marie (*see* Voltaire)
Ashville, Alabama, 199
Atascosito Road, 15, 264
Audubon, James J., 81, 87, 237 (n. 39), 268
Austin County, Texas, 51
Austin, Stephen Fuller, 1, 5, 8, 203, 222, (n. 2), 223 (n. 9), 266, 267
Austin, Texas, xx, 89, 143, 145, 202, 203, 205, 211-213
Auxiliary Volunteer Corps, 7, 263
Ayres, Ann, 50, 51
Ayres, David, 50, 223, 232 (n. 30)

B

"Babe of the Alamo" (*see* Dickinson, Angelina)
Bagby Street (Houston), 170
Baker rifles, 26
Baker, M. (acquaintance of John Hunter Herndon), 206
Baker, Moseley, 80, 106, 206
Baldwin, Col. ____ (proprietor of Houston House), 84, 85, 238 (n. 44)
Baltimore, Maryland, 205, 272
Barker, Eugene C., 101, 222 (n. 2), 235 (n. 16), 240 (n. 2), 246 (n. 11)
Barnard, Dr. Joseph Henry, 15, 27
Barr, Robert, 267
Barragán, Miguel, 5
Barrett, Don Carlos, 13, 264
Basic Texas Books, An Annotated Bibliography of Selected Works for a Research Library (1983), 243 (n. 30), 247 (n. 18), 259 (n. 11), 260 (n. 31)
Bassett, Clement N., 175

Bath, New York, 130, 245 (n. 8)
Bauer, Dr. John H., 77
Bayard, Pierre Terrail, seigneur de, 104
Bayland Guards, 207
"Bayou City" (*see* Houston, Texas)
Bee, Bernard, 272, 273
Bell, Joseph T., 68
Bellows, Peter, 202
Bellville, Texas, 51
Benavides, Plácido, 14, 20
Bernardo Plantation, 40
Béxar (*see* San Antonio de Béxar)
Béxar, Siege of, 17, 150, 170, 223 (n. 10), 264
Bierce, Ambrose, 187, 257 (n. 43)
"Big Bugs" (Houston) (*see* Gentry)
Billingsley, Jesse, 41
Bird, Capt. John, 273
Birdsall and Gazley (Houston law firm), 142
Birdsall, John, 142
Birdsall, Maurice L., 178
Black Bean Episode, 197, 256 (n. 37)
"Black Vomit" (*see* Yellow fever)
Blister flies, 75
Body Snatchers, 161, 183, 187
Boerne, Texas, 198
Bond, Miss ____ (acquaintance of John Hunter Herndon), 190
Bonham, James Butler, 7, 223 (n. 13)
Borden, Gail, Jr., 81, 131, 132
Borden, John P., 58
Borden, Thomas, 74, 131, 132
Boston, Massachusetts, 79, 186
Boswell, James, 139, 246 (n. 17)

INDEX   291

bounty certificates, 48, 51, 52, 231

Bowie knives, 56, 97, 119, 120, 123, 155, 164, 244 (n. 40)

Bowie, James, 10, 18, 263

Bowie, Rezin P., 100, 266

Bowles (Cherokee chief), 271

Boyce, Capt. Robert, 66, 67, 234 (n. 12)

Brashear, _____ (shooter of Algernon Thompson), 123

Brazoria County (Texas), 197

Brazoria Male and Female Academy, 197

Brazoria, Texas, 52, 233 (n. 5)

Brazos River (Texas), 1, 8, 37-40, 51, 57, 58, 71, 75, 197, 266

Breckinridge, John C., 205

Brenan, William, 38, 39, 43, 225 (n. 28), 229 (n. 3)

Brigham, Moses W., 171

Briscoe, Andrew, 178

Brooklyn, New York, 211

Brooks, Zachariah S., 229 (n. 3)

Brown, John Henry, 211

Brown, Samuel T., 228 (n. 3)

"Brown Bess" musket, xli

Brutus (Texas schooner), 58

Buckeye Rangers, 130

Buffalo Bayou, 41, 42, 58, 62, 63, 74, 78, 82, 93, 131, 142 (map), 197, 203, 210, 214, 234 (n. 7)

Buffalo Bayou, Brazos and Colorado Railway Company, 197

Burke, David N., 15, 229 (n. 3)

Burleson, Edward, 200, 272

Burnet, David G., 7, 51, 68, 100, 101, 130, 131, 141, 143, 144, 223 (n. 13), 232 (n. 32), 265-267

Burr, Aaron, 155

Burr–Hamilton Duel, 155

Bury St. Edmunds, England, 257 (n. 40)

Butler, Bennett, 229 (n. 3)

Bynum, Alfred, 225 (n. 28)

C

Caldwell, Matthew "Old Paint," 200

California, 9, 209

Callithumpian (definition), 261 (n. 40)

"Callithumpian Society" (Houston), 213

Calvit, Alexander, 197

Calvit, Barbara Makall Wilkinson (Mrs. John Hunter Herndon), 197

Camino Real, 14

Camp Harrisburg, 265

Camp Victoria, 46, 53

Campana, Texas, 38

Capitol building (Houston), 59 (map), 69-72, 92, 123, 141, 235 (n. 17), 249 (n. 35), 268-270

Carbajal, Mariano, 225 (n. 28)

Carlos, John, 123, 271

Carlos' Saloon (Houston), 123

Carolina Street (Houston), 170

Carrer, Charles J., 225 (n. 28)

Cartwright, Jesse H., 234 (n. 15)

Cass, James M., 225 (n. 28)

Cavanaugh, _____ (one of the Houston grave robbers), 161, 183, 256 (n. 37)

292   INDEX

cazadores, 26

Cedar Bluff, Alabama, 199

centralistas (*see* Centralists)

Centralists, 4, 5, 19

Chance, Joseph Bell, 40, 42, 43, 265

Charles II, King of England, 184

Charleston, South Carolina, 205

Cheng, Maria, 255 (n. 36)

Chenoweth, John, 14

Cherokees, 10, 203, 273

cholera, 71

"Citizen" (nom de plume of a correspondent in the *Telegraph and Texas Register*),
193-195, 210

Clarksville, Texas, 113

Clements, Joseph D., 13

code duello, 150, 153, 155, 157

Coleman, Robert M., 38, 230 (n. 11)

Coleto Creek, 24, 26, 35

Coleto Creek, battle of, 19, 47, 52, 265

College of Physicians and Surgeons, 184

Colorado River (Texas), 25 (map), 36, 212

Columbia, Texas, 40, 58, 59, 61, 66, 82, 115,
131, 233 (n. 5), 234 (n. 9), 267

Comanches, 200, 207-208, 233 (n. 2), 271,
273

"Come and Take It" fight (*see* Gonzales,
battle of)

Company H, First Regiment of Texas
Volunteers, 43-44

Company J, Second Regiment of Texas
Volunteers, 39

Concepción, battle of, 263

Confederacy, 205, 211

Confederate States of America, 105

"Congestive fever" (*see* malaria)

Congress Avenue (Houston), 69, 86

Connecticut, 52, 70

Constitution of 1824 (Mexican), 2, 4-5

Constitution of 1836 (Texan), 48

Consultation of 1835, 8, 234 (n. 15)

consumption, 149, 204

Convention of 1845 (Texan), 210

Cooke, Alistair, 257 (n. 43)

Cooke, William Gordon, 14-17, 165, 225 (n.
28), 250 (n. 5)

Cooper, Dillard, xli, 229 (n. 3)

Copano Bay, 13-14, 264

Corder, William, 185

Córdova, Vicente, 272

Corpse Thieves, 257 (n. 43)

Cos, Brig. Gen. Martín Perfecto de, 5, 263

Council House Fight (1840), 208

county surveyors, 49

Cox, C. C., 75-76, 237

Cox, Harvey, xli

Crane, Ichabod (fictional character in
Washington Irving's The *Legend of
Sleepy Hollow*), 135

"Crescent City" (*see* New Orleans)

Crockett, David, 15

Cruger, Daniel, 133

Cruger, Jacob W., 130, 132-134, 245 (n. 7)

Cruger, James F., 130

Cummings, John, 37-38

Cummings, Rebecca, 37

D

Daily Picayune (New Orleans), 251 (n. 7),
269, 276

INDEX   293

Dalberg-Acton, Lord John Emerich
    Edward (*see* Lord Acton)
Dalton, S., 185
"Dancing the hempen jig," 183
"Dancing the Tyburn jig," xxxv
Darden, Fannie A. D., xli
Davenport, Harbert, 15, 224 (n. 27), 225
    (n. 28), 288
Davis, Andrew, 113
Davis, Jefferson, 105, 205
Desanque, Francis J., 27
"Dead man's hand," putative effects of,
    xxxv
The Devil's Dictionary (1911), 187
Dickinson, Almaron, 88
Dickinson, Angelina, 202
Dickinson, Noah, 225 (n. 28)
Dickinson, Susanna, xxvii, 88-90, 201-
    203, 259 (n. 18-20, 22), 269, 283
Dickson, Abishai, 7, 28, 223 (n. 13), 228
    (n. 57)
Duluth, Minnesota, 211
dissection, 183-187, 189-190
District Court (Houston), 120, 174, 196,
    204
Douglas, Stephen A., 205
Douglass, Rep. Kelsey H., 73, 97, 116, 137,
    203-204, 212, 236-238, 243, 246, 259,
    269
Dresel, Gustav, 76, 83, 84, 112, 116, 167,
    199, 236, 242, 251, 259
dueling, 136, 150, 153-157
dueling ground, 151, 153, 157, 249 (n. 35)
Duval, Burr H., 21, 28, 227 (n. 39)

Duval, John Crittenden, 28, 227-228, 276,
    286
Dylan, Bob, xxvii
dysentery, 48, 71

E
Edinburgh Guild of Surgeons and
    Barbers, 184
Edinburgh, Scotland, 184
eggnog, 91, recipe for, 239 (n. 54)
Ehrenberg, Hermann, 24, 227 (n. 47),
    229 (n. 3)
El Paso, Texas, 209
"Elegy Written in a Country Churchyard"
    (1751), 220 (n. 2)
Eliot, T. S., 217, 261 (n. 44)
Elliott, Capt. W. J., 48, 266
"Empire State" (*see* New York)
empresarios, 1, 3, 52
England, 184, 207
English Common Law, 186
Erath, George B., 49, 231 (n. 29)
Escott, ____ (private, San Antonio Greys),
    225 (n. 28)
Everitt, Stephen H., 207
Exchange Hotel (Houston), 213

F
Fannin, James Walker, Jr., 10, 14-16, 18-27,
    47, 224 (n. 27), 226 (n. 30), 227 (n. 38),
    263-264
Fannin Massacre Ball, 180
"Father of Houston" (*see* Allen, John
    Kirby)

294 INDEX

"Father of Texas Medicine" (*see* Smith, Ashbel)

"Father of Texas" (*see* Austin, Stephen Fuller)

"Father of the University of Texas" (*see* Smith, Ashbel)

federalistas (*see* Federalists)

Federalists (Mexican), 4-5, 9, 14, 226 (n. 33)

Ferguson, Joseph G., 21

filibusters (American), 1, 222 (n. 1)

Fisher, S. Rhoads, 267

Fisher, William S., 109, 242 (n. 20-21), 268

"Fishermen" (*see* Body Snatchers)

Floyd's Hotel (Houston), 65, 84, 120, 180, 190

"Fog of battle," 33

"Forks of the Road" incident, 41, 230 (n. 14)

Forsyth, John, 269

Fort Bend, Texas, 42, 154, 233 (n. 5)

Fort Defiance (*see* Presidio La Bahía)

Fort Delaware, 205

Fort Parker, 266

Fourth Judicial District (Republic of Texas), 175

Fowler, Rev. Littleton, 69, 147-148, 235 (n. 16), 247 (n. 23), 248 (n. 27-29), 269

France, 207, 273

Frankenstein, Victor (fictional character in Mary Shelley's *Frankenstein; or, The Modern Prometheus*), 94

Frankenstein; or, The Modern Prometheus (1818 novel), 94

Frankenstein's "creature," 94

Frazer, Hugh McDonald, 27

Free Blacks, 52, 243 (n. 35)

G

Gall, Dr. Franz Joseph, 188

gallows, 255 (n. 36)

Galveston Bay, 42, 58, 142 (map)

Galveston County, Texas, 210

Galveston Hurricane of 1900, 214

Galveston Island, 66, 140, 148, 207, 244

Galveston, Texas, 25 (map), 124, 140, 142 (map), 209, 214

gambling, 103, 115, 117, 120, 121, 147, 168, 171-172, 177, 180, 182, 250 (n. 50), 254 (n. 27)

Garray, Col. Francisco, 20

General Council, 8, 12, 224 (n. 21), 234 (n. 15), 263-264

General Land Office (*see* Texas General Land Office)

gentry, xxxvii, 50, 56, 86, 118, 121, 125, 127, 129, 144, 146, 149, 157-158, 179, 216

Georgia, 205, 241 (n. 11)

Georgia Battalion, 22, 265

Gerlach Family, 84

German Community (Houston), 84

Germany, 199, 202

Gibbeting (*see* hanging in chains)

Gilland, George M., 225 (n. 28)

Globalization and World Cities Group and Network, 214

Goliad Campaign (1835), 170

Goliad Campaign (1836), 19-29, 170, 224 (n. 27)

Goliad garrison, 15, 20, 23, 24, 45, 264

Goliad Massacre, xix, xli, 16, 19, 31, 33, 34, 46, 47, 52, 179, 227 (n.39), 228 (n. 3), 265, 270

Goliad survivors, 38, 43

Goliad, Texas, 9, 13-15, 17-18, 20-24, 25 (map), 31, 38-40, 44-46, 52, 108, 195, 209, 224 (n. 26), 233 (n. 5), 264-266

Gonzales, battle of, 5, 100, 223 (n. 10)

Gonzales, Texas, 5, 22, 25 (map), 36, 263, 271

Goodrich, Dr. Chauncey, 151-156, 158, 215-216, 269

Goodrich–Laurens Duel, 158, 269

Gouge, William M., 116, 240 (n. 2), 252 (n. 14)

Gould, ____ (private, San Antonio Greys), 225 (n. 28), 238 (n. 45)

"Grabs" (*see* Body Snatchers)

Grace, John, 16-17, 225 (n. 28)

Grand Lodge of Texas, 148, 203, 270-271

Grant, Dr. James, 14, 20, 226 (n. 33)

"Grave Robbers" (*see* Body Snatchers)

Grave Robbing, 161, 257 (n. 43)

"Grave Watchers," 187

Graves, John, xxvi

Gray, Millie (Mrs. William Fairfax Gray), 93, 213, 236 (n. 22), 239 (n. 56), 260 (n. 39)

Gray, Thomas, 220 (n. 2)

Gray, William Fairfax, 71, 102, 141, 236, 236, 249, 260

Great Comanche Raid of 1840, 200

Greece, 207

Green, George, 225 (n. 28)

Green, Thomas J., 106, 231(n. 23), 240 (n. 5)

Green-Wood Cemetery (Brooklyn), 211

Griffin, Peter, 225 (n. 28)

Griffith, John Maynard, 202

Groce, Jared, 38, 40

Groce's Retreat, Texas, 233 (n. 5)

Guadalupe County, Texas, 197

Guadalupe River (Texas), 22, 25 (map), 35, 45

H

Hadden, William, 229 (n. 3)

Hall, C. K., 124

Hall, Robert, 47, 201

Hamad al-Bandar, Awad, 255 (n. 36)

Hamilton, Alexander, 155

Hamilton, Isaac D., 229 (n. 3)

Hamilton, Gen. James, 105

hanging, effects of, xxxv-xxxvii, 255 (n. 36)

hanging in chains, 256 (n. 38)

Hanging not Punishment Enough (1701 pamphlet), 184

Hangman's noose, xxxiv, xxxv, 221 (n. 5)

Hangman's rope, putative effects of, selling of, xxxvi

"Hangmen's Grove," 64-65 (map), 196

Hannan, A. B., 14

Hannig, William, 202

Hardwicke, Charles S., 15

Harpe, Micajah "Big," 256 (n. 38)

296 INDEX

Harpe's Head, Kentucky, 256 (n. 38)

Harper, William, 225 (n. 28)

Harris County, Texas, 201, 204, 207

Harris, Dilue Rose, 68, 234 (n. 15)

Harrisburg County, Texas, 68, 89, 90, 142
(map), 234 (n. 14), 254 (n. 27)

Harrisburg Rail Road and Trading
Company, 210

Harrisburg Town Company, 210

Harrisburg, Texas, 25 (map), 40-41, 44, 52,
58, 62, 170, 142 (map)

Hazen, Nathaniel, 14-15, 38, 239 (n. 3)

headright grants, 48-51

Heath, Ebenezer Smith, 225 (n. 28)

Hedenberg, Charles, 123-124

Hedenberg, Maggie, 124

Hempstead, Texas, 198

Henderson, James Pinckney, 267

Henry VIII, King of England, 184

Herndon, John Hunter, 79, 80, 84, 87, 92,
120, 127, 139-141, 161, 175-180, 182-183,
189-191, 197, 219 (n. 1), 220 (n. 2), 242
(n. 27), 246 (n. 17), 255 (n. 36), 259 (n.
8), 270-271

Heroes of San Jacinto, The (1932), 196, 233
(n. 2)

Herring, Francis P., 201

Hidalgo, Texas, 233 (n. 5)

Highland Lick, Kentucky, 256 (n. 38)

Hill, Stuart, 225 (n. 28)

Hill, William Warner, 43

Hodge, Nathan, 225 (n. 28)

hogs, 36, 67, 74, 75, 199

Holland, Benjamin H., 225 (n. 28), 229,
(n. 3)

Holland, Capt. James, 24

Holland, Miss _____ (acquaintance of
John Hunter Herndon), 190

Holley, Mary Austin, xxvii, 67, 70, 79, 81,
90, 91, 170, 203, 234 (n. 14), 235 (n. 18),
239 (n. 54) 270

Holliday, John, 228 (n. 3)

Holloway, John, 185, 220 (n. 1)

Holman, James S., 138

Holmes, Oscar, 202

horse-and-cart hanging, xxxiv, 220 (n. 3)

horseracing, 121

Horseshoe Bend, battle of, 157

Horsham, England, 181

Houston and Texas Central Railroad, 74

Houston Chronicle, 255 (n. 36)

Houston House (hotel), 84-85, 171, 238
(n. 44)

Houston Jockey Club, 121

Houston Ship Channel, 214

Houston, Sam, 6-7, 9, 20, 22, 38, 39
(portrait), 45, 68, 101, 105, 137, 142,
145-146, 204,
206-209, 223 (n. 13), 235, 237, 241

Houston, Texas, mention of, xxv, xxviii,
53, 57, 81-82, 84, 99, 111, 112, 131-133,
138-140, 143, 155-156, 166-168, 175,
179-180, 189-190, 197-198, 203-207,
210-211, 270-271; character of, 66,
80-81, 85, 87-93, 97, 110, 117 118,
124-125, 127, 129, 132, 136, 149, 152, 157,
161, 165-167, 173-174, 177, 179, 201-202,
206, 211, 213-216; crime in, 68, 118-124,
128, 163-165, 167-168, 171, 173-177, 181,
211-217, 221 (n. 11), 269, 270-271; disease

in, 71, 93, 213-214; gambling in, 69, 120, 167; horse racing in, 121-122, 163; inflation in, 66-67, 116-117; maps of, 59, (bird's eye view), 64-65; origins of, 58-61, 266, 268; rapid growth of, 69-72, 83-84, 117, 225 (n. 16), 269; reacts to Quick–Jones hanging, xxxi, xxxiii, xxxvi, xxxvii, 183, 193-196, 271; refinement in, 90-91, 129, 131, 139-141, 147, 179, 214-215, 268, 270-271; saloons in, 56, 66, 69, 86, 87, 97, 120, 122-123, 215; as seat of government, 58-62, 70-71, 92, 130, 138, 143, 213, 267-269, 273; squalor in, 56, 71-76, 80-82, 136-137, 210, 212, 216, 269; travel to, 62-63, 66, 71-74, 140-141, 149; violence in, 92, 97, 117-123, 136-137, 149-150, 152, 154-157, 164-165, 167-168, 171, 173, 175, 177, 200, 212-214, 249 (n. 35), 269; vermin in, 74-76, 80, 199; weapons in, 97, 118-123, 136-137; weather in, 70, 76-80, 84, 180, 199, 268-270

Houstoun, Matilda, 84-85, 119, 237 (n.30), 240 (n. 1)

Hubbard, Z., 136

Humphreys, Mrs. ____ (acquaintance of John Hunter Herndon), 189

Hunchback, The (1832 stage play), 271

Hunt, Memucan, 269

Hunter, William, 225 (n. 28), 229 (n. 3)

Hurst, Capt. Stephen, 24

Hussein, Saddam, 255 (n. 36)

Huston, Felix, 101 (portrait), 100-105, 199, 201, 240-242, 266-268

Huston–Johnston Duel, 105-106

I

Ibra him, Barzan, 255 (n. 36)

indentured servants, 52

Independence Convention (1836), 16, 165, 265

Indiana, 8

influenza, 71

Invincible (Texas schooner), 266

Irion, Robert A., 68, 141, 235 (n. 16), 239(n. 52), 268

Irish, Milton, 2 25 (n. 28), 229 (n. 3)

J

Jackson, Andrew, 6, 267-268

James I, King of Scotland, 184

James, ____ (Third sergeant of San Antonio Greys), 225 (n. 28)

Jenkins, John H., 207, 223(n. 13), 230 (n. 4), 243 (n. 30)

Jerry ("black porter" and "great thief"), 85

Jetty, Rufus K., 15

Johnson, Francis (Frank) W., 10, 19, 21, 263-264

Johnson, William P., 225 (n. 28)

Johnston, Albert Sidney, 101, 105 (portrait), 108, 109, 207, 240-242, 245, 268

Jones, Dr. Anson, 61 (portrait), 141, 168, 207, 238 (n. 52), 270-271

Jones, David James, mention of, xviii-xxviii, 1, 15, 33-34, 52-53, 137, 167, 172, 196-197, 201, 209; as Texas volunteer, 6-8, 13-17, 264; as member of Goliad garrison, 17, 21-22, 36, 264; at battle of Coleto Creek, 23-27, 265; as Mexican

298 INDEX

prisoner, 27-28; escapes Goliad Massacre, xli, 29, 33, 265; joins other Massacre survivors, 36-38; arrives at Houston's camp, 38; in San Jacinto army, 40, 42-43, 265; fights at San Jacinto, 43-44, 265; in Texas army following San Jacinto, 44-45, 48, 266-267; returns to Goliad, 31, 46-47; discharged from Texas army, 48; sells bounty and headright certificates, 48-49, 51-52, 170; in Houston, Texas, 53, 99, 121, 139, 158; as rowdy loafer, 163-165, 173, 212-213, 215-217; murders Wood, 164, 269; trial of, 174-177, 194-195, 270; suicide attempt of, 177, 270; hanging of, xxv, xxxi, xxxiii, xxxvi xxxvii, 1, 180-183, 195, 219 (n. 1), 247 (n. 18), 253 (n. 27), 270; disinterment and decapitation of, 161, 183-184, 258 (n. 46), 270-271; name left off San Jacinto monument, 196, 258 (n. 5)

"Julian" (an Indian), 186

K

Karnes, Henry, 41

Kaufman, David S., 141

Kelcy, L., 136

Kemp, Louis Wiltz, 196

Kemp, Thomas, 38, 40, 43, 229 (n. 3)

Kennedy, William, 240 (n. 3), 243 (n. 30)

Kenny, David J., 226 (n. 28)

Kentucky, 34, 79, 100, 117, 135, 139, 179, 197, 203, 224 (n. 26), 256 (n. 38)

"Kentucky Wine Club" (Houston), 140

Kessler, Henry, 86, 116-117

Kessler's Round Tent, 59 (map) 86, 116

Kichais, 266

King, Amon B., 14, 22, 227 (n. 40), 264

King, Florence, 152, 249 (n. 39)

Kiowas, 266

Kittredge, Susan Cooke, 257 (n. 43)

Knowles, Sheridan, 271

Kuykendall, Jonathan Hampton, 41, 230 (n. 14)

L

"L" (nom de plume of correspondent in *Telegraph and Texas Register*), 171-172

"Labaca" River (*see* Lavaca River)

La Branche, Alcée, 268

La Fayette Battalion (*see* Second Battalion)

Labadie, Nicholas, 38, 230 (n. 11)

Labranche, Hermogene, 203

"Lady Justice" (allegorical symbol), 194-195

Lamar, Mirabeau Buonaparte, 100, 141, 143 (portrait), 212, 214, 246 (n. 11), 266, 272

Lapham, Moses, 58, 115, 232 (n. 2), 243 (n. 32)

Larson, Andrew (*see* Lawson, Andrew)

Laura (steamboat), 62, 267

Laurens, Levi L., 151 156, 158, 269

Lavaca River, 36, 106

Law of April 6, 1830, 3

Law of Nations (1793), 190

Lawrence, A. B., 78, 237 (n. 34)

INDEX 299

Lawrence, William, 175

Lawson, Andrew, 168, 178

Led Zeppelin (British rock group), 255 (n. 36)

"Lessons of the gallows," 181, 195, 213

Levenhagen, Robert, 83

Lewes, England, 185

Lewis, Dr. _____ (drinking companion of Dr. Robert H. Watson), 141

Lexington, Kentucky, 203

Liberty County, Texas, 210

Liberty, Texas, 52, 142 (map), 167

"Ligeia" (1838, short story), 272

Lincoln, Abraham, 205

Linley, Charles, 14-15 Little River (Texas), 273

Liverpool, England, 272

Livingston County, New York, 130

Lockhart, Dr. John Washington, 63, 72, 74, 78, 120, 234 (n. 8), 244, 251

Lockhart, Texas, 200, 202

Logan, John C., xli, 17, 226 (n. 28)

London, England, xxxv, 85, 139, 220 (n. 1)

Long Row (Houston), 59 (map), 69

Long-drop hangings, xxxiv, xxxv, 221 (n. 5)

Lord Acton (Sir John Emerich Edward Dalberg-Acton), xxvii

Louisiana, 1, 25 (map), 40, 199, 203

Lubbock, Adele (Mrs. Francis R. Lubbock), 75, 80

Lubbock, Francis R., 62-63, 66, 71, 75, 79-81, 110, 138, 204-205, 207, 233 (n. 5), 81 (portrait), 235 (n. 16), 242 (n. 22), 245 (n. 1), 267

Lynch, Nathaniel, 42

Lynch's Ferry, 42, 265

Lynchburg, Texas, 62, 142 (map)

Lyndon B. Johnson Space Center (Houston), 214

M

Machiavelli, Niccolò di Bernardo dei, 4

Magruder, Maj. Gen. John Bankhead, 205

Mahoney, Dennis, 226 (n. 28)

Maillard, Nicholas Doran P., 88, 114, 238 (n. 48), 243 (n. 30)

Main Street (Houston), 69, 71, 86, 123, 221 (n. 3), 244 (n. 47), 249 (n. 35), 268

Maine, 70, 72

Malaria, 73, 93

Manford, Rev. Erasmus, 88, 238 (n. 48)

Mann, Pamelia, 38

Mansion House (Houston boarding house and brothel), 65 (map), 88, 152

Martindale, Daniel, 229 (n. 3)

Mason, William, 228 (n. 3)

Masonic Order, 147, 197, 204, 270-271

Massachusetts, 130, 134, 137, 155, 186

Matagorda County, Texas, 197

Matagorda, Texas, 233 (n. 5)

Matamoros Expedition of 1836, 7, 9, 14, 16, 102, 108-109, 264

Matamoros Expedition of 1837, 109

Matamoros, Mexico, 14, 16, 19, 25 (map), 102, 263-264

Mather, Cotton, 136

Matthews, Rev. Z. H., 90

Maverick, Mary, 73

300 INDEX

Maverick, Samuel, 72, 73 (portrait)
Maxey, David, 225 (n. 27)
McCrory, Hugh, 90, 238 (n. 52)
McCulloch, Ben, 200
McCullough, David, xxviii
McHenry, Lydia Ann, 51
McWhiney, Grady, xvii, xx, xxi, 215
Medical and Surgical Society of Houston,
247 (n. 22), 255 (n. 37)
Medina County, Texas, 197
Mercantile Row (Houston), 69
"Merry Boys" (see Rowdy Loafers)
Mexican Army, 36, 41, 44-45, 90, 228,
265
Mexican Congress, 44, 108
Mexican prisoners of war, 97, 236 (n. 23),
Mexicans, 1-5, 9, 16-17, 23-27, 35, 37, 42,
44-45, 73, 100, 173, 236 (n. 23)
Mexico City, Mexico, 267
Mexico, 2, 4, 25 (map), 97, 101-102, 105,
142, 198, 208, 236 (n. 23)
Mier Expedition, 197, 256 (n. 37)
Mier y Terán, Gen. José Manuel, 3
Milam Guards (Houston), 213
Milam, Ben, 150
Mill Creek (Texas), 37
Minnesota, 211
Mississippi, 100-101, 104, 108, 121, 152,
199, 253 (n. 27)
Mobile Grays, 15
Montville (home of David and Ann
Ayres), 51
Moody, Edward, 226 (n. 28)
Moore, Commodore Edwin Ward, 273

Moore, Dr. Francis, Jr., mention of, xxvii,
62, 74, 81-82, 175, 233 (n. 7); portrait
of, 137; youth of, 129-30, 155; loses
arm, 129-130; practices medicine,
129, 153; in Texas army, 129-130; as
Burnet supporter, 129-130; supports
Texas annexation, 130, 136, 210;
unpopularity of, 134, 136, 138, 156-157,
170, 198, 216; fashion sense of, xxxi,
137, 246 (n. 10); as Houston mayor,
xxxi, 74, 139, 165-166, 170,
178, 181, 195-196, 198, 210, 213,
216-217, 272; partnership with
Jacob Cruger, 132-134, 245 (n. 8);
as newspaper editor, 131-132, 138-139,
153, 165, 171-172, 193, 209, 245 (n. 6),
250 (n. 1); describes rapid growth
of Houston, 70; editorializes against
dueling, 151, 156-157; editorializes
against moving capital, 138, 212;
editorializes against carrying
weapons, 136; editorializes
against drinking, 136; editorializes
against rowdy loafers, 168-169,
173-174; editorializes against
Quick and Jones, 172-173, 175-177,
270; at hanging of Quick and Jones,
xxxi, 182-183; reports hanging of
Quick and Jones, 182-183, 195, 255
(n. 36); criticizes Texas Emigrant,
198; marries, 210; rapprochement
with Sam Houston, 210; as Unionist,
210; as Texas State Geologist,
210-211; moves to New York, 211;

INDEX   301

State Representative, 210, 273;
death of, 211; resting place of, 211

Moore, Dr. Francis, Sr., 129, 260 (n. 37)

Moore, John W., xxxi, 68, 177, 234 (n. 15)

Morales Battalion, 23

Morgan, Able, 26, 228 (n. 51)

Morgan, James, 51

Morning Star (Houston), 77, 196

mosquitoes, 75, 78

Muir, Andrew Forest, xxvi, 247 (n. 18)

Murphy, Daniel, 14-15, 35, 38, 229 (n. 3)

N

Nacogdoches, Texas, 3, 7-8, 25 (map),
40, 42, 97, 141, 204, 233 (n. 5)

"Napoleon of the West", 42

NASA, 214

Natchez, Mississippi, 100-101, 121, 201

Neches, battle of the, 203, 273

New England, 203

A New History of Texas (1847), 199

New Jersey, 50-51, 123, 221 (n. 8)

New Orleans Greys, 15, 17, 165

New Orleans, Louisiana, 17, 45, 66-67, 72,
77, 107, 139, 165-6, 199, 203

New Washington Association, 52

New Washington, Texas, 42, 52, 142 (map)

New York, 51-52, 58, 66, 130, 165, 210-211,

New York, New York, 51-52, 58, 66, 165,
211

New York Daily News, 165

New York Sunday School Union, 51

Nichols, James Wilson, 200, 259 (n. 13)

Noland, James, 226 (n. 28)

North Carolina, 52, 152-153, 207,
240 (n. 4)

Nueces River, 19, 51

O

Oak Grove Cemetery (Nacogdoches), 204

Oakwood Cemetery (Austin), 203

Ohio, 75, 104, 150, 198

"Old Leather-Breeches" (see Huston,
Felix)

"Old Long-shanks" (see Huston, Felix)

"Old States" (see United States of America)

"Ol' San Jacinto" (see Houston, Sam)

Old Testament, xxxvi

"One-armed Proteus"
(see Francis Moore, Jr.)

Orozimbo, Texas, 233 (n. 5)

P

Paine, Thomas, 141

Panic of 1819, 2

Panic of 1837, 165

Pattillo, George A., 13

Patton, William, 40, 43

Parker, John A., 89-90, 238 (n. 51)

Peckinpah, Sam (film director), xxvi

"Peculiar institution" (see Slavery)

Pennsylvania, 171, 234 (n. 15)

Perkins, _____ (private, San Antonio
Greys), 226 (n. 28)

Perote Prison, 256 (n. 37)

Pettus, Samuel O., 17-18, 25-27,
225 (n. 28), 264

Petty, Rufus K. (see Jetty, Rufus K.)

INDEX

Phi Beta Kappa, 143-144

Philadelphia, Pennsylvania, 116, 151

Philosophical Society of Texas, 141, 143-145, 214, 247 (n. 23), 248 (n. 24, 28), 270

Phillips, Charles, 226 (n. 28)

phrenology, 188, 258 (n. 44)

"Pissing when you can't whistle," xxxvi

Pittman, James F., 14-15, 224 (n. 26)

Plum Creek (Texas), 200

Plum Creek, battle of, 201

Poe, Edgar Allan, 272

Post Oak Race Track, 121, 151

Potomac River, 4

Presidio La Bahía, 14, 16, 27, 47

Preston Street (Houston), 69

Preusch, William G., 226 (n. 28)

Price, Dr. J. Hervey, 161, 183, 187, 190, 225 (n. 37)

Price, Norman, 34

"Present Mindedness," 215

prisoners of war (*see* Mexican prisoners of war)

prostitutes, 88, 213

Provisional Government, 7-8, 58, 99

public education, 208, 272

Puerto de Los Cuates de Agua Dulce, 264

"Proteus" (Greek mythology), 135, 137, 169, 210, 246 (n. 11)

Q

Quick–Jones hanging, xxxi, xxxiii, xxxiv, xxxvi, 180-183; weather as a non-factor in, 253 (n. 27)

Quick, John Christopher Columbus, xxv, xxxi, xxxiii, xxxvi-xxxvii, 137, 161,

171-173, 175-178, 180-183, 188-191, 194-197, 201, 209, 213, 215, 220 (n. 2), 253-254 (n. 27), 270-271

Quintana, Texas, 233 (n. 5)

R

Ramey, Lawrence, 68

rats, 74, 76, 80, 86, 97, 125, 199

Red River (Texas), 113

Redd, William D., 135, 246 (n. 11)

Redlands, 8, 203

Rees, John, 226 (n. 28), 229 (n. 3)

Refugio, Texas, 10, 14, 22-23, 25 (map), 233 (n. 4), 264-265

Remington, Frederic, xxv, 219

Republic of Texas, xxviii, xxxiii, 61, 85, 131, 181, 193, 204, 206-207, 212, 220 (n. 1), 234 (n. 15), 236 (n. 23), 243 (n. 30), 265, 267-268, 270

"Resurrectionists" (*see* Body Snatchers)

Richmond Convention (1860), 205

Richmond, Texas, 143, 197

Richmond, Virginia, 205, 239 (n. 54)

Riddell, Dr. John Leonard, 67, 234 (n. 14)

Riddle, Joseph P., 226 (n. 28)

Rio Grande (Texas), 9, 14, 25 (map), 45, 90, 263-265

Robinson, James W., 8, 12-13, 39, 43, 175, 208, 224, 226 (n. 28), 263, 270

Robinson, Mary Isdell, 8

Robinson, Sarah Snider, 8

Romanticism, Age of, 93

Romantics, 93

Rome, 70, 207

INDEX   303

Rossetta ("a negress"), 85

"Rowdy loafers," xxviii, xxv, xxvii, 97, 99, 101, 168, 177, 182, 194-195, 199, 215, 217

Rowe, Joseph, 141

Runaway Scrape, xix, 38, 51, 80, 107

Rusk, Gen. Thomas Jefferson, 31, 45-47, 100-101, 143, 241 (n. 8), 266-267

S

Sabine River, 1

"Sack-'em-up-men" (*see* Body Snatchers)

Salem, Massachusetts, 129

Saligny, Alphonse de, 273

San Antonio de Béxar, Texas, 5, 7, 10, 14-18, 25 (map), 73, 150, 155, 165, 170, 223, 233, 263, 264, 271

San Antonio Greys, 15-17, 225 (n. 28), 264

San Antonio River (Texas), 25 (map), 29, 35

San Bernard (Texas schooner), 256 (n. 37)

"San Bayard" River (*see* San Bernard River)

San Bernard River (Texas), 37

San Diego, California, 209

San Felipe de Austin, Texas, 10, 13, 17, 25 (map), 36-38, 264

San Jacinto Ball, 268

San Jacinto, battle of, 7, 41-42, 45-46, 48, 51-53, 97, 100-101, 106, 116-117, 130, 146-147, 157, 170, 175, 195-196, 233 (n. 2), 235 (n. 16), 236 (n. 23), 265

San Jacinto battleground, 65 (map), 141, 142 (map)

San Jacinto Monument, 196, 258 (n. 5)

San Jacinto River (Texas), 42, 52, 57, 142, (map)

San Luis Battalion, 23

San Patricio, Texas, 10, 14, 17, 19-20, 25 (map), 51, 233 (n. 5), 264

Santa Anna, Antonio Lòpez de, 4-5, 14, 18, 23, 31, 33-34, 41-44, 100, 104, 209, 227-228, 264-267

Sargent, Charles, 226 (n. 28)

Scott County, Kentucky, 139

Scott, R. J., 226 (n. 28)

Second Battalion, 35

Second Militia District, 234 (n. 15)

Second Regiment (Sherman's) of Volunteers, 39-40

Second Texas Infantry (C.S.A.), 207

Seevy, ____ (assailant outside Kessler's Round Tent Saloon), 123

Seguin, Texas, 67

Shackelford, John ("Jack"), xli, 14, 23, 227 (n. 44), 229 (n. 3)

Shain, Charles B., 38, 44, 50-51, 228 (n. 57), 229 (n. 3-4)

Sharp, V., 229 (n. 3)

Shelley, Mary Wollstonecraft, 94, 187

Shepherd, Dr. ____ (acquaintance of John Hunter Herndon), 190

Sheridan, Francis C., 119-120, 122, 244 (n. 40)

Sherman, Sidney, 40, 42-43

Shiloh, battle of, 105, 207

short-drop hangings, xxxv, xxvi

Simpson, Wilson, 229 (n. 3)

304 INDEX

skulls, 127, 140, 190

Smith, Judge ____ (acquaintance of John Hunter Herndon), 190

Smith, Miss ____ (acquaintance of John Hunter Herndon), 190

Smith, Mrs. ____ (acquaintance of John Hunter Herndon), 190

Smith, Ashbel, 70, 72, 77, 86, 141, 143 (portrait), 154, 166, 206-207, 213-214, 235-238, 247-248

Smith, Benjamin Fort, 235 (n. 16)

Smith, Erastus "Deaf," 41, 232 (n. 2)

Smith, Henry, 7-8, 9 (portrait), 10-12

Smith, Jackson, 84

Smith, Mary, 90, 238 (n. 52)

Smith, Sam S., 89, 238 (n. 51)

"Snatches" (*see* Body Snatchers)

Snow, Dr. Charles B., 161, 183, 187, 256 (n. 37)

Somervell Expedition, 197

South Carolina, 62, 105, 205

Space Center Houston, 214

Spain, 1, 222 (n. 1)

Sprague, Samuel, 13-15, 38-39 224 (n. 26), 229 (n. 3)

St. Louis Cemetery (New Orleans), 203

Stanley, Cicero Marcus, 153

State Geologist (*see* Texas State Geologist)

State House Press, xvii, xxiii, xxviii

Stegall, Moses, 256 (n. 38)

Sterett, Capt. ____, 63

Sterne, Adolphus, 204, 259 (n. 25)

Stevenson, Robert, 44

Stiff, Edward, 77, 86, 125, 135, 137, 198, 210, 233 (n. 5), 241 (n. 10), 246, 251, 259

stitchdowns (shoes), xxxi, 135, 246 (n. 10)

Suffolk General Hospital, 185

Supreme Court (Texas), 141, 175

Sussex County, England, 186

Swisher, John Milton, 44, 231 (n. 19)

"Sword of San Jacinto", 39, 68, 92, 210, 248

T

Teal, Henry, 107, murder of, 108, 241-242

Tejanos, 4, 14, 23, 223 (n. 6)

Telegraph and Texas Register, 15, 58, 62, 65 (map), 81, 131, 193, 209, 219-221, 251 (n. 1)

Texana, Texas, 176, 253 (n. 26)

Texas, in American imagination, 1-2, 222 (n. 1)

Texas Army, 46, 110, 152, 242 (n. 19), 267 (n. 20)

Texas Avenue (Houston), 70, 268

Texas Emigrant, The, Being a Narration of the Adventures of the Author in Texas, and a Description of the Soil, Climate, Productions, Minerals, Towns, Bays, Harbors, Rivers, Institutions, and Manners and Customs of the Inhabitants of That Country; Together With the Principal Incidents of Fifteen Years Revolution in Mexico; And Embracing a Condensed Statement of Interesting Events in Texas From the First European Settlement in 1692 to the Year 1840 (1840), 246 (n. 10)

Texas Congress, 61, 92, 147, 267-269

Texas General Land Office, xv, 42, 269

Texas Medical Association, 206

INDEX   305

Texas Medical Center (Houston), 214

Texas National Anthem, 271

Texas Navy, 256 (n. 37), 276

Texas Revolution, 25 (map), 51

Texas State Cemetery (Austin), 208, 260

Texas State Geologist, 211

Texas State Historical Association, xx, 115

Texas Supreme Court, 141, 175

Texas, The Rise, Progress, and Prospects of the Republic of Texas (1841), 240 (n. 3), 243 (n. 30)

Texas veterans, 49-50, 53, 56, 116-117, 120, 170, 195

Texian War for Independence (see Texas Revolution)

"Texians," 5

Thompson, Algernon, 123

Thomson, Alexr, 13

Thomson, John W., 14-15

Tomkins, Augustus M., 155, 252-254

Town of Washington, Texas, 20, 37, 51, 209, 264 (map), 227 (n. 36)

Trans-Pecos region (Texas), 211

Transylvania College, 139

Travis, Charles, 50-51

Travis, William Barret, 18, 22, 50, 230 (n. 9), 232 (n. 30), 234 (n. 15)

Treaties of Velasco, 265

Tres Villas Battalion, xli, 34

Trinity River, 25 (map), 142 (map)

"Triple Tree," xxxv

Trollope, Frances, 103, 113, 241 (n. 10)

tuberculosis, 71

typhus, 71

U

Unionists, 210

United States of America, xxviii, xxxiv-xxxv, 1-3, 6, 12, 28, 34, 46, 52, 58-59, 61-62, 67, 93, 105, 109-110, 112, 131-132, 136, 165-166, 181, 187, 201, 210, 267, 269, 272

United States Military Academy at West Point, 19, 105

United States Navy, 273, 267

United States' volunteers, 6-7, 10, 13, 18, 21-22, 33, 40, 43, 45-48, 50, 99, 100-101, 143, 169, 216, 223 (n. 13), 263-264, 266

University of Texas, 145, 208

University of Texas Board of Regents, 208

Urrea, Brig. Gen. Juan José Cosme, 14, 19-23, 26-27, 44, 226, 236 (n. 23), 264-265

V

Vattel, Emmerich de, 190

Velasco, Texas, 25 (map), 130, 165, 198, 233 (n. 5), 265

Vera Cruz, Mexico, 273

Veterans (see Texas veterans)

Vicksburg, battle of, 207

Vicksburg, Mississippi, 152

Victoria Advocate, 255 (n. 36)

Victoria, Texas, xv, xxi, 22-26, 45, 255 (n. 36) 265

Vince's Bridge, 233 (n. 2)

Virginia, 1, 93, 205

Voltaire (pen name of Francois Marie Arouet), 134

Vose, George, 226 (n. 28)

W

Walker Street (Houston), 170

Wallace, A. J., 226 (n. 28)

Wallace, Benjamin C., 15, 35

War Party, 52

Ward, Thomas William "Peg-leg," 70, 1
50, 268

Ward, William, 22

Washington (*see* Town of Washington,
Texas)

Washington County, Texas, 44, 50

Washington, DC, 267

Washington-on-the Brazos (*see* Town
of Washington, Texas)

Washington Guards, 40

Water Street (Houston), 74

Waterloo, battle of, 42

Waterloo, Texas, 211, 272

Waters, Esq. _____ (acquaintance of John
Hunter Herndon), 190

Watrous, J. C., 175-176

Watson, Dr. Robert H., 127, 140, 161, 183,
187, 247 (n. 22), 256 (n. 37), 270

Webster Street (Houston), 221 (n. 3)

Wells, Lysander, 43, 230 (n. 17)

West, Emily D., 52, 232 (n. 33)

West, James, 226 (n. 28)

West Point (*see* United States Military
Academy at West Point)

Whig Society (Transylvania College), 139

White Oak Bayou, 66, 142 (map)

Williams, John (Goliad survivor), 35

Williams, John (Susanna Dickinson's
husband), 90, 201, 269

Williamson, Robert McAlpin "Three
legged Willie," 182

Wilson, Robert, 272

Winthrop, John, 58

Woll, Gen. Adrian, 208

Wood, Benjamin, 165, 245 (n. 8)

Wood, Elizabeth Mofat (Mrs. Francis
Moore, Jr.), 210, 245 (n. 8)

Wood, Fernando, 165

Wood, John, 226 (n. 28)

Wood, Mandred, 163, 269

Woodruff, John, 178

Wynns, Archibald, 175

Y

Yale College, 143-144

Yellow fever, 71, 195, 199, 203, 206, 213-214

"Yellow Rose of Texas" (*see* West, Emily D.)

Yellow Stone (steamboat), 40, 62, 82, 131,
234 (n. 7)

Yucatán Battalion, 34

Z

Zavala, Lorenzo de, 52, 267

www.ingramcontent.com/pod-product-compliance
Lightning Source LLC
LaVergne TN
LVHW041737281224
800028LV00012B/138/J